ONTARIO
To Clayton and Ogdensburg
Fort Ontario
OSWEGO
Oswego Beach
Oswego Jc.
MEXICO BAY
Mannsville
Hooker
N. Boylston
Lacona
Monteola
Smartville
Orwell
Pulaski
Richland
Salmon River
Daysville
Altmar
New Haven
Fernwood
Osceola
Kasoag
Mexico
Howardsville
Florence
Scriba
Sala
Parish
Williamstown
Fruit Valley
E. Florence
Minetto
Bundy
Amboy Center
Hastings
West Camden
Palermo
N. Sterling
N. Constantia
Camden
Sterling
Fulton
Mallory
Gayville
Poultneyville
Sodus Point
Fairhaven
Hinmanville
Central Square
Williamson
Martville
Constantia
Bernards Bay
Webster
Union Hill
Fruitland
Ontario
Lake Bluff
Great Sodus Bay
Redcreek
Phoenix
Brewerton
Cleveland
W. Vienna
North Bay
Frenchmans Island
East Williamson
Sodus
Wallington
Sta.
Alton
Bay Resort
Westbury
Ira
Cigarville
ONEIDA LAKE
Sylvan Beach
Sagamore
Oneida Lake Navigation Co.
West Webster
Lincoln
W. Walworth
Wolcott
Victory
Little Utica
Cicero
Euclid
Sodus Center
N. Rose
Cato
Meridian
Belgium
South Bay
Baldwinsville
Bridgeport
Lakeport
Walworth
Marion
S. Sodus
Rose
Butler Cen.
Plainville
Woodward
Fairport
Fairville
Wayne Center
Spring Lake
Van Buren
North Syracuse
Egypt
S. Butler
Conquest
Long Branch
CROSS LAKE
Lake Shore R.R.
SYRACUSE
Macedon Center
Newark
Lyons
Lock Berlin
Clyde
Savannah
Montezuma
Port Byron
Weedsport
Jordan
Peru Jc.
ONONDAGA L.
E. Syracuse
Minoa
Kirkville
Chittenango
Oneida
Macedon
Palmyra
Port Gibson
SYRACUSE & EASTERN
Memphis
Warner
Marcellus
STATE FAIR
ONEIDA RY.
To Utica
Canastota
Manlius Center
Clockville
DeWitt
Fayetteville
Cottons
Manlius
Thompsons
Tyre
Throop
Split Rock
Edwards Falls
Chittenango Falls
Victor
Manchester
Phelps Jc.
Jamesville
Mertensia
Shortsville
Phelps
AUBURN
Skaneateles
Cazenovia
Navarino
Paddlefords
Seneca Falls
Waterloo
Cayuga
Marietta
Rippleton
Amber
Pompey
Canandaigua
Hopewell
Seneca Castle
Cayuga Lake Park
Lakeside Park
Ten Mile Point
OTISCO LAKE
Collingwood
Geneva
Geneva Jc.
Cayuga Jc.
Owasco
Borodino
Otisco
New Woodstock
Spangles
Canoga
Lakeside
MacDougall
Union Springs
Niles
SKANEATELES LAKE
Spafford
Stanley
SENECA LAKE
CAYUGA LAKE
OWASCO L.
Apulia Sta.
Gorham
Halls Sta.
Varick
Farleys
Merryfield
Kelloggsville
Tully
Lebanon
Rushville
Earl
Venice Center
Bellona Sta.
Romulus
Aurora
Cascade
Glen Haven
Deruyter
Vine Valley
CANANDAIGUA LAKE
Angus
Kendaia
Genoa
Moravia
Middlesex
AUBURN & SYRACUSE ELEC. R.R.
AUBURN ELEC. R.R.
NEWARK & MARION RY.
SYRACUSE LAKE SHORE & NORTHERN R.R.
NEW YORK CENTRAL & HUDSON RIVER R.R.
LEHIGH VALLEY
DEL. LACK. & WEST'N R.R.
NEW YORK ONT. & WEST'N

TROLLEY TRIPS IN CENTRAL NEW YORK

ISSUED BY

ROCHESTER SYRACUSE & EASTERN R.R.
AUBURN & NORTHERN ELECTRIC R.R.
AUBURN & SYRACUSE ELECTRIC R.R.
SYRACUSE LAKE SHORE & NORTHERN R.R.
SYRACUSE & SOUTH BAY ELECTRIC R.R.
SKANEATELES LAKE TRANSPORTATION CO.

AMERICAN COLORTYPE CO. N.Y. CHI.

TRAVELECTRIC

The Story of the Rochester, Syracuse & Eastern Railroad and Associated Lines

by James R. McFarlane

Bulletin 143 of the Central Electric Railfans' Association

travElectric

The Story of the Rochester, Syracuse & Eastern Railroad and Associated Lines

by James R. Mc Farlane

Bulletin 143 of the Central Electric Railfans' Association

An Illinois Not-for-Profit Corporation
Post Office Box 503, Chicago, Illinois 60690, U.S.A.

CERA Bulletins are technical, educational references prepared as historic projects by members of the Central Electric Railfans' Association, working without salary due to their interest in the subject. This bulletin is consistent with this stated purpose of the corporation: To foster the study of the history, equipment and operation of electric railways.

travElectric was designed by Jack Sowchin. Production was coordinated by Bruce Moffat.

ISBN: 978-0-915348-43-5

Library of Congress
Control number: 2009942315

Preceding page:
Pen and ink sketch by George Krambles - 1943.

Introduction

"The Rochester, Syracuse & Eastern Railroad is a double-tracked high speed electric line, directly connecting Syracuse and Rochester, a distance of 86 miles. It is planned and equipped to maintain a fast and frequent service. It rivals in point of time many of the steam trains, excels most of them in convenience and all in economy. As the road traverses the main streets of numerous villages and towns, the traveler may alight at the very door of block, bank or residence without the annoyance of a long and costly transfer, while through passengers find central terminals in the heart of the principal cities. It should be a matter of congratulation that the interconnecting lines of the various electric railroads mentioned in this folder afford unusual facilities for cheap, safe and rapid travel, thus bringing into close touch the great population of Central New York."

Thus was the Rochester, Syracuse & Eastern described in the opening paragraph of the company's most elaborate travel folder, *Trolley Trips in Central New York,* issued in 1911. Most of the so-called Beebe Syndicate interurban lines appear to have fit into the somewhat theoretical category of an "electric interurban railroad" about as well as any electric railroad ever did. They connected two large centers of population and they operated predominately passenger service at high speeds over well-graded private right-of-way except for typical street operation in the terminal cities and through portions of intermediate towns and villages.

Most of the Beebe lines were designed for double-track operation and were built to steam road specifications. Passenger cars weighing 40 tons or more were to be the norm. Only two of the lines were finally completed as double-track roads, the 12-mile Syracuse & South Bay and the 86-mile Rochester, Syracuse & Eastern. The $184,000 per mile cost to construct and equip this latter line was more than the average cost of interurbans built in central and western New York state at that time. The carrying charges for such heavy capital costs were undoubtedly a contributing factor in the demise of all of the Beebe interurbans within a span of twenty-five years. An engineer from one of the bridge companies who supervised the dismantling of some of the steel bridges in the early 1930s remarked, " I am sorry to see these electric railroad companies going out of business after such a short life. I am sorry that we built them as well as we did. We might have saved some money by making all their structures of temporary construction."

It was mostly an uphill struggle for all the Beebe lines for three main reasons: First, the lines were built in direct competition with existing steam roads and, except for the South Bay line, their layouts prevented their handling quantities of carload freight in interchange with the steam roads. Second, the capital investment in each interurban was far too great for the road's earning capacity. Lastly, the electric interurban industry as a whole had the misfortune of being born in the same decade as the internal combustion engine. It has been said by some that if the electric interurban railroads had been able to get their feet solidly on the ground before the arrival of the automobile and hard-surfaced roads, they might have been a part of our national economy for a longer period of time.

Even so, interurbans like those of the Beebe Syndicate made their place and left their mark on American life. It was the electric railway that first introduced city people to the advantages of suburban living, and first offered farmers a chance to become better acquainted with their nearby towns.

The traveling salesmen early saw the conveniences offered by the interurban for expanding their territories into the smaller towns and villages. The interurbans offered a service filled with personality in a way the larger steam roads never could equal.

Here, then, is the story of the several Beebe Syndicate electric railways in central and western New York state during the first third of the twentieth century. They all added to the development of the area through which they ran.

This book's title ***TRAVELECTRIC*** [pronounced trav' electric] was created by the Beebe Syndicate's advertising department in 1915 when the syndicate's control of its interurban railroads was at its peak. ***TRAVELECTRIC*** continued to appear on timetables of the Rochester & Syracuse Railroad through 1925 and on those of the Empire State Railroad until the end of service in 1931.

I wish to dedicate ***TRAVELECTRIC***
to my late wife Sally (1928-2006),
my companion for over 56 years.

Acknowledgements

The major elements of this history were developed and written in the late 1950s and were included in a 1961 long out-of-print history of the Rochester, Syracuse and Eastern Railroad that I coauthored with the late William R. Gordon of Rochester, New York. I am grateful for a recent gift of Bill's copyright in his 1961 publication. With the recent encouragement of several interested friends, I have dusted off, updated and expanded some data that has developed since 1961. The electric interurban railroads in central and western New York state were high-class properties and their stories need to be told and recorded.

My present work is based on visits in the late 1930s and early 1940s with as many employees as I could find who still had keen memories of their association with the interurbans, including a few who were in service when the roads were first opened. Surviving railroad papers and reports of the individual lines have furnished technical data and statistical information. Early archaeological excursions through the car shops at Lakeland (near Syracuse) and Newark, a trip through the mostly vacant former general office space in Syracuse plus the then unoccupied Weedsport station together yielded many treasures.

Pictures and artifacts included here are from my collection unless otherwise identified. The photographers, if known, are noted.

1 wish to particularly thank the following individuals for their invaluable and enthusiastic assistance in making this work possible:

Shelden S. King, David S. Lanni, Charles R. Lowe and Charles C. and Carol Robinson, all associated with the New York Museum of Transportation (NYMT) at Rush, NY, George W. Shaw, Esq. of Penfield, NY, the late Edwin W. Leary, Esq., Cayuga County Attorney and finally my four late departed companions of the search for interurban lore, Jim Barstow, Larry Meloling and Bob Waters, all of the Syracuse area and Ray Gale of West Hartford, Connecticut.

Celia B. Jackson of Newark Historical Society and Tom Kirn of Rochester both kindly furnished material in connection with the operation of Rochester & Syracuse cars in the Rochester Subway.

Holly Sammons, Librarian at the Onondaga County Public Library in Syracuse provided much background information about the principal investors of the Beebe Syndicate lines.

Staff at the Registry of Deeds in Cayuga, Monroe, Onondaga, Oswego and Wayne Counties in New York state were helpful in making available old interurban railroad right-of-way plans and profiles.

Staff in the public libraries in Kalamazoo, MI and Liverpool, NY, and staff in the following historical societies were all most helpful in supplying important details and photographs: Old Brutus Historical Society, Weedsport, NY, Onondaga Historical Association, Syracuse, NY, Perinton Historical Society, Fairport, NY and Wayne County Historical Society, Lyons, NY.

James R. McFarlane
Cape Elizabeth, ME

The Beebe Syndicate

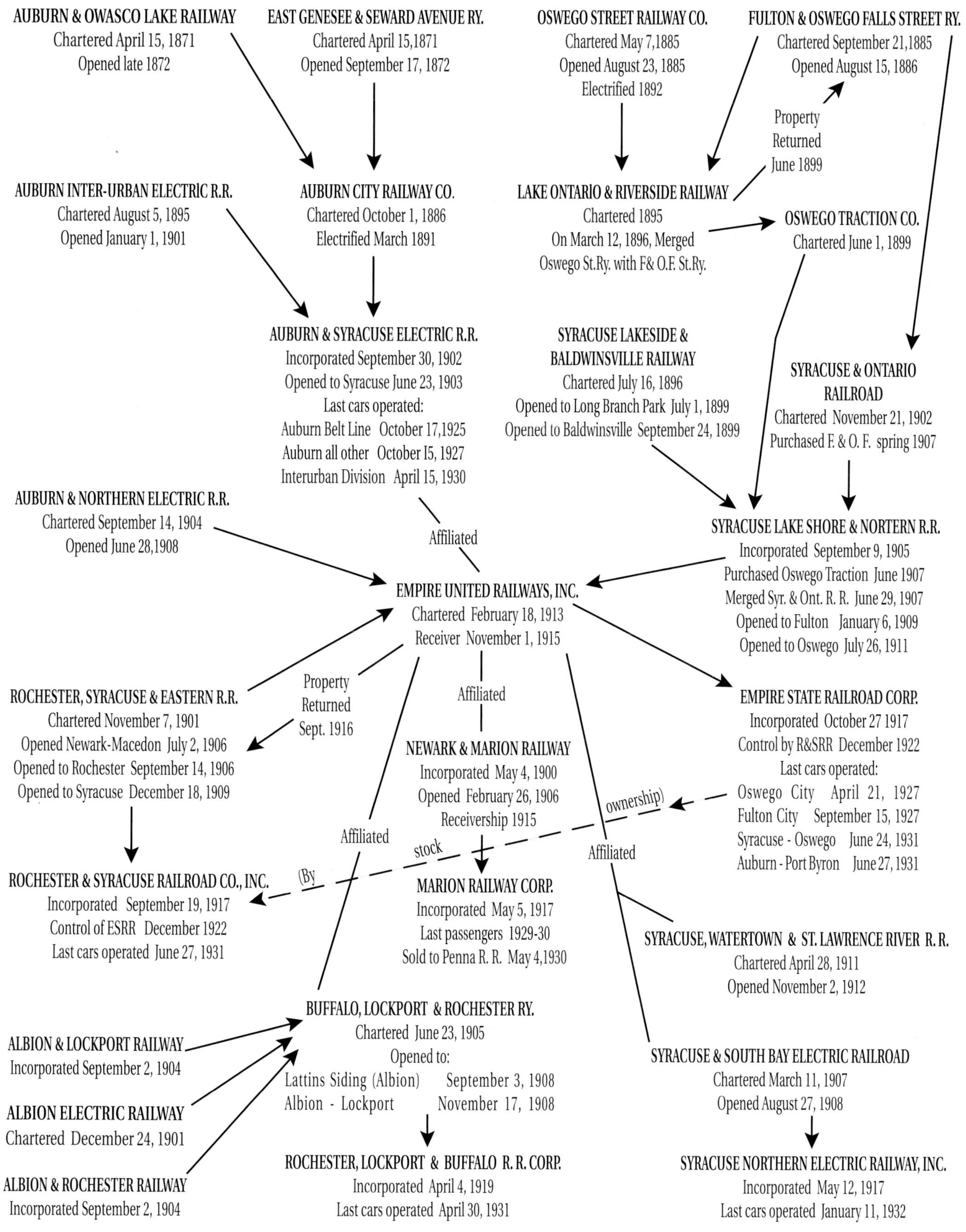

Table of Contents

Here Comes the Trolley 1

Rochester, Syracuse & Eastern Railroad
Empire United Railways
Rochester & Syracuse Railroad

Students of our country's transportation systems recognize that the route of the Erie Canal across the middle of New York state, between Albany on the Hudson River and Buffalo on the Great Lakes, opened one of the principal corridors for commerce between the east coast and the developing mid-west.

The 363-mile canal opened through in 1825. Many villages sprang up along the canal and quickly became part of the canal economy. The people, who lived and worked along the canal, and the local farmers, were generally content with their lot. Since the average speed of a canal boat was 1.5 miles per hour, the locals had little incentive to travel beyond a neighboring village.

All this life along the canal began to change in the1840s with the arrival of the railroads. By the 1890s, things were beginning to change considerably. The telephone was coming into common use which drew people and villages closer together. Small electric light plants were being built in the villages for local lighting purposes. Larger towns and cities were electrifying their horse car lines and people in small neighboring villages were having visions of local electric car lines along their main streets.

In the early 1900s, well-informed electrical engineers were learning how to generate large quantities of direct current electric power for street railway use, converting the dc to high voltage alternating current for transmission to distant points and then reconverting ac to dc for local street car use. Eventually, most of the local electric plants were replaced by purchasing power from nearby railways or by connections with long distance high tension transmission lines bringing power generated at Niagara Falls.

The desire by local citizens along the canal to improve their transportation facilities between Syracuse and Rochester came early. They made two attempts to connect the villages of Newark and Lyons by trolley. The Newark and Wayne County Traction Company was the first, being incorporated in June of 1894. The second was the Wayne County Traction Company, incorporated in August 1896 with a total capital of $60,000. Each company was organized by local people but neither developed beyond the planning stage. April 1900 saw the incorporation of the Newark Electric Railway. This was to be a local 5-mile line. A year later the Palmyra Electric

Facing page: *RS&E looking west as the tracks leave Main Street, Palmyra for Macedon, the next station west. Overhead is not in place in this 1906 view because of road relocation under way. Note the high-tension transmission line detour around the village is seen returning to the railway right-of-way at the eighth pole on the right-hand side. The Erie Canal and its tow path can be seen on the right.*

Above: *This is an interesting view of the old and new modes of transportation in 1906. In the background can be seen a "change bridge" over the Erie Canal. These bridges were located where the tow path changed from one side of the canal to the other. The bridges and ramps were designed so the mules hauling the boats could transfer from one side of the canal to the other without being unhitched from the tow line. In the foreground, westbound RS&E car 114 has just left Main Street, Palmyra, soon after the line was opened in the summer of 1906.*

The east span of RS&E Bridge 7 over the Erie Canal at Lyons, NY was under construction in early 1906 when this picture was taken. The false work in the canal left little room for barges to drift through. The towing mules were led through the timber maze on the tow path after which they were reattached to the tow line. Construction of a second span over adjacent Ganargua Creek had not yet begun.

Stop 12, Connor Road or Basket Road, was just due west of Fairport. The Erie Canal is just out of camera range on the right. The RS&E was brand new in this accident view dated October 15, 1906, just one month after the line was opened to Rochester (April 14, 1906.)

Railway with capital of $45,000 started building a 4.5-mile line east and west of town. Macedon, not to be left behind, raised $30,000 on paper to build a one-mile line from the village north to its West Shore Railroad station. The Newark and Macedon projects never went beyond the paper stage and no work of consequence was done at Palmyra.

Next came Charles A. Lux, a local business man in Clyde, New York, a village on the Erie Canal, midway between Rochester and Syracuse. He was interested in the coming use of electricity to light villages like Clyde and his interests soon expanded to include the new emerging electric railways. Lux became an agent for an unnamed syndicate early in 1901 and began acquiring street railway franchises for the syndicate, first in Clyde in March 1901, then in Lyons, Newark, Palmyra and Macedon. Finally, on November 4, 1901, a franchise for his newly formed Fairport Electric Railway was granted by the thriving village of Fairport (with a year 1900 population of about 2500.) The unnamed syndicate turned out to be the group of Syracuse businessmen and investors that became known as the Beebe Syndicate. They were the driving force that, in late 1901, created the Rochester, Syracuse & Eastern Railroad (RS&E). The syndicate's chief advance agent, Charles Lux, became an original director of the new railroad. He also was named Secretary of the company and remained in that position for the next 14 years. After agent Lux obtained the Fairport Electric franchise, it was turned over to the RS&E.

Charles Lux had competition during his efforts to acquire a satisfactory street railway franchise in Fairport. Local interests and Rochester investors had chartered the Monroe County Electric Belt Line (MCEBL) on July 5, 1901. The new company issued $230,000 worth of stock to construct an electric railway between Rochester and Fairport in the form of a loop through the intermediate towns of Brighton, Pittsford, Despatch (now East Rochester), and Penfield. The total planned line was to be 20 miles in length. The only track actually laid was for a few blocks in South Main Street, Fairport. However, no cars were ever operated over it. The RS&E was particularly interested in the MCEBL franchise for its 1.39 miles of right-of-way between the east village limits of East Rochester and the west village limits of Fairport and for its special right-of-way in Fairport village. In August 1902, "Consent from the State of

Just west of Fairport station, the RS&E tracks were adjacent to the Erie Canal tow path. This view shows the high board fence that was built so faster moving electric cars would not spook the mules towing barges. The canal can be glimpsed through the break in the fence.

New York Superintendent of Public Works" was granted for MCEBL to build within the Blue Line of the paralleling Erie Canal as far east as Mill Street. The Blue Line was the outer boundary of Erie Canal property. Village franchises to MCEBL covered the rest of Mill, John and Main Street occupancy. This "consent" from the state of New York solidified the RS&E position with respect to a clear route through Fairport. Stock control of the MCEBL was acquired by the RS&E in 1904.

Of interest is a portion of a revised franchise to operate through Fairport. Dated September 1905, it read in part, "that one car shall be run over the line on Main Street controlled by the Rochester, Syracuse & Eastern Railroad Company as far as Church Street not less than once each hour from six o'clock in the forenoon until eleven o'clock P.M., and that no extra fare shall be charged passengers of said Main Street line who are going to or from the main line of said company through Mill and John streets in said village and the service over said Main Street from John to Church Street shall commence within three months of the service over said Mill and John Street." The franchise finally granted by the village the following November did not contain the above clause, so that was as close as Fairport ever came to having local street car service.

The original route of the RS&E through Fairport was planned to make use of the MCEBL trackage in South Main Street. Cars from the west were to turn south into Main Street from Mill Street and run to a point just south of Church Street, thence easterly over private right-of-way for about a mile to a meeting with the line as actually built, just a few feet south of the bridge over the Erie Canal. Before construction had progressed very far, the main line route was changed to the John Street alignment and a major bridge was built to carry the electric cars over the Erie Canal just east of town. This route turned out to be far superior to the original street-running Main Street line with short radius curves at each end of the street and the prospects of a schedule-interrupting Main Street lift bridge over the developing Barge Canal alignment. John Street is now known as Lift Bridge Lane East and the 240-foot long Mill Street has become Lift Bridge Lane West.

For a very short distance just west of the RS&E's Fairport station at Mill Street, the car tracks ran very close to the Erie Canal. A high board fence was constructed along the towpath so the faster moving electric cars would not scare the mules pulling barges. In this same area, a mill and five houses were so close to the canal that only a single track could be laid. The property owner was reluctant to sell a 20-foot wide strip of land for anything less than $30,000 so the strip was condemned and the matter was settled in court for $5,064. The land owner was very slow to abide by the April 18, 1908 court order so eventually Track Supervisor Helmer Snow cut the offending buildings in half and had his work train clear the area. The second track was finally placed in service May 18, 1909. In May of 1916, the Monroe County Electric Belt Line was formally purchased by the Empire United Railways (successor to the RS&E) for $24,175.

During the electric railway construction through Fairport, everyone was in a hurry. Crews were hired to work nights preparing the grade for the west approach to the Erie Canal bridge just east of town. Many of the workmen lived in the area and while they liked being paid for night work, they also liked their sleep. So shortly after 9 P.M. and a couple of hours work, they would all walk home for the night. They would return shortly before 6 A.M. and

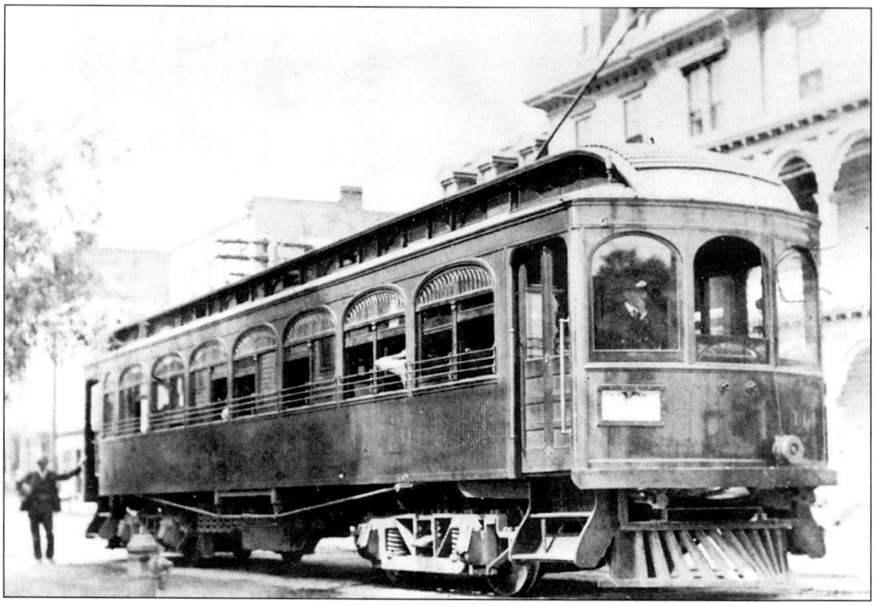

On opening day, August 18, 1906, the track in Lyons ended at the foot of Water Street. RS&E car 114 is standing in front of the Congress Hall House. By 1922, this house of lodging had been renamed Hotel Wayne.

The first Lyons passenger station was a leased store-front type. Note the baggage truck parked on the sidewalk. This eastbound RS&E car will proceed north one more block before turning east on Canal Street through a close clearance curve. Lack of autos in this view would suggest a 1906 or 1907 date.

shovel for a while. This went on for about ten days till the contractor sent a supervisor around to see why so little was being accomplished on this red-hot project. The party was over.

The RS&E was not the first suburban or interurban line to be built in the central and western New York area. The Syracuse, Lakeside & Baldwinsville Railway opened its 13-mile single-track side-of-the-road electric line from Syracuse, along the west shore of Onondaga Lake to Baldwinsville on September 24, 1899. The Rochester & Sodus Bay Railway opened its 39-mile mainly a side-of-the-road line from Rochester to Sodus Point on Lake Ontario in the summer of 1900. Finally, the 41-mile substantially-built Rochester & Eastern Rapid Railway ran its first heavy interurban cars to Canandaigua on November 15, 1903 and to Geneva on Seneca Lake June 15, 1904.

The Rochester, Syracuse & Eastern Railroad was incorporated under New York laws on November 7, 1901 for the purpose of constructing a high-speed double-track electric railroad between Rochester and Syracuse in central New York state. The line was promoted by Clifford D. Beebe of Syracuse and about a dozen prominent Syracuse business men, together known as the Beebe Syndicate. Location surveys were first run in 1902 and construction was begun in August of 1904. The road was opened in sections for regular scheduled service beginning with the 12-mile portion between Newark (32 miles east of Rochester) and Macedon on Monday July 2, 1906. Charles Soper was conductor and Morris Clark was motorman on car 110 on the initial trip. The first paying passenger was O. E. Fisk, for many years ticket agent for the RS&E at Palmyra.

Construction of the road was continued toward Rochester and at the same time was pushed eastward toward Syracuse. The line was completed and placed in operation as follows: Macedon to Egypt August 6, 1906, Lyons to Fairport 12 days later, Fairport to East Rochester (then called Despatch)

Bridge 13 - A 1908 picture of the bridge carrying the RS&E over the Erie Canal about two miles west of Port Byron. This view was looking east. For some reason the canal had been drained so the rip-rap along the off side of the canal can be clearly seen. This stonework helped protect the embankment from wash created by passing boats. It was about ten years before this section of the old Erie would be abandoned, to be replaced by the New York State Barge Canal on a different alignment several miles to the north.

on September 1, 1906, to Brighton one week later and finally to the Rochester city line at Culver Road on September 14, 1906. Here passengers made connection with the University Avenue cars of the Rochester Railway Company for the three-mile ride into the heart of the Flower City. RS&E cars began operating on Rochester streets July 1, 1907. The first 35 miles of line, from Lyons to Culver Road was now complete.

Building eastward from Lyons, the first cars were run to Clyde on September 1, 1907, to Savannah June 27, 1908 and finally across the treacherous Montezuma Marsh to Port Byron, 22 miles east of Lyons, on July 23, 1908. Connections were made at the latter point with the newly completed Auburn & Northern Electric Railroad for the 8-mile trip to Auburn. Syracuse-bound passengers then changed to cars of the Auburn & Syracuse Electric Railroad for the balance of the trip into Syracuse. On August 10 of the same year, the signal system on the single-track A&N was completed and operation of through RS&E cars between Rochester and Auburn was begun.

Through cars were never operated between Rochester and Syracuse via Auburn except in special service. The first of these special runs was made shortly after the road was opened. On July 29, 1908 at 5 A.M., a car in charge of conductor Jacob Loos and motorman Morris Clark left Rochester carrying a number of officers and guests of the railroad. The run to Syracuse was made in four hours. One purpose of the trip was to make running tests with an RS&E car under the new catenary construction of the associated Syracuse, Lake Shore & Northern Railroad south of Baldwinsville.

That these tests were satisfactory is evidenced by the fact that this type of overhead construction was used on 17 of the remaining 22 miles of the RS&E between Port Byron and Syracuse. RS&E cars entered Syracuse over the tracks of the Syracuse, Lake Shore & Northern from a connection at Lake Shore Junction, on the shore of Onondaga Lake, 4.4 miles northwest of the city. The RS&E was pronounced open for business Saturday December 18, 1909. The crew of the first car out of Syracuse consisted of Frank Emmel, motorman, and Walter Loos, conductor. The cars that day ran as far west as Port Byron where connections could be made with the then operating through cars between Auburn and Rochester. The first through cars between Syracuse and Rochester began the following day. Hourly service of local or Limited cars was scheduled.

The occasion of the line's completion called for a special car of the first order. On Thursday December 16, two days before the regular opening, a car loaded with nearly 50 railroad officers, engineers, bankers, newspaper men and other citizens left Syracuse for Rochester. Among those present were: Lyman C. Smith, President of the RS&E; Clifford D. Beebe, Vice President and General Manager; Willis A. Holden, Treasurer; Charles A. Lux, Secretary; William Nottingham, Attorney for the company; R. A. Dyer, Jr., Assistant General Manager; Senator Hendrick S. Holden and W. K. Pierce, both directors; J. Stanley Moore, General Passenger Agent and Thomas H. Mather, Chief Engineer. Some sort of speed record was set by this first official trip for they left Syracuse Terminal on Clinton Square at 10:30 A.M. and reached Culver Road in Rochester at exactly 12:49 P.M. The standard running time for Limiteds was first set at two hours and thirty minutes. This was later increased by ten minutes in the Empire United days.

An even faster time was recorded shortly after the Syracuse end of the RS&E was opened. According to *Electric Traction Weekly* for August 6, 1910, Mr. Dyer operated this special to test the speed possibilities of the main line. The train left the Rochester city line at Culver Road at 12:20 P.M. and made Lake Shore Junction at the Syracuse end, a distance of 80.25 miles in 1 hour and 46 minutes. This included one full stop and nine slowdowns in addition to slow running through eleven villages. One mile was clocked at 54 seconds (66.6 mph) and a continuous run of twelve and a half miles was made at an average speed of 64.75 miles per hour. This was done without laying out regular trains in any way.

Clifford D. Beebe
1866 - 1937

From W. R. Gordon Collection

Beebe Syndicate 2

and the Empire United Railways

Although the first president of the Rochester, Syracuse & Eastern Railroad was Lyman C. Smith of Syracuse typewriter fame, the chief promoter of the road was Clifford D. Beebe, also of Syracuse. Born in Sandusky, Cattaraugus County, New York state in 1866, Beebe grew up in Kalamazoo, Michigan. After about eight years of local banking experience in nearby Hastings, Michigan, Beebe arrived in central New York state in 1894. He cut his electric railway financing teeth as president and general manager of the Syracuse & East Side Railway, a 10-mile local street railway line in Syracuse. Beebe was just 28 years old at that time.

During the next few years, Beebe became active in several local trolley lines such as the Schuykill Valley Traction in Norristown, PA and the Geneva, Waterloo, Seneca Falls & Cayuga Lake Traction line in the Finger Lakes area of New York state. However, his interest in Syracuse local transit was soon dropped in favor of the electric interurban railroad field. The first member of Beebe's new railway family was the Auburn City Railway (a forerunner of the Auburn & Syracuse Electric Railroad) in 1899. Beebe entered into the affairs of other interurbans being promoted in the Syracuse and central New York area becoming associated with: the Syracuse, Lake Shore & Northern Railroad, the Syracuse & South Bay Electric Railroad, the Syracuse, Watertown & St. Lawrence River Railroad, the Auburn & Northern Electric Railroad, the Newark & Marion Railway and, in time, a couple of steamboat lines operating on neighboring Oneida and Skaneateles lakes. From 1911 to 1917, the Buffalo, Lockport & Rochester Railway was also under control of the Beebe offices in Syracuse. The entire operation was never gathered into one corporation but was loosely known as the Beebe Syndicate with common management.

In the case of all these roads, the Beebe Syndicate acquired control of virtually bankrupt companies. Beebe reorganized them and at the same time he improved and extended their physical properties. The Rochester, Syracuse & Eastern was different from its neighbors in that it was built from scratch by the Syndicate. It was Beebe's pride and joy. Unfortunately, for several reasons, it was the least successful financially.

Before going further into the history of the Beebe Syndicate, it would be well to learn more about the principal men who supported Beebe with their time and treasure. The original 1901 list of ten directors and major stockholders of the RS&E included Clifford Beebe and seven men of industry

Courtesy of The Old Brutus Historical Society

RS&E car 119, westbound, is approaching the Weedsport station, probably in the spring of 1910. The freight siding had not been constructed at that time.

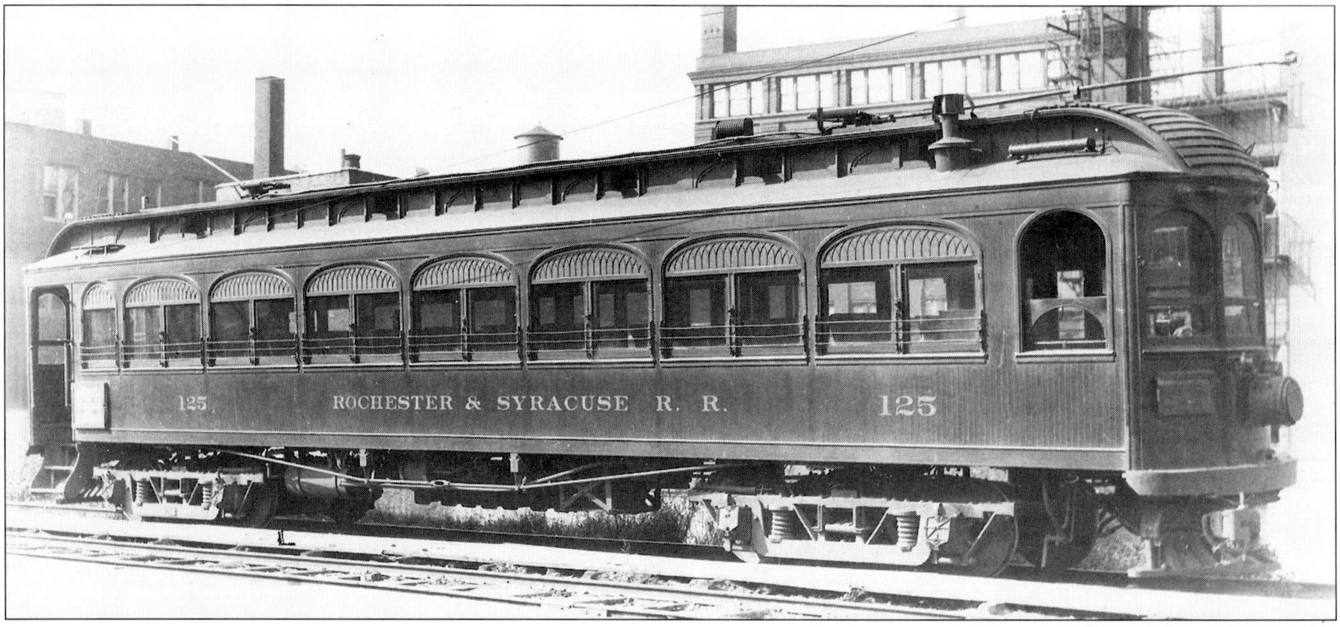

Walter A. Lucas, photographer

and financial prominence in the Syracuse area. Two directors hailed from other parts of New York state and one was from New Jersey. They were the nucleus of the Beebe Syndicate. Membership on the syndicate board changed from time to time. Some were active in the management of one or more of the six railroads until the syndicate collapsed late in 1915.

Lyman C. Smith, first president of the Rochester, Syracuse & Eastern Railroad, first became engaged in the manufacture of breech-loading firearms in 1877. In 1890, he left that type of business to organize the Smith Premier Typewriter Company. After his company had been purchased by a larger typewriter concern, Smith and his brothers organized the L. C. Smith & Brothers Typewriter Company in 1903. This later became the L. C. Smith & Corona Typewriter Company with head office and plant in Syracuse. Smith was a director of the local Halcomb Steel Company and president of a number of companies in New York state including Hudson Portland Cement Company of Hudson, NY and the National Bank of Syracuse. L. C. Smith was extremely interested in affairs involving Syracuse University. He was named Trustee of the University in 1896 and three years later was elected First Vice President of the Board. He completely funded and equipped a four-story limestone building to house the newly formed L. C. Smith College of Applied Science. The building was opened in 1904. Three years later, Smith funded and equipped the adjacent three-story Machinery Hall. L. C. Smith died November 5, 1910 at age 60.

Albert K. Hiscock was a son of the former United States Senator from New York, Frank Hiscock. He was an original member of the Beebe Syndicate and was first treasurer of the Rochester, Syracuse & Eastern, the Auburn & Syracuse, the Syracuse, Lake Shore & Northern and the Syracuse & South Bay railroads. Hiscock was also a managing director of the Auburn & Northern Electric Railroad and of the Oswego Traction Company. In addition, he was active in the Syracuse banking interests. He was president of the State Bank of Syracuse and vice-president of the Trust & Deposit Company of Onondaga. Albert Hiscock died unexpectedly on April 7, 1908 from complications following an operation. He was only 50 years old.

Willis A. Holden was also an original member of the Beebe Syndicate in 1901. He was made treasurer of the Rochester, Syracuse & Eastern, the Auburn & Syracuse, the Syracuse, Lake Shore & Northern and the Syracuse & South Bay railroads following the untimely death of treasurer Albert Hiscock. Holden was active in these positions until the collapse of the Empire United Railways in the fall of 1915. Willis Holden graduated from Syracuse University in 1880 with a B.S. degree and was in the coal business in Syracuse with his father and an uncle until 1905. With his older brother, State Senator Hendrick S. Holden, he took part in the advancement of banking and commercial enterprises both locally and in the western part of the country. Willis Holden was in his sixty-first year when he died of a heart disease September 28, 1916.

Hendrick S. Holden, the older brother of Willis, was a man of many interests in the industrial world, railroading, banking and publishing. He was owner of a large local coal business begun by his father, he was a director of the Solvay Process Company near Syracuse and was president of the Commercial National Bank of Syracuse. He owned docks and tidewater properties in Seattle, Washington and land on the Calumet River in the Chicago area. Holden had strong interests in Syracuse University and he was

Facing page: *Rochester & Syracuse car 125 is seen on the layover track at Erie Railroad station, Rochester, September 14, 1919. New lettering has been applied to the car but the old type destination boards have not been replaced with roller destination signs.*

Right: *A "last day" photograph taken in front of the R&S office building at Newark shops on the afternoon of Saturday, June 27, 1931. Reading from the left: Jess Elliott, Motorman, David E. Crouse, Chief Engineer, William C. Felton, Chief Substation Operator, Fred G. Mathes, Dispatcher, Alan P. Norris, Superintendent of Transportation and James M. Delaney, Chief Dispatcher.*

Courtesy of A. P. Norris, superintendent. D. E. Crouse Jr., photographer

instrumental in the establishment of the New York State College of Forestry at Syracuse. Holden Observatory on the university campus was named after him. Senator Holden served one term in the state legislature at Albany. As a director in the Beebe syndicate group, he was also active in the management of several of the syndicate lines. His last railroad related responsibility was as Receiver of the Syracuse – Oswego interurban line during its reorganization in 1916-17, and for a brief period he was president of the newly formed Empire State Railroad (1917-1918.) Senator Holden died November 10, 1918. He was 69 years old.

William Nottingham was a prominent lawyer and a partner in the firm Nottingham, Nottingham & Edgcomb in Syracuse. He was general counsel for the syndicate and was active in the legal affairs of all the Beebe lines from their 1901 beginnings through its reorganization period of 1917-1918. Nottingham was an 1876 graduate of Syracuse University. He was a president of the New York State Bar Association. He was a Trustee of the University from 1892 to 1902 and then became a member of the State Board of Regents. His particular interest at the University was promoting a College of Home Economics. William Nottingham died on January 23, 1921 from heart failure. He was 68 years old. His memory continues to this day in the form of the William Nottingham Junior-Senior High School in Syracuse.

William K. Pierce was active in the industrial development of Syracuse. In 1876, he entered the crockery manufacturing business with his father. Later, wholesale gas, water and steam fittings supplies were added, and by 1876 cast-iron boilers and radiators for home heating became the mainstay of Pierce Butler & Pierce Manufacturing Company. William Pierce organized the first electric light company in Syracuse in 1882. Afterward he became president of the Syracuse Heat and Power Company. In 1901, Pierce became associated with Clifford D. Beebe in the development of the Rochester, Syracuse & Eastern Railroad. Pierce served on the board of directors of several of the Beebe syndicate lines until his untimely death in April 1915. He was only 64 years old.

Albert E. Nettleton was founder and president of the A. E. Nettleton Shoe Company in Syracuse. As makers of fine men's shoes, the company enjoyed world wide sales up to the time of the Great Depression. Nettleton became a director of the Paragon Plaster Company in 1888 and of the Empire Savings & Loan Association in 1892. A year later he became president of the nearby Fulton Paper Company. He was a director of the National Bank of Syracuse and the Syracuse Trust Company. Nettleton was vice president of the Great Lakes Steamship Company and was a trustee of the Onondaga County Savings Bank. He was an original stockholder of the RS&E and was on the Beebe Syndicate's board from 1908 through 1915. Albert E. Nettleton died November 2, 1939 at age 89.

One of the original stockholders and directors of the RS&E was Ferdinand W. Roebling of Trenton, New Jersey. He was of the John A. Roebling family, the large wire and wire rope-making firm of Brooklyn Bridge fame. Perhaps Mr. Roebling's interest in the Beebe Syndicate was due to the 1600 plus miles of various sizes of wire that would be strung over the syndicate's five electric interurban lines being built in central New York state. Mr. Roebling was also listed as vice president of the Rochester, Syracuse & Eastern, the Empire United Railways and Syracuse & South Bay lines in the period 1908 – 1915. Ferdinand W. Roebling, and his elder brother Washington A. Roebling, took over the Roebling Wire

Onondaga Historical Association Museum & Research Center, Syracuse, NY.

Talmadge C. Cherry
1875 - 1941

Rope Works upon the death of their father John A. Roebling in 1869. In dividing the responsibilities for the work, Washington was the engineer and Ferdinand handled the commercial and administrative functions. He became secretary and treasurer of the company, renamed John A. Roebling's Sons Company and continued in that position as long as he lived. The business interests of Ferdinand Roebling were widespread. He was president of the Mercer Automobile Company, the Trenton Brass & Machine Company, Union Mills Paper Manufacturing Company and Universal Paper Bag Company. He was a director of the Otis Elevator Company, several local banks and the Trenton Hall & Building Association. His son, Ferdinand W. Roebling, Jr. followed in his father's footsteps in all of the above, and beginning in 1912, sat on the boards of all the Beebe Syndicate roads including the Buffalo, Lockport & Rochester Railway. As late as 1918, Roebling, Jr. was listed on the boards of the Auburn & Syracuse and the Syracuse Northern Electric railways. Ferdinand Roebling, Sr. died March 16, 1917 at age 75 and his son passed away May 29, 1936 at age 58.

Edwin D. Metcalf, a prominent manufacturer in Auburn, was an active member of the Beebe Syndicate board of directors between 1908 and 1914. He was a director and first president of the Auburn & Northern Electric Railroad, the 8-mile short line connecting Auburn with the RS&E at Port Byron. He was a director of the Auburn & Syracuse Electric Railroad and when the Empire United Railways was formed in 1913, Metcalf was made a vice-president and sat on its board. He resigned from his railroad duties in October 1914 because of ill health. He died December 31, 1915 at age 67. Edwin Metcalf had come to Auburn from Massachusetts in 1890 to be treasurer and general manager of the local D. M. Osborne Company, manufacturer of farm machinery. This company was later acquired by the International Harvester Company and Metcalf was made a member of its executive department. Metcalf was president of the Columbian Cordage Company and the Columbian Rope Company. He was a director of the Brown, Lipe, Chapin Gear Company of Syracuse and the Cayuga County National Bank of Auburn.

In 1911, General Manager Beebe replaced L. C. Smith, then deceased, as president of the RS&E. R. A. Dyer, Jr., Assistant General Manager, and really the chief operating officer of the company since its inception, was continued in that capacity. Beebe was a promoter and a financier, not really an operating man.

One supreme effort was made to relieve the RS&E financial plight by coupling it with the more successful Syracuse, Lake Shore & Northern and the Auburn & Northern lines. The Empire United Railways, Inc. (EUR) was formed February 18, 1913. Beebe was the new company's president and Dyer became the general manager. In April 1914, Dyer was replaced by Ernest Gonzenbach, brought in from the Sheboygan Railway & Electric Company of Sheboygan, Wisconsin.

At its height in 1915, the Beebe Syndicate controlled 28 different companies. Each had been organized for a different purpose. The system was designed so financial problems of any one company would not affect the financial structure of the others. This was typical in railroad construction where the failure of a branch line would not bring down the main line. Here are the 28 companies under Beebe Syndicate control on May 1, 1915:

- American Light, Power & Transportation Company
- Auburn & Northern Construction Company
- Auburn & Syracuse Construction Company
- Auburn & Syracuse Electric Railroad Company
- Buffalo, Lockport & Rochester Railway Company
- Edgecliff Park Company
- Electric Terminal Association
- Empire United Railways, Inc.
  - Auburn & Northern Electric Railroad Company (*)
  - Rochester, Syracuse & Eastern Railroad Company (*)
  - Syracuse, Lake Shore & Northern Railroad Company (*)
- Inter-State Financing and Construction Company
- Newark & Marion Railway Company
- The Hudson Finance Company
- The Monroe County Electric Belt Line Company
- The Ontario Construction Company
- The Syracuse Railroad Construction Company
- Warren Street Realty Company
- Interurban Publishing Company
- Newark, Williamson & Northern Railroad Company, Inc.
- Oneida Lake Terminal Company
- Onondaga Amusement Company
- Rochester Belt Line Company
- Sagamore Navigation Company
- Skaneateles Lake Transportation Company
- Syracuse & South Bay Electric Railroad Company
- Syracuse Terminal Association
- Syracuse, Watertown & St. Lawrence River Railroad Company

(*) These companies did not lose their corporate identity when they were folded into the Empire United and they actually outlived the EUR.

The Empire United was still way overcapitalized and on November 1, 1915 it found itself in receivership. Former State Senator Hendrick S.

Holden and C. Loomis Allen of Allen & Peck, Inc. (engineers and utilities managers) were appointed Receivers. At this time both Beebe and Gonzenbach retired from the active management of the Syndicate lines. Talmadge C. Cherry replaced Gonzenbach as general manager. Beebe remained in the Syracuse area until 1919 when he left to pursue real estate development interests in the New York City area. In 1935, he returned to Kalamazoo. He suffered a sudden heart attack and died at his home February 17, 1937. Beebe was 71 years old.

In 1916, Gonzenbach was appointed manager and then receiver of the faltering Syracuse & South Bay Electric Railroad and the Syracuse, Watertown & St. Lawrence River Railroad. His services ended a year later when these lines were reorganized as the Syracuse Northern Electric Railway, Inc.

In September 1916, the RS&E property had been taken out of the Empire United receivership and was reorganized separately. Loomis Allen remained as receiver until the new company was formed. The engineering firm of Allen & Peck took over R&S management. The Allen & Peck team was headed by Talmadge C. Cherry. He brought with him several key railroad men who remained with the reorganized Rochester & Syracuse, the Auburn & Syracuse, the Syracuse Northern Electric and, after December 1922, the Empire State Railroad. Alan P. Norris was in charge of train operations and David E. Crouse was head of roadway, power and equipment departments as Chief Engineer. A third key member of the Cherry team was Walter K. Zinsmeister. He started as an auditor for the Beebe Syndicate in 1910 and continued in various financial capacities including Treasurer through the end of all electric railway operations in 1932.

On March 15, 1918, the Allen & Peck firm was reorganized as Peck-Shannahan-Cherry, Inc. engineers and managers of public utilities. Cherry became the central figure in the management of all the reorganized companies and he remained so until the end of their liquidations in 1936. Cherry, born in 1876, was a civil engineer. His previous railroad experience, mostly management, included service with the Syracuse Rapid Transit Railway in their Track Department, and in management positions on the Buffalo & Lake Erie Traction, the Utica & Mohawk Valley, the Schenectady Railway and the Annapolis Short Line in Maryland.

The Empire United was sold at foreclosure on August 28, 1917 and its component roads were reorganized separately. On September 19, 1917, the Rochester-Syracuse Division became the Rochester & Syracuse Railroad, Inc. On October 27, 1917, the Syracuse-Oswego and Auburn–Port Byron Divisions became the Empire State Railroad Corporation.

Charles R. Lowe collection

RS&E car 112 is westbound at an unknown local stop in the Rochester - East Rochester area. The conductor appears to be standing in the front end behind the partially closed door. This suggests that the car was being held for an early and a great photo-op.

Courtesy of New York Museum of Transportation

Left: *Westbound R&S car 100 loading passengers at Lyons station in the mid 1920s. The blank panel behind the motorman indicates that this car was originally built with two sliding baggage doors at one end.*

Facing page: *R&S line car 64 is seen standing on the westbound main at Newark shops. The car and crew patrolled the line for about a month after the June 27, 1931 cessation of service to discourage theft of copper wires. Shown from left are Fred Mathes, Dispatcher, Joe Romer, Lineman and Bert Garrett, Master Mechanic. The photographer was W. C. Felton, Chief Substation Operator.*

RS&E Finances

As originally chartered, the Rochester, Syracuse & Eastern Railroad was authorized to issue $1,000,000 of capital stock. In 1905, the New York State Board of Railroad Commissioners consented to an increase in capital stock to $3,500,000. At that time, it was found necessary to bond so $5,000,000 of 5% gold bonds was issued. The bonds were, of course, secured by a first mortgage on the entire physical property including rolling stock. These stock and bond figures were increased as construction proceeded. The total assets of the company as of June 30, 1912 were $14,775,000 of which $14,600,000 represented the cost of road and equipment. Against these assets the company had outstanding $6,000,000 in common stock and $2,500,000 in 6% preferred stock. It had $5,000,000 in 5% gold bonds and $950,000 in three-year notes. Revenues increased rapidly as sections of the road were completed and placed in operation. During the twelve month period ending June 30, 1912, more than 4,337,000 revenue passengers were carried. The gross revenue for the period was a shade over three quarters of a million dollars. Operating expenses accounted for 49 cents of each dollar earned and the balance was taken up by interest on the bonded indebtedness and three-year notes (totaling $318,750 annually), taxes and rental for track and terminal facilities. This left nothing for the stockholders except a $68,000 deficit which had accumulated over the previous five years. The company had a bottom line net income for only three years – 1908, 1910 and 1911 – and then only in the neighborhood of $2,000 per year.

The RS&E was consolidated with the Syracuse, Lake Shore & Northern Railroad and the Auburn & Northern Electric Railroad on February 18, 1913 to form the $22,500,000 Empire United Railways, Inc. The new company assumed the bond and short term obligations of the three underlying roads totaling $9,237,000. Old stock certificates were replaced with new EUR certificates for total capital stock of $11,600.000. In this exchange, the value of RS&E stock was written down by about 13%. The holders of A&N common received only 12.5 cents on the dollar in new certificates. Since the SLS&N was considered by management to be the strongest road of the three being consolidated, their stock holders received new certificates of the same value as the old.

The new company spruced up its passenger service. It became more active in soliciting freight movements, both local and interline. It worked on containing its operating expenses. For the year ending June 30, 1913, the Empire United carried 8,936,000 passengers. Revenue from passengers was $1,291,000, from milk and express $68,000 and from all other operating sources $57,000 for a total operating revenue of $1,416,000. With all of this, however, the Empire United simply couldn't generate enough income to cover expenses including the quarterly mortgage payments of $123,000. The result was receivership and sale of the company at a foreclosure sale on August 28, 1917 for $1,000,000.

Rochester & Syracuse Railroad

On September 19, 1917, the Rochester & Syracuse Railroad Company, Inc. came into being with a much more realistic financial structure. Capital values were slightly less than half of those of the RS&E in 1912. Outstanding stocks and bonds of the new company totaled $6,500,000. Properties and franchises were valued at slightly less than $7,000,000. Annual interest charges on the bonded indebtedness was $125,000. On this basis, the company soon showed a modest profit. During the four year period beginning with 1921, it paid a 1% quar-

W. C. Felton, Lyons, NY, photographer

terly dividend on the nearly $2,500,000 of preferred stock. The holders of common stock of the R&S received nothing during the life of the company.

In December 1922, the Rochester & Syracuse acquired control of the neighboring Empire State Railroad (successor corporation to the foreclosed Empire United Railways) through stock purchase. This acquisition was a common sense move that was mostly a transfer of stock ownership. The two railroads had a great deal in common such as joint property use, trackage rights and common managers at the operating level, but because of separate reorganization plans, each company had a different engineering-management firm. Some savings were immediately possible. The managers of the R&S, Peck-Shannahan-Cherry, Inc., assumed the ESRR work and Ford, Bacon & Davis, managers of the Empire State were dismissed. Alexander H. Cowie, president of the R&S then became president of the Empire State Railroad as well.

Alexander H. Cowie was a Syracuse attorney and an outstanding authority on corporation law. A partner of the firm Hiscock, Cowie, Bruce and Lee, Cowie was a general counsel for many central New York businesses including the Syracuse Savings Bank, Bank of East Syracuse and First Trust & Deposit Corporation. He was local counsel for the New York Central Railroad. He was also a director of the Auburn & Syracuse and the Syracuse Northern Electric lines. Cowie was actively involved in the 1931-1939 liquidations of both the Rochester & Syracuse and the Empire State railroads. Alexander H. Cowie remained active as an attorney in Syracuse until shortly before his death July 6, 1948 at age 75.

By 1927, deficits were again beginning to creep into the books of the R&S and on May 12, 1930, T. C. Cherry was appointed its receiver. The end came on June 12th in the following year when the company was sold under foreclosure proceedings to the R&S Liquidating Corporation for $115,000. Right up till the end there were flickers of hope for the employees and patrons of the line. Some talk was heard of the Pennsylvania Railroad purchasing the property so as to gain access to both Rochester and Syracuse from their Northern Central line at Newark but nothing came of it. As a last-ditch effort to save the company, the officers and employees all took a 10% cut in wages and the operating men seriously considered purchasing the business. It was all too late. The revenue traffic was just not there and the carrying charges were too great. All operations were discontinued with the running of the last cars on June 27, 1931 and the property was dismantled.

The overhead was kept "hot" for a few months to discourage pilferage of the copper. The railway was torn up from Rochester eastward toward Newark and from Port Byron westward. Line car 50 and various freight motors hauled gondolas from the West Shore Railroad track interchange east of Newark to pick up rail and scrap. The line east of Port Byron was dismantled eastward toward Syracuse by gangs out of Lakeland shops. The scrap metals in that section were hauled to a freight interchange with the Lackawanna Railroad at Lake Shore Junction.

In the summer of 1932 the work was completed. By the end of 1937, the last of the assets had been distributed and the R & S Liquidating Corporation was dissolved.

LOCAL
FOR
ROCHESTER
117

3 A Great Interurban Is Built

The Rochester, Syracuse & Eastern Railroad was one of the finest examples of electric interurban railroad construction to be found anywhere. The entire line was double-tracked, and apart from street operation through eight villages and the terminal cities, the roadway was located entirely on private right-of-way. Generally speaking, the right-of-way strip was 100 feet or more in width and it was owned in fee simple. There were no grade crossings with steam railroads except for one crossing of a New York Central industrial spur on John Street in Fairport. A grade crossing with the New York Central RW&O (later St. Lawrence) Division in Syracuse was on Syracuse, Lake Shore & Northern tracks over which RS&E cars operated. There were ten grade separations with highways, three with the principal east-west New York state highways, five were road underpasses and two were road overpasses.

Grades on private rights-of-way were in accordance with the best steam railroad practices. The average of the grades across the whole line was 1%. Only three short approaches to major bridges were as steep as 4%.

The RS&E was exceptionally free from sharp curves thus making a high-speed operation possible. Although over 56 miles of the road were straight, the longest single tangent was only 4.16 miles between Warners and Lake Shore Junction. There were thirteen locations where the road was straight for over a mile.

The sharpest curves on the line were one of 55-foot radius from Water Street onto the canal bridge at the west end of Lyons and one of 75-foot radius at Main and Union streets in Newark. The majority of curves outside the municipalities were under 4 degrees with a few scattered exceptions of 6 or 8 degrees, there was only one at 10 degrees. This latter curve was part of a reverse curve as the electric road passed under the West Shore Railroad just west of Fairport.

The Syracuse Railroad Construction Company (one of the Beebe syndicate companies) was the general contractor for the entire job of building the RS&E. Sub-contractor J. G. White & Co. of New York City did the grading, track laying and overhead work between Rochester and Lyons with subcontracts going to Fred T. Ley & Co. of Springfield, Massachusetts and John Shields Construction Company of New York for parts of White's work. I. M. Luddington

Facing page: *RS&E car 117, westbound at Warners station, was signed "Local for Rochester." Line car 50 and crew joined in this picture. Warners was an open agency station 10 miles west of Syracuse.*

Charles R. Lowe collection

This is a Beebe Syndicate portrait of its brand new cars on its brand new railroad. This picture of cars 123 and 126 was taken in the spring of 1910 on the RS&E westbound main at mileage 73.86 (measured from Rochester), just west of Stop 91, Memphis, or about 12 miles west of Syracuse. The caption of a July 1910 company publicity piece stated: "The Rochester, Syracuse & Eastern Railroad is now operating trains by multiple unit control systems, as shown in the above cut. This gives a train with one thousand horsepower, capable of going sixty-three miles an hour."

Courtesy of Perinton Historical Society

This eastbound car has just passed under the West Shore Railroad and is climbing a 2.5-percent grade toward Fairport. The West Shore embankment can be seen in the background. The structural steel frame work in the distant left supported the RS&E duplicate transmission line over the West Shore right of way.

This 1920s right-of-way scene is looking west toward Stop 94. Warners village is seen in the far distance. Tie replacements were scattered here. Tie plates were not generally used on the Rochester & Syracuse.

Here the RS&E ducked under the West Shore Railroad main line on a 10-degree curve, about a mile west of Fairport station. The view is looking toward East Rochester.

David S. Lanni collection

One of the RS&E "short cars" (97-99 series) in the Rochester - Fairport stub or suburban service. Stop 7 was at Maplewood, an old-time picnic area close by East Avenue Extension, Rochester. This picture probably dates close to the road's opening, September 14, 1906. Several of the centerline grade stakes and freshly cut embankments can be seen.

RS&E car 116 is westbound approaching Stop 17 (Hogan's Alley), 2.7 miles east of Fairport. Block signal 14 and Egypt village are in the background. Note the light box on the near pole for patrons to flag passing local cars.

Charles R. Lowe collection

of Rochester constructed the roadbed east of Lyons to Stop 86, east of Jordan. I. A. Hodge & Company completed the line to a connection with the Syracuse, Lake Shore & Northern Railroad at Lake Shore Junction.

As was pointed out, plans of the RS&E called for a heavier class of construction than was found on many steam roads. On sections of the road where grading was light, the work was done with horses, wheel scrapers and wagons. On heavier sections, steam shovels were employed. Gravel for ballast was obtained for the most part from pits located along the line. The major one at Egypt was in service as long as the company existed.

As sections of the new electric road were

Concrete pavements came early to village streets along the Rochester & Syracuse Railroad. In the summer of 1921, the New York State Commission of Highways paved the entire length of Palmyra's Main Street. The railroad's portion, 19 feet wide and 0.9 miles long, was paved with brick. Single-track operation prevailed during the construction work.

Paving on Water Street, Lyons, in July 1921, looking east toward Williams Street. This was one of the recurring expenses of having interurban tracks in village streets.

graded, the first track was laid in skeleton form. Steam locomotives were very much in evidence all up and down the line hauling ties, rail, other track material, ballast, poles and finally stringing the overhead wires. The second track was built completely, after which the first one was finished.

Tracks were laid on 12-foot centers (10-foot centers in the village streets), the steel rails coming in 60-foot lengths. Each weighed 70-pounds-to-the-yard. Rail in village streets was 90-pounds-to-the-yard. ASCE section T-rails, connected with "continuous joint" angle bars, were standard on the RS&E. Joints were laid staggered. The paving around the track in the villages was brick on ballast of local stone or poured concrete. Originally the cross ties were untreated longleaf yellow pine laid on 24 inch centers. The rails were bonded with 300,000 cm (circular mils) copper bonds soldered to each rail head.

Tracks through the villages were generally laid down the center of the streets. One interesting variation of this alignment was found in Macedon. As the two tracks entered the village from the west, they were laid to each side of the street and were about 32 feet apart. The traveled way was down the middle for a half mile through the residential section of town. Then the tracks resumed their 10-foot centers through the "downtown" section. Total occupancy of the public way through Macedon was only eight tenths of a mile. Possibly this variation from standard track location was due to local political pressure.

The numerous highway and country road crossings at grade were protected by a rather distinctive metal crossing sign, common to all the Beebe lines. Normally there was only one sign at each crossing. At the time the line was being constructed between Lyons and Clyde, a rather unique method of rail distribution was used by contractor I. M. Luddington. He completed the subgrade before snow time. Then, teams and bobsleds hauled the rails over frozen grade to proper location. This method proved to be less expensive than using locomotives to push strings of rail cars. When con-

Top picture courtesy of Wayne County Historical Society

There were two close clearance curves in the village of Lyons, one at each end of Williams Street. Here are views looking west up Water Street from the corner of Williams Street - top in 1906 and bottom in 1908. The 1922 track relocation in the old Erie Canal bed eliminated both sharp and close clearance curves.

Edgar Y. Pattison, photographer

Where possible, street running through the villages east of Lyons was avoided. This is a 1922 view of the R&S right-of-way, looking east across Main Street, Port Byron.

This real photo postcard shows the RS&E right-of-way slicing through Port Byron village. The passenger station, fronting on Main Street, is in the center of the image on the left-hand side of the tracks. A westbound car shown was making a station stop and an Auburn & Northern car was standing next to the station. The Erie Canal is seen diagonally across the upper right-hand corner of the picture.

Westbound RS&E car 117 is seen leaving the short stretch of street running in Weedsport village near Brutus Street station. This picture was taken about 1910, before the motorman's operating position was moved over to the right-hand side of the vestibule.

Courtesy of The Old Brutus Historical Society

This 1910 postcard view shows a westbound RS&E car about to leave Clinton Street in Jordan for its private right-of-way. Note the company's two high-tension transmission lines accompanied the 500 feet of track through the streets of the village.

struction reached Clyde, and car service from Rochester first began, a temporary wye was constructed east of the station to turn the cars because, where possible, the company preferred to operate their double-end cars with the smoking compartment forward.

One of the most miserable and unexpected pieces of construction difficulty encountered was a sink hole east of Clyde where the line crossed Black Creek at Bridge 8, MP 49. In this marshy area, over 100,000 cubic yards of material was dumped into a seemingly bottomless hole a half-mile long. So much fill was used to gain a solid foundation that the muck displaced raised the level of the marsh all around the fill for a considerable distance. Curiously enough, the second crossing over Black Creek two miles further east offered no such resistance.

The crossing of the Montezuma Marsh (now known as Montezuma National Wildlife Refuge), east of Savannah was costly but was at least planned for. In addition to an extensive earth and rock fill at the west end, a 28-span deck plate girder bridge on concrete piers carried the tracks across 1512 feet of swamp and the Seneca River.

Street operation was more prevalent on the

western end of the line. RS&E cars operated through Commercial and Chestnut streets in East Rochester, through Mill and John streets in Fairport, along practically the entire length of Main Street in both Macedon and Palmyra, for nearly a mile-and-a-half in South Main and Union streets in Newark, as well as approximately a half-mile through Water, Williams and Canal streets in Lyons. This last street running was considerably shortened in 1922 when a relocation of the line through the abandoned Erie Canal bed left only 1000 feet of track in Water Street. East of Lyons, street running was limited to one block on Brutus Street in Weedsport so as to pass under the Lehigh Valley Railroad and to a few hundred feet in Clinton Street, Jordan. Of course, cars ran in the streets of both Rochester and Syracuse but not over their own tracks.

As the RS&E was being built, three physical track connections were established with the neighboring West Shore Railroad. One was at Stop 12 west of Fairport village, the second was nearly 2 miles east of Newark and the third was just west of the long bridge across the Montezuma Marsh. Materials for the construction of the road were delivered at these

One of the RS&E "short" cars (97,98 or 99), eastbound, making a station stop in Macedon. It is always amazing to see how wide the main streets of these villages were. This post card was postmarked September 30, 1908, over a year before the railroad was completed to Syracuse.

Facing page: *A postcard view of a westbound RS&E car that had just left Jordan station, was crossing Main Street and would enter Clinton Street for a few hundred feet before entering its private right-of-way.*

Right: *RS&E freight and express car 68 is seen in work train service at the Egypt gravel pit, just 0.8 miles east of Egypt village. Of several gravel pits opened during the road's construction, this one at Egypt was the only one in continuous service during the life of the railroad.*

David S. Lanni collection

points. The Fairport and Montezuma interchanges did not last long after the line was completed. The one east of Newark was used extensively for coal delivery to the Newark car shops and the delivery of rolling stock. It was the last piece of the Rochester & Syracuse Railroad west of Port Byron to be torn up in 1932.

When sidings and crossovers on the RS&E were laid out, they were so arranged that cars operating with the current of traffic on the double track would always trail through the switches. Station sidings were located in nearly every village and there were approximately 32 crossovers along the line. The location of these latter varied somewhat depending on the needs of the service, but in all possible instances, facing point movements were avoided. Adherence to this policy created some complicated track work, particularly at Savannah, Weedsport and Jordan. At these stations, the buildings were so located with respect to the main line that it was necessary for freight motors to make a switchback move in order to come alongside the freight platforms. The standard turnouts on the RS&E had 15-foot points and number 8 spring-rail frogs.

Eastbound car passing Egypt (Stop 18). Building on the left of the shelter was the Egypt Cannery. This was the only on-line industry served by a siding on the RS&E. The cannery was later owned by the Comstock Canning Company of Newark, NY.

David S. Lanni collection. Brunner Brown, photographer.

This appears to be a special eastbound move somewhere between Egypt and Macedon on the RS&E, c1908.

There were few sidings along the line other than those at the stations. There was, of course, one at the Egypt gravel pit. There was also a siding into the Egypt Canning factory. A short storage track was located at Stop 24 just west of Macedon. A short spur at Stop 49 ran into the tie yard where ties brought in by canal boat were stored. In the early years, a siding served Horton gravel pit just west of Stop 62 and there was a short spur at Stop 69 at Montezuma. These last two were removed before World War I.

With the exception of the Egypt Canning factory track, there were no industrial sidings on the RS&E. The Syracuse, Lake Shore & Northern road had a physical track connection with the Lackawanna Railroad at Lake Shore Junction. There were a number of steam road freight connections in the Rochester Subway system , but none of these connections were of much use to the RS&E because it could not handle revenue carload freight traffic.

When the RS&E was first projected, its promoters announced that they wanted the shortest possible route between Rochester and Syracuse. They wanted one that could be maintained at minimum cost and still give the steam roads a run for their money in terms of elapsed time between terminals. They saw some measure of success. The RS&E was only 6 miles longer than the New York Central main line and it was 2 miles shorter than the highway routes, yet the electric was the last to choose its location. The interurban's Limited running time of 2:43 in the period 1917-1927 compared very favorably with the time of New York Central trains making a comparable number of intermediate stops. Thus the RS&E was aptly labeled "Electric Short Line."

The caption on this 1922 company photograph reads: "Unloading 35,000 creosoted long-leaf yellow pine ties at Lock 28A Barge Canal." The ties arrived by steamer and barge from Jacksonville, Florida. In this view looking southeast from the canal,the R&S main line lies just beyond the piles of ties. Lyons station is two miles to the east. 3500 of these ties were used in the construction of the main line relocation through Lyons. The rest of them were for general track maintenance across the system.

Track Changes

Only two track changes were ever made to improve alignment and reduce running time on the R&S. The first was at Lyons in the fall of 1922 when a 3066-foot long diversion was constructed in the abandoned bed of the Erie Canal through the village. This new route eliminated three sharp curves and considerable street running so that 4 minutes were cut from the cars' schedule. Fill for construction of the double-track road bed came from the extensive accumulation of cinders at the company's nearby power house. A 1700-foot spur was built along the company's power line detour right-of-way from the main line to the cinder pile. Four side-dumping ballast cars were leased to move the 12,000 cubic yards of cinders. An additional 8000 yards of earth were required to complete the job. The total cost of the improvements was about $40,000, of which $10,000 represented the cost of the new combination passenger and freight station. The project was completed and opened for business in late December 1922.

The second change was a 1928 track diversion that brought the R&S passenger cars into the City of Rochester's new $12,000,000 City Subway. A 500-foot long double-track tunnel was constructed under the New York Central's Auburn Branch and East Avenue, beginning at the R&S Rockwood Street (City Line) stop. R&S cars entered the subway at its Winton Road station. The $190,000 cost of the tunnel, its approaches, track, overhead wires and signal work was borne by the City. All train movements

Pictures presented in pairs on pages 33-38 show work in progress as the R&S constructed a 3,066-foot diversion of its main line around the street running through Lyons village. New tracks and a station were placed in the abandoned bed of the Erie Canal. The pictures show the project beginning at the west or Williams/Water street end and advancing eastward to a connection with the original main line east of the village. The top pictures of each pair were taken in September 1922 and the lower views were made in following April. The new line was placed in service in December 1922.

Only half of the canal's width was required to accommodate the first class double-track line.

Most of the necessary fill for the new road bed came from the cinder piles at the company's power house, little more than one track mile away.

in the Subway were governed by block signals including those on the R&S at its Rockwood Street point of main line divergence. Eight minutes were sliced off the running time and four miles of street running in Rochester were eliminated for the passenger cars. The official mileage of R&S cars on subway tracks were:

Rockwood St. connection with R&S main line	0.00	mile
Winton Road station connection with subway main line	0.36	mile
Monroe Avenue station	1.93	mile
City Hall station	3.83	mile
Center of Oak Street turning loop	4.41	mile

Looking east from Church Street toward Geneva Street and the site of a standard RS&E type "A" passenger and freight station. This type building had a bay window facing the tracks.

Looking west across Geneva Street toward the freight house end of the new station in April 1923. The floor plan of the standard station is from Electric Railway Journal V61 N5 1923.

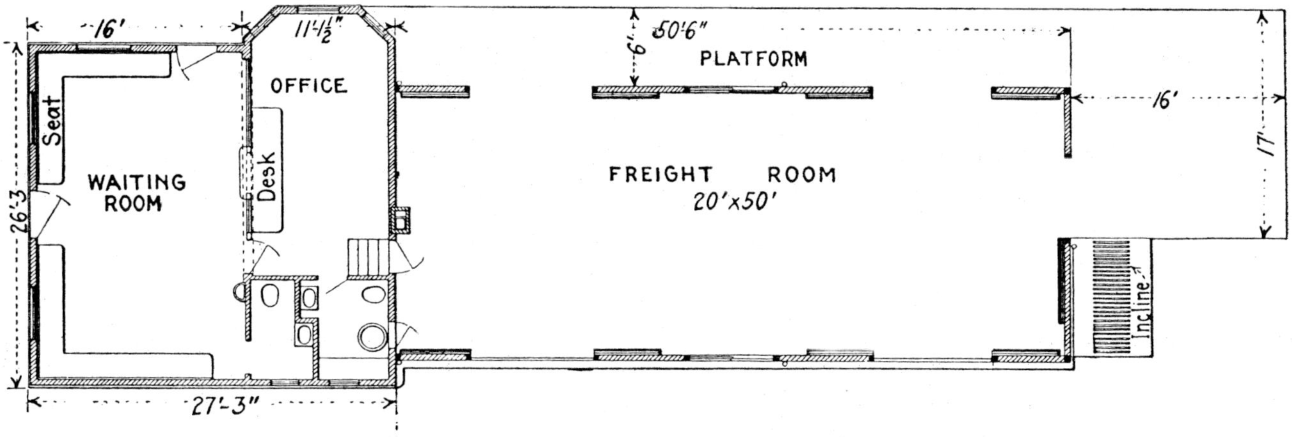

Plan of Passenger and Freight Station, Standard for Certain Types of Station on R. & S. R.R.

Track space was available at City Hall station for the storage of R&S cars during layover times. The first R&S car entered the Rochester Subway on April 15, 1928. Electric freight cars of all of Rochester's interurban lines, including the R&S, continued to use Rochester city streets in order to reach the joint Electric Freight Terminal located on Frank Street at the rear of the New York State Railways State Street car barn.

The Rochester Rapid Transit & Industrial Railway (Subway), first opened on December 1, 1927, consisted of tracks laid in the abandoned bed of the old Erie Canal through the city. The subway had been designed and built to relieve traffic congestion in the downtown area by reducing some of the local street car traffic and by removing the passenger cars of three interurban lines from the city streets. The subway layout consisted of a double-

The side track reaching the freight house was longer than usual because of the Geneva Street crossing and curve required to reach the freight platform. In the distance can be seen the main line crossover that always accompanied side tracks on the Beebe lines.

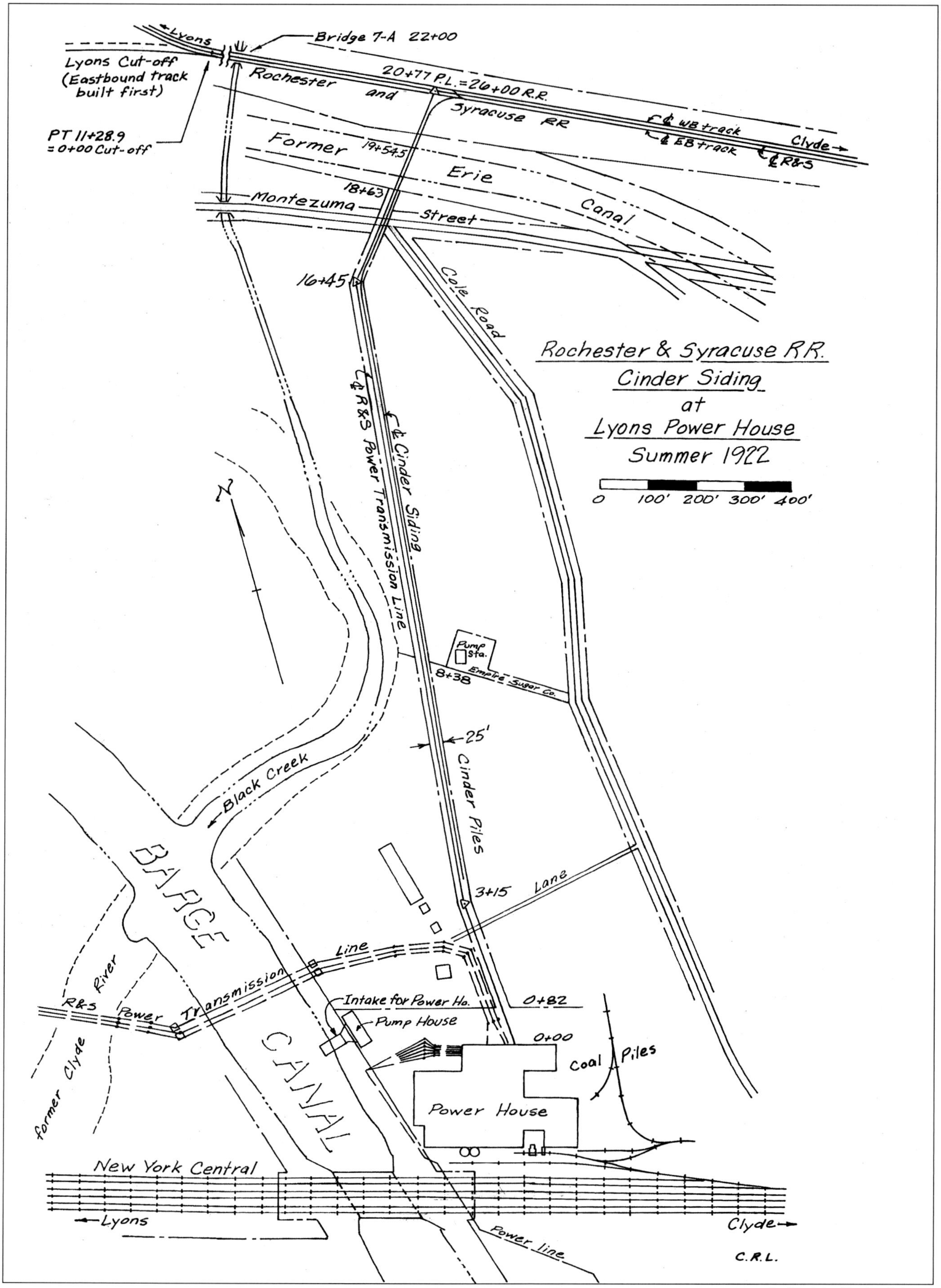

Art Work by Charles R. Lowe

Courtesy of New York Museum of Transportation.

R&S cars entered the Rochester Subway at Winton Road after passing through a tunnel under East Avenue and the Auburn Branch of the New York Central Railroad. This picture of the subway, looking east from Winton Road station shows the track layout for converting right-hand operation on the R&S to left-hand running in the subway. The two tracks in the center of the picture show R&S tracks emerging from its tunnel. The two switches where the three men are standing were spring operated. The only power switch was located at the station where eastbound R&S cars were diverted from the subway's eastbound main. The entire layout was protected by signals. An eastbound Rochester & Eastern car is seen leaving the Winton Road station. The subway freight main is at far right against the retaining wall. The westbound passenger main and a short passing track are seen between the freight line and the R&S tracks.

Courtesy of New York Museum of Transportation.

This view of the Rochester Subway is looking east at Meigs-Goodman station with an eastbound New York State Railways 2000-series car at left and a gasoline driven locomotive on loan from General Electric on the freight main at right. The picture was taken in early 1928, a few months before the Rochester & Syracuse cars would be passing this station.

track line for passenger cars and one or two freight tracks through most of the system. These latter tracks were connected with five of the steam railroads entering Rochester. Track interchange facilities enabled the electric line to serve a number of industries located along the old canal bed. Construction was open cut except for the Genesee River crossing on the old Erie Canal's stone viaduct and

ROCHESTER SUBWAY SIGNAL SYSTEM

Sections on route of Rochester & Syracuse Railroad cars

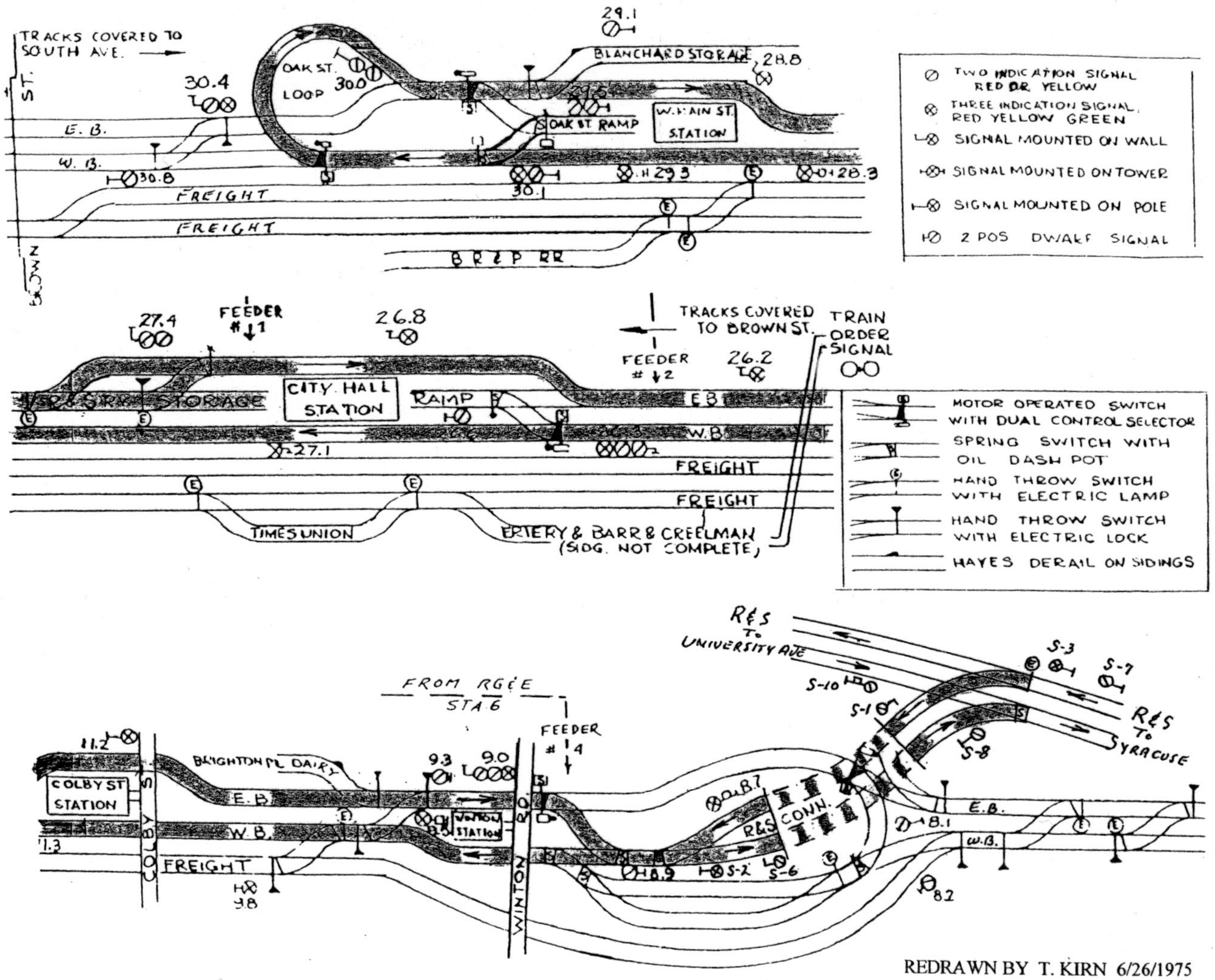

REDRAWN BY T. KIRN 6/26/1975

Additions by R. J. Gustafson 10/11/1975

Additions by Jim McFarlane 5/12/2007

for a few blocks in the center of the city. At these locations, the railroad was covered over, paved and called Broad Street. Thus Rochester could boast of 1.9 miles of genuine subway.

The subway system was operated by the local New York State Railways under a service-at-cost contract with the City. The 8.15-mile line extended from Rowlands in the southeast corner of Rochester via City Hall station to Driving Park Loop in the northwest section of the city. Left-hand operation was used in the subway as there was only one island platform at each station and it was located between the two passenger tracks. Shelters were provided for passengers at the end loops and at each intermediate stop. The only station with a waiting room and ticket office was at City Hall. Frequent local car service was offered. The interurbans were not permitted to do inter-station business in the subway.

There were two minor track adjustments made throughout the life of the R&S. In 1927, a wye off the main line was constructed at the rear of the Newark shops to turn the chair cars because their new seats could not be turned. In 1930, a short connection was installed at Port Byron to permit a through "Chair Car" service between Syracuse and Auburn after the associated Auburn & Syracuse electric line folded. A similar connection was installed by the Empire State Railroad at its Syracuse freight terminal on West Belden Avenue creating a wye at that point because R&S chair cars were often stored in the three-track freight yard between revenue trips.

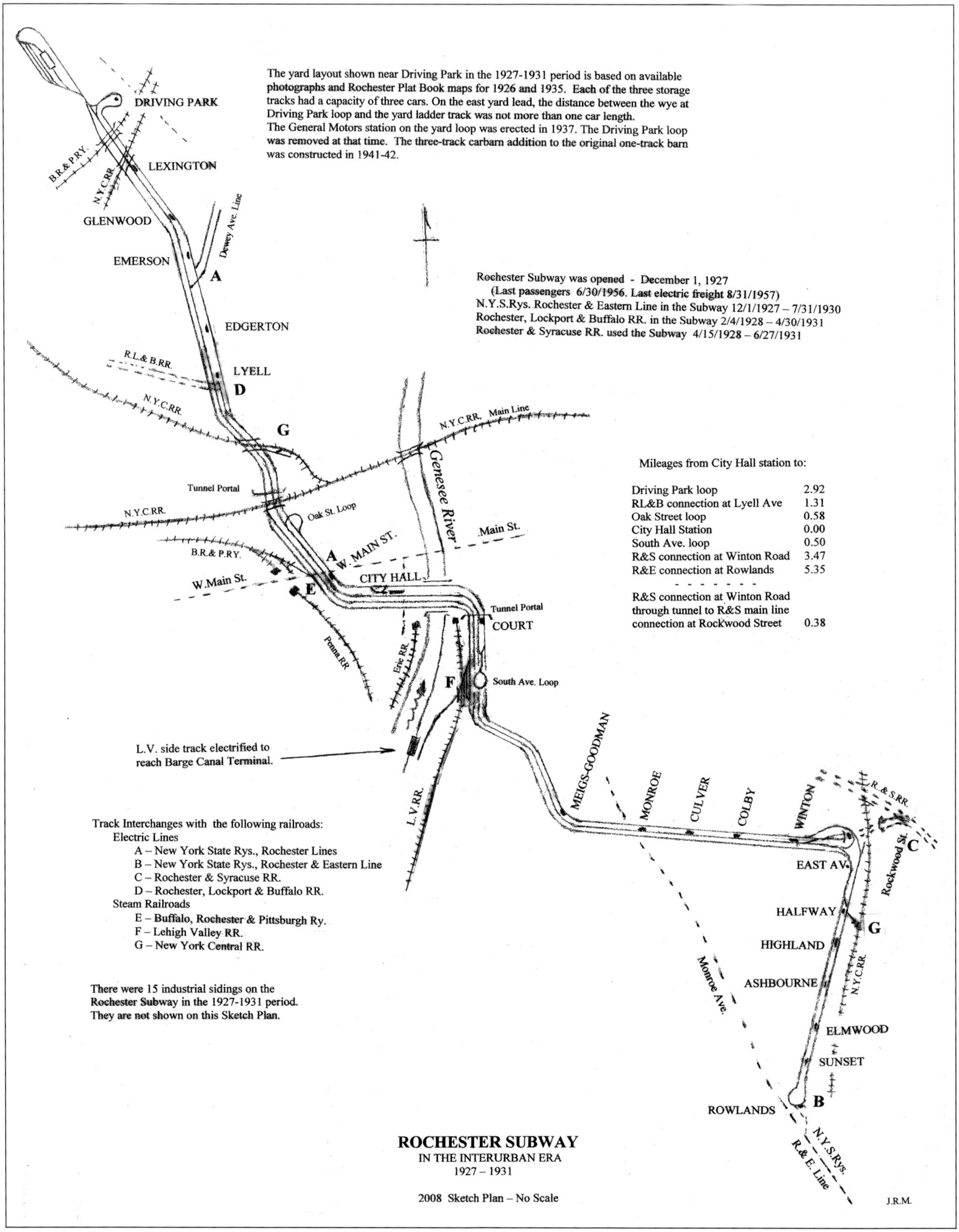
The yard layout shown near Driving Park in the 1927-1931 period is based on available photographs and Rochester Plat Book maps for 1926 and 1935. Each of the three storage tracks had a capacity of three cars. On the east yard lead, the distance between the wye at Driving Park loop and the yard ladder track was not more than one car length.
The General Motors station on the yard loop was erected in 1937. The Driving Park loop was removed at that time. The three-track carbarn addition to the original one-track barn was constructed in 1941-42.
Rochester Subway was opened - December 1, 1927
(Last passengers 6/30/1956. Last electric freight 8/31/1957)
N.Y.S.Rys. Rochester & Eastern Line in the Subway 12/1/1927 – 7/31/1930
Rochester, Lockport & Buffalo RR. in the Subway 2/4/1928 – 4/30/1931
Rochester & Syracuse RR. used the Subway 4/15/1928 – 6/27/1931
DRIVING PARK
B.R.& P.RY.
N.Y.C.RR.
LEXINGTON
GLENWOOD
EMERSON
Dewey Ave. Line
A
EDGERTON
R.L.& B.RR.
LYELL
D
N.Y.C.RR.
G
N.Y.C.RR. Main Line
Genesee River
Mileages from City Hall station to:
Driving Park loop 2.92
RL&B connection at Lyell Ave 1.31
Oak Street loop 0.58
City Hall Station 0.00
South Ave. loop 0.50
R&S connection at Winton Road 3.47
R&E connection at Rowlands 5.35
R&S connection at Winton Road through tunnel to R&S main line connection at Rockwood Street 0.38
Tunnel Portal
N.Y.C.RR.
Oak St. Loop
Main St.
W. MAIN ST.
B.R.& P.RY.
A
W.Main St.
E
CITY HALL
Tunnel Portal
COURT
Penna.RR
Erie RR.
F
South Ave. Loop
L.V. side track electrified to reach Barge Canal Terminal.
L.V.RR.
MEIGS-GOODMAN
MONROE
CULVER
COLBY
WINTON
R.& S.RR.
C
Rockwood St.
EAST AV.
Track Interchanges with the following railroads:
Electric Lines
A – New York State Rys., Rochester Lines
B – New York State Rys., Rochester & Eastern Line
C – Rochester & Syracuse RR.
D – Rochester, Lockport & Buffalo RR.
Steam Railroads
E – Buffalo, Rochester & Pittsburgh Ry.
F – Lehigh Valley RR.
G – New York Central RR.
HALFWAY
G
HIGHLAND
ASHBOURNE
N.Y.C.RR
Monroe Ave.
There were 15 industrial sidings on the Rochester Subway in the 1927-1931 period. They are not shown on this Sketch Plan.
ELMWOOD
SUNSET
ROWLANDS
B
N.Y.S.Rys.
R.& E. Line
ROCHESTER SUBWAY
IN THE INTERURBAN ERA
1927 – 1931
2008 Sketch Plan – No Scale
J.R.M.

Major bridges on the RS&E were substantial structures. This railroad company photo shows bridge number 1 crossing over the Auburn Branch of the New York Central at Brighton (later Rochester). This viaduct and bridge was built on a 2-degree curve. The total structure was 860 feet long and the 9 sections at each end supported the double tracks on 4% grades.

Bridges

The bridges of the Rochester, Syracuse & Eastern Railroad were designed and built in accordance with the best steam road standards. They were built to last. As a general rule, reinforced concrete culverts were used where possible and where spans were short. Deck plate girder bridges were designed for spans of 50 to 80 feet, and through steel trusses were specified for longer spans. All bridges were designed to carry two 3-car trains weighing 60 tons per car when loaded, passing each other on the structure with each train traveling 60 miles per hour. All bridges were fabricated and erected by American Bridge Company with the exception of three smaller ones which were supplied by the Oswego Bridge Company. There were thirteen major structures carrying the electric railway over the various railroads and canals encountered. At Fairport, Newark and in two places at Weedsport, the RS&E passed under existing steam railroads.

The man who knew the most about the bridges on the RS&E was Washington E. "Wash" Ferris. He went to work for the road as Bridge Inspector in 1905 when construction was just getting underway. In 1906 he was made Bridge and Building Inspector of all the Beebe roads, and later the Buffalo, Lockport & Rochester Railway was added. On the Syracuse & South Bay line, "Wash" was involved in building its underpass of the Syracuse Junction Railroad at Syracuse and in the construction of the railway's

This 276-foot skewed broken top chord through truss span carried the RS&E cars over the New York State Barge Canal just east of Fairport station. This company photograph, looking north, was taken in 1906, soon after the road was opened to Rochester. Note the triangular shaped steel panels added to the truss on diagonally opposite corners. These were necessary because the railroad 's concrete abutments were parallel with the canal centerline and were not at right angles to the track centerline.

Looking up the 2.5 percent grade on the westerly viaduct approach to bridges over Ganargua Creek and the Erie (later New York State Barge) Canal . Total length of the two bridges and the viaduct was 1077 feet. The village of Lyons is in the background.

Here is a 1906 company photograph of the completed viaduct and two pin-connected through-truss bridges over Ganargua Creek and Erie Canal at Lyons. Note that the canal has apparently been drained for the season. The abutment and piers of these structures contemplated sufficient overhead clearance for the old Erie, soon to be converted to the New York State Barge Canal.

A 1908 RS&E company photograph of Bridge 10 over the double-track West Shore Railroad. The view is looking east toward Syracuse. This is another example of the extra triangular steel panel in diagonal corners of the through truss bridge because the RS&E crossed over the West Shore at an angle of 45 degrees rather than 90 degrees. The two steam roads were diverging at this point and the RS&E Bridges 9 and 10 were only 320 feet apart.

A 1908 RS&E company photograph of Bridge 9 over the New York Central Railroad's four-track main line just one half mile east of the electric line's Savannah station. View is looking east toward Syracuse.

Courtesy of The Old Brutus Historical Society

Just west of its Weedsport station, the RS&E passed under the double-track West Shore Railroad (New York Central & Hudson River Railroad). Note the two special steel towers carrying the RS&E twin transmission circuits over the steam road. This view was looking east about 1910.

This 1909 company photograph shows the RS&E tracks passing under the Lehigh Valley Railroad bridge over Brutus Street, Weedsport, NY. Note the street surface had just been lowered to provide overhead clearance for the electric cars. The view is looking east shortly after the RS&E was opened between Port Byron and Syracuse.

Bridge 15 - A 1909 company picture of the RS&E bridge crossing over the double-track West Shore Railroad 1.77 miles east of Weedsport village. The entire bridge and viaduct structure was about 610 feet long. This view is looking toward the east.

steamboat pier at South Bay. He was in charge of erecting all the catenary towers on the RS&E between Weedsport and Lake Shore Junction and on the Lake Shore road from Long Branch to Oswego. In 1916, "Wash" was made roadmaster of the Beebe roads in addition to his other duties. He resigned from the company April 1, 1917 to go into business for himself.

The only major alterations ever made to bridges on the RS&E were in 1910 during construction of the new State Barge Canal system. RS&E Bridge 11, about three miles east of Savannah, was a 1512-foot-long steel structure, which crossed the Montezuma Marsh, the old Erie Canal and the Seneca River on a level grade only 15 or 20 feet above the marsh level. A new RS&E Bridge 12 over a new canal channel was located on the railroad's alignment about 300 feet east of the east end of Bridge

Bridge 16 - A 1909 company picture of the RS&E crossing over the Erie Canal. The small hamlet of Peru can be seen through the bridge structure. Cars crossing this bridge from right to left would be heading in an easterly direction for Syracuse, 15 miles away.

Bridge 17 - A 1909 company photograph of the 2-span through-truss structure carrying the RS&E cars over the 4-track New York Central main line (near span) and the double-track West Shore Railroad. Cars crossing from right to left in this view were headed for Syracuse 14 miles to the east.

A 1908 RS&E company photograph of Bridge 11, a 1512-foot long 28-span deck plate girder structure across the Montezuma Marsh, three miles east of Savannah. This view is looking west. Counting from near end, the Seneca River passed under the bridge at spans 8 through 11. A dredged channel passed through span 17. In 1910, the New York State Barge Canal was dug across the RS&E right-of-way just 500 feet east of the east abutment seen here.

Bridge 12 was thus created. No picture of Bridge 12 has ever turned up.

This is a faded view of a handsome RS&E express car 68 at Gravel Pit siding Stop 69, a quarter mile east of Bridge 11 over Montezuma Marsh and 4.5 miles west of Port Byron. The siding was removed in 1917.

11 and on solid ground east of the marsh. The tracks on the new canal bridge were to be at a higher elevation to allow for proper canal boat clearances. Therefore, Bridge 11 had to be raised on a steady grade to meet the new bridge elevation. Bridge 11was raised 6 inches on the west end and 6 feet on the east end. With these dimensions, the bridge grade matched the 0.4% grade of the western approach to Bridge 12. This made a constant-grade approach to the new bridge over the canal. The 28-span structure was actually two single-track deck plate girder bridges side by side on concrete piers so it was possible to raise one track at a time and thus permit continuous rail service. A "shoo-fly" (short track detour) carried rail traffic around the new bridge site. The RS&E bridge-raising job took a year to complete. The new Barge Canal channel was dug out after the new Bridge 12 had been constructed.

J. J. McCarthy, R&S Engineering, photographer

R&S right-of-way looking east at Stop 78, the first stop west of Weedsport. This picture was taken from a weed sprayer train on August 3, 1920. There was no road crossing here, just a path from a nearby local road that is seen to the right of the shelter. The parallel Erie Canal was just out of view on the left.

Overhead Construction

The overhead construction on the Rochester, Syracuse & Eastern Railroad was as substantial as the roadbed, track and bridges. Between Culver Road (Rochester) and Weedsport (61+miles), pole and span construction was used. On the section between Weedsport and Lake Shore Junction (18 miles), the overhead was supported by steel towers. On the western portion of the line, the standard wood poles were 35 feet long, set 6 feet into the ground and 8 feet from the centerline of the nearest track. The poles were raked sufficiently so as to properly resist the pull of the span wires. Poles were set every 80 feet on tangents. This distance was shortened on curves depending on the degree of curvature, with a minimum spacing of 50 feet. The trolley wire (4/0 copper) was directly suspended from steel span wires and was 18 feet above the track at the hangers. Two 500,000 cm bare copper feeder cables were carried on the poles on the south side of the tracks from Culver Road to the first steel tower just east of Weedsport. In later years, a third feeder was added between the East Rochester substation and Rockwood Street at the Rochester city line. Trolley taps from the feeders were spaced about 1000 feet apart and were connected across both trolley wires.

Duplicate 3-phase (No. 2 copper) 33-kV transmission wires were strung, one set on each line of poles between East Rochester substation and Lakeland substation at Lake Shore Junction. In addition, the poles on the north side of the tracks carried four telephone wires from one end of the line to the other, and one No. 10 shelter light wire off and on for practically the entire distance. The high voltage transmission lines were detoured around Fairport, Macedon, Palmyra, Newark, Lyons and a portion of Weedsport rather than carry them through the streets of these villages.

Pictured here is the RS&E catenary bridge or steel tower just east of Weedsport village. These steel bridges, spaced every 300 feet, carried the duplicate high-tension transmission lines and trolley wires from this bridge 18 miles east to Lake Shore Junction on the Syracuse, Lake Shore & Northern Railroad near Syracuse. Note how the two 500,000cm bare copper feeder cables (seen on the left-hand pole line) became catenary messengers to support the trolley wires, beginning at this dead-end bridge. Note, also, the first two wood poles beyond the catenary bridge where the two transmission lines left the railroad right-of-way to be detoured southerly and westerly around Weedsport village. This view dates to around 1910.

East of Weedsport the 4/0 trolley wire was suspended by a single catenary and was carried 18 feet above the top of the rail. Here the copper feed-

This right-of-way scene of the Rochester & Syracuse Railroad is looking west from Armstrong Road, Stop 97, 1.49 miles west of Lake Shore Junction and a connection with the Empire State Railroad to Syracuse. Note how the duplicate high-tension transmission lines were lifted off the steel catenary towers to meet the required clearance at the highway crossing. This view is looking at the longest stretch of tangent track on the R&S, 4.16 miles. Date of the picture c1928.

Edgar Y. Pattison, photographer

Looking east on the RS&E at the approach to Bridge 18 over the Lackawanna Railroad at Lake Shore Junction, 4.40 miles north of Syracuse. The catenary towers on the RS&E were 300 feet apart. On all curves, two wood poles were placed on the outside of the curve and were equally spaced between the towers. These poles supported pull-offs to draw the catenary trolley wires to a position more nearly parallel to the center lines of the tracks below. This photo was dated July 15, 1922.

ers acted as messengers. The steel towers were spaced 300 feet apart on both tangents and curves. The trolley wires were supported by steel hanger rods spaced 60 feet apart. On the sharper curves, wood pull-off poles were used with pull-offs to each hanger rod, these latter being spaced every 30 feet. The towers carried all wires except the telephone circuits which were strung on their own wood pole line along the north side of the tracks. There were 317 catenary bridges or towers on the line. Originally designed for the Beebe lines, they were built by the Archbold-Brady Company of Syracuse.

The first installation of these catenary bridges was on the Syracuse, Lake Shore & Northern between Long Branch and Baldwinsville in 1907. Duplications of these towers were later to be found on the Boston & Maine's Hoosac Tunnel electrification, on portions of the Fonda, Johnstown & Gloversville RR and on the Northern Ohio Traction & Light Co. The initial cost of this type of installation on the RS&E was only a few hundred dollars per mile more than the wood pole and span type, and the savings in maintenance proved to be considerable. The estimated installed cost of the pole and span type exclusive of copper wire and cable was $3325 per mile while that of the catenary towers was $3425. To the latter was added $160 per mile to cover cost of the separate telephone pole line. When later abandoned by the power company, sixteen of these RS&E towers were donated to the Seashore Trolley Museum at Kennebunkport, Me. and eight have been re-erected on its main line. Two of the museum's towers originally stood just east of the Peru substation and fourteen were west of the substation.

The telephone system operated by the RS&E consisted of four circuits. Line 31 connected the Newark car house with the Syracuse general office and the nine intermediate ticket offices. Line 33 connected the Newark car house with the five ticket offices west to Culver Road, Rochester. Line 32 connected the Newark car house with the Syracuse general office and the intermediate substations plus the Lyons power house and the chief substation operator at Lyons. Line 34 connected the Newark car house with the three substations west of Newark. There was also a local inside telephone line in Rochester that connected the R&S freight house with the R&S ticket office and the car inspector at the passenger terminal.

This 1912 view looking westerly, shows the RS&E tracks leaving Main Street in Macedon and signal 18, the first of nine to be encountered by Rochester-bound cars. The company's duplicate high-tension transmission lines were customarily detoured around towns and villages such as Macedon. In this view, the detoured transmission lines, which had been routed south of the village, are seen returning to the right-of-way on the fourth pole beyond the block signal.

Signals

In 1908, the Rochester, Syracuse & Eastern Railroad installed six block signals on the westbound track between Stop 4, two miles east of Culver Road, and Fairport station. It was felt necessary to space the Rochester-bound cars in this area because of the frequent local commuter service being offered west of Fairport. These signals were controlled by a 10 volt ac (alternating current) track circuit designed after steam railroad standards of the day. Two No. 8 and two No. 14 signal wires were carried on the adjacent pole line. At the time of installation, the signals were considered to be the first such on any electric railroad. The equipment was designed, built and installed by Union Switch & Signal Company of Pittsburgh. The signals were two-position light and semaphore type mounted on high steel masts. They were so wired that failure of any part would cause them to display a STOP aspect.

In September 1911, three more US&S signals were added to the system extending the westbound protection as far east as Macedon.

Timetable instructions advised motormen to come to a full stop when approaching a block showing red. If the signal did not clear after waiting 5 minutes, they could proceed under full caution to the next block. The waiting time between Fairport and Brighton (just east of Culver Road, Rochester) was reduced to 3 minutes.

Additional signals were added to the property in 1928 when main line tracks and cars were routed into the Rochester Subway. These signals were at Rockwood Street and were connected to the Subway signal system. They also provided protection when westbound R&S main line cars crossed over the old eastbound main on a diamond as they entered the subway underpass. At the point of diversion by westbound cars, the hand-thrown switch was normally aligned for the subway route. Since there was no switchman on duty at Rockwood Street, the conductors of westbound local cars destined for Culver Road performed that task. Local cars eastbound from Culver Road entered the main line through a spring switch and were governed by signal indications.

Courtesy of New York Museum of Transportation

Left: *Block signal 14 looking west from Egypt village, Stop 18. Signal wires were carried on the bottom cross arm, telephone wires next above. Picture was taken in July 1912.*

Right: *Block signal 18 was the last of nine (even numbered) signals governing westbound train movements on the 15 miles of the RS&E between Macedon and the Rochester city line at Culver Road. The rule book read: "When approaching a block set at danger, car must come to a full stop. If, after waiting five (5)minutes, signal does not clear, car may enter the block at full caution - - - ." Between Fairport and Culver Road, the wait time was three minutes.*

Power

When the RS&E was originally built, the company generated its own power at a large steam station located adjacent to and just north of the New York Central Railroad main line on the east side of the Clyde River just east of Lyons. The coal consumed was delivered to the plant on a NYC siding which ended on a timber trestle adjacent to the boiler room of the building. The steam station itself was of considerable proportions for it occupied over a half-acre of ground and was from 36 to 40 feet high. Even the chimney was of generous size – 20 feet in diameter at the base and 250 feet high. The plant contained three 1500-kW (kilowatt) 3300-volt Westinghouse-Parsons turbo-generators. Transformers stepped up the 3300-volt 2-phase power to 33000-volt ac 3-phase 25 cycle for transmission to the six substations on the RS&E as well as to four substations on the Syracuse, Lake Shore & Northern. The northern section of the Auburn & Northern was powered from Lyons with the balance coming from the Auburn & Syracuse power house in Auburn. The RS&E also sold small amounts of power to several of the communities through which it operated.

The standard brick substation on the RS&E was indeed a handsome building. It was designed by Scheaff & Jaastad of Boston who also designed the Lyons power house. Except for the Port Gibson substation, which also housed a waiting room and ticket office, each building contained just two rooms, a rotary room and a transformer room. Equipment consisted of two rotary converters, each of 400- or 500- kW capacity and four 200-kW 33,000 to 390-volt transformers. The East Rochester substation had an additional 750-kW rotary. The rotary converters at each location changed the transformed high transmission voltage to 650 volts dc (direct current) for distribution through the feeders to the trolley wires. Substations were located at East Rochester, Macedon, Port Gibson, Lyons (in the power house), Savannah, Port Byron, Peru and Lakeland. The Lakeland substation was owned by the Syracuse, Lake Shore & Northern but it contained two rotaries and the necessary transformers owned by the RS&E. It was located just north of Lake Shore Junction. In 1920, serious consideration was given by management to installing automatic equipment in their substations. Because of lack of

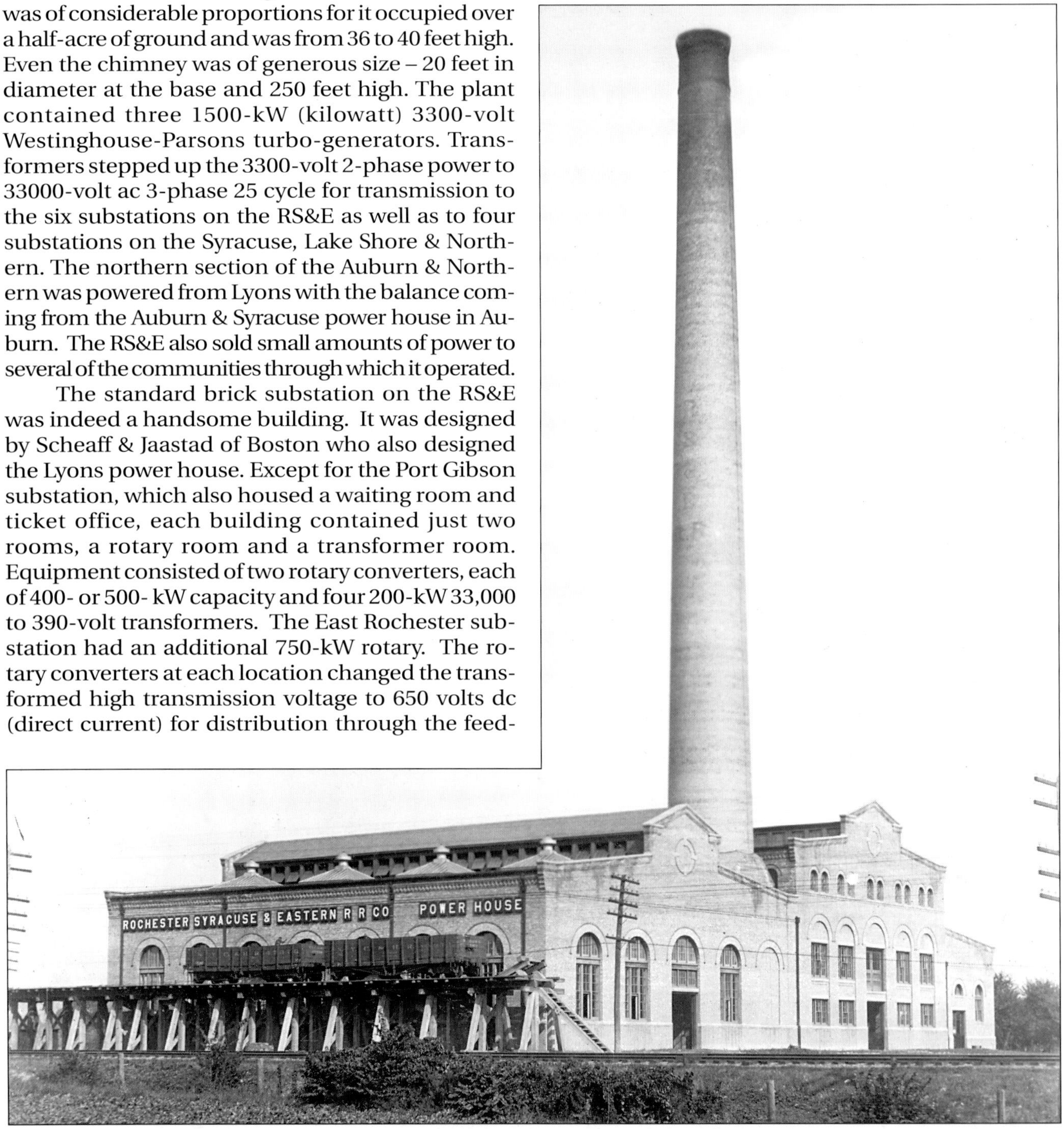

This early company view of the RS&E power house and coal delivery trestle at Lyons, NY was widely used in its early advertising brochures. The New York Central Railroad's main line is seen in the foreground.

All substations on the RS&E were identical except at Port Gibson where a 12 by 12-foot brick ticket office was added. Everything in this view appears to be brand new, c1906.

capital funds, only Macedon received Westinghouse automatic switchgear in 1923.

In November 1912, the Lyons steam plant was sold to the Niagara, Lockport & Ontario Power Company for $600,000. According to the 20-year contract beginning December 1, 1912, the power company paid $5500 per year rental to the RS&E (and $1800 to the SLS&N) to transmit power over the railroads' 33,000-volt high tension circuits. The RS&E, the SLS&N and the Syracuse & South Bay purchased power at each of their substations as measured by meters connected to the high tension side of their transformers. Each road paid seven mills ($.007) per kWh (kilowatt-hour) delivered. In the course of this ownership changeover, the RS&E was provided substation space in the Lyons power house for its two 400-kW rotary converters. At this location, the railroads' power was metered at the alternating current terminals of its rotaries because the rotaries were being fed directly from the power house transformers.

Courtesy of Perinton Historical Society

This RS&E standard substation was located at East Rochester. The room on the left contained three rotary converters and the switchboard. The taller wing housed four 33,000 to 390-volt transformers. Standard substations, spaced approximately 10 miles apart, were also located at Macedon, Port Gibson, Lyons (in the company power house), Savannah, Port Byron, Peru, east of Jordan, and at Lake Shore Junction, near Syracuse.

This picture of Macedon substation was made in 1923 on the occasion of the installation of Westinghouse automatic switchgear. Macedon was the only Rochester & Syracuse substation to receive this update.

The finishing touches were being applied to the Port Byron substation. It was ready to distribute power when the Auburn & Northern line opened June 28, 1908. The first RS&E car reached Port Byron from the west 25 days later.

Richard Pearson collection

Peru substation of the RS&E looking east toward Bridge 17 over the New York Central and West Shore Railroads. This view shows some of the outdoor pole and wire work required at substations. The building was 10 miles west of Lake Shore Junction on the Syracuse, Lake Shore & Northern Railroad.

Onondaga Historical Association Museum & Research Center, Syracuse, NY.

RS&E car 126 is eastbound on Main Street, Palmyra. This view shows the standard type "B" station erected when the building and freight house occupied a village lot. Note the track crossover in the street. There was always a crossover at each siding so it could be serviced by cars headed in either direction.

Stations

The standard village station on the RS&E was a very substantial and impressive looking structure. There were eight such stations on this line as well as three on the Lake Shore road and one on the associated Buffalo, Lockport & Rochester Railway. They were all constructed with the idea that the electric railroads were going to last far beyond their actual 25-year life.

Designed by Gordon A. Wright, a Syracuse architect, the buildings were of frame construction on poured concrete foundations. The exterior finish was 1-5/8-inch Georgia Pine vertical siding separated by panels of rough cast Portland cement. Interior walls had a 4 ½-foot wainscot of white oak with a "fumed oak" stain. The balance of the walls and the ceilings were plaster. Roofs were slate. Heat was supplied by a coal-fired furnace in a small basement.

Each station was divided into two sections; a 16- by 25-foot waiting room seating 35 people at one end and a 20- by 50-foot freight room at the other.

The RS&E station in Newark was a standard type "B" building because it was set on a downtown lot at right angles to the street. Note there was no bay window for the agent's office. The station was less than two years old when this card was purchased for mailing.

Courtesy of The Old Brutus Historical Society

This early 1910 view of the Weedsport station was taken before the siding beside the freight platform had been built. Note this was a type "A" station, built parallel to the main line tracks. It included a ticket office bay window. Weedsport was 23 rail miles west of Syracuse.

Onondaga Historical Association Museum & Research Center, Syracuse, NY.

Westbound local RS&E car 115, its train crew and local assorted citizens have posed for this early 1910 real photo postcard. The railroad was so new that the siding to the freight house platform had yet to be installed.

The waiting room included a 10- by 14-foot ticket office and suitable rest room facilities. The freight room floor was at the same level as the freight car floors. On one side of this room, two 9-foot sliding doors opened onto a loading platform adjacent to the side track. Wagons (and later trucks) were accommodated at similar doors located on the opposite side of the freight room. There were two styles of stations designed. Type "A" buildings were set parallel to the main line and had an office bay window facing the track. Type "B" buildings were set on a downtown lot at right angles to the street and had no bay window. The only type "B" stations on the RS&E were at Palmyra and Newark. Fortunately, a set of blueprint plans, elevations and sections of these great station buildings has been saved from the ravages of time.

These handsome stations were located at Fairport, Palmyra, Newark, Lyons, Clyde, Port Byron, Weedsport and Jordan. Palmyra station was opened in 1910, Fairport in 1911 and Newark in 1912. The others were opened as the line was completed. When these stations were built, they cost around $6,000 apiece. By 1922, when the Lyons cut-off was

RS&E car 111, westbound, has made a station stop in Macedon, 20 miles east of Rochester. The company rented store-front space for a ticket office both here and in East Rochester. The sign on the pole reads: "R.S.& E. Limited Cars Stop Here." This post card view was postmarked March 20, 1915.

Courtesy of Wayne County Historical Society

The original station at Savannah was a standard octagonal cross-road waiting shelter. The Springstead Hotel was conceived by its owner and was built with the idea of leasing most of its ground floor to the RS&E for its passenger and freight station. Note the siding adjacent to the raised freight platform and the raised platform in the foreground for handling milk shipments. This building was still in place and in use in the mid 1970s. Two characteristics of its railroad use still remained - the canopies over the two train-side doors.

constructed, the cost of the same station building had risen to $10,000. The company rented space for ticket offices at Rochester Terminal, Culver Road, East Rochester, Macedon and Syracuse Terminal. At Savannah, a local resident built a 2-story concrete block hotel adjacent to the RS&E tracks. He leased ground floor space to the railroad for their freight and passenger station. The two terminal stations shared space with the other interurban lines in the area. The RS&E owned land in East Rochester and Macedon on which standard stations were to have been built. These works were never carried out, however, and storefront stations were leased.

The local passengers who waited for cars at

Looking north at Linden Road crossing, Town of Brighton, 2.87 miles east of Culver Road, Rochester. Note an extra panel on opposite sides of the standard RS&E octagonal shelter to accommodate larger numbers of Rochester-bound passengers. The standard Beebe system crossing sign shows clearly in this view.

This right-of-way view, looking east from Stop 6, Linden Road, Town of Brighton, shows the RS&E main line on a 3-degree curve. Note the two pole-mounted signal boxes by which waiting passengers could signal local cars in either direction.

This RS&E standard octagonal crossing shelter was seen at many of the country cross roads. They were all built of chestnut and were, indeed, very handsome buildings. Stop 18 at Egypt.

many of the country crossroads were equally well cared for but on a much smaller scale. There were approximately 100 intermediate stops between Rochester and Syracuse not including the major stations or storefront stations. A few stops were at street intersections in the various villages but the majority of the stops were at local intersecting crossroads. Sixty-four of these latter locations were provided with standard shelters, 8 more with non-standard shelters and a number with only landing platforms.

The standard shelters, also designed by Gordon Wright, were works of art, very possibly unequalled on any other electric line outside of the Beebe Syndicate. They were built of chestnut in a true octagonal shape, each side panel being 50 inches in width, every joint being mitered. The buildings measured 10 feet across and were 14 feet high with 8-foot ceilings inside. They had hardwood

This is a view of a standard RS&E shelter at Stop 25, Macedon. It shows how the octagonal shaped building, occupying a 10-foot square base, was placed on a standard 15- by 20-foot platform. Built of chestnut, each panel was 50 inches wide. Each building had but one door. The interior seating could accommodate eight to ten people.

Courtesy of The Old Brutus Historical Society

Brutus Street was an in-village station stop on the RS&E. This view is looking railroad west. The building and grounds are nearly new. That suggests a photo date of summer 1910. Brutus Street station was also the point of interchange for passengers to and from the nearby Lehigh Valley Railroad station on Willow Street. Willow Street is seen passing behind the RS&E shelter.

floors and oak seats with a capacity of 8 to 10 people. A few shelters, like the ones at Warners, Memphis and Stop 6 near Rochester, had one extra panel on opposite sides to increase the capacity for waiting patrons. All buildings were electrically lighted. Three electric car heaters were placed under the seats to keep the passengers comfortable even in the most strenuous weather. Electric signal boxes with levers were installed on poles outside so patrons could signal cars approaching from either direction.

The shelters were placed on 15- by 20-foot wood platforms, and since there was usually only one building at a crossing, it was generally placed beside the inbound track to the closest city or village. This was to avoid the necessity of the majority of passengers having to cross the tracks from the shelter to reach the boarding side of the approaching car.

Each standard shelter represented an initial investment of about $400 when built and, on the average, it required about $100 a year to maintain. It was soon found that some people showed their appreciation for the heaters by stealing them or destroying them so that portion of the project was soon abandoned and the heaters were removed. The lights and signals remained until the end of the road, however. The few shelters built in later years were of a more simple design yet they served their purpose just as well. The Newark shop forces built portable shelters in 1921 for the use of flagmen who were obliged to work out on the line during severe weather. The shelters were made in sections that could be hooked together - four sides, a roof and a floor. The only window was in the door. Electric heaters were provided in cold weather. These shelters were of such a size that they could be dis-

Eastbound RS&E car 121 was entering Brutus Street in Weedsport. This is another close-up view showing details of the Beebe Syndicate's handsome way stations.

Courtesy of The Old Brutus Historical Society

A new Rochester Union Freight Terminal was built in early 1921 to accommodate freight trains of the interurban lines entering the city. This 1926 view shows Rochester & Syracuse express car 61 loading up for a mid-day local run east to Port Byron and Auburn. Cars of the Rochester, Lockport & Buffalo used docks where the truck is standing. Cars of the New York State Railways Rochester & Eastern and Rochester & Sodus Bay lines were spotted on the opposite side of the freight house.

mantled, loaded into an express car and moved from place to place.

The first RS&E freight house in Rochester was a modest frame building adjacent to the Erie Railroad freight house on Exchange Street. The Buffalo, Lockport & Rochester line shared these quarters. This arrangement was discontinued November 1, 1914 when the electrics moved into one end of the new Erie freight house adjacent to its passenger station. Early in 1921, the New York State Railways in Rochester opened a new Union Freight Terminal on Frank Street at the rear of their State Street car barn. It was intended for the use of the interurban lines entering Rochester, and its cost of operation was distributed among the tenants on the basis of tonnage handled. Electric freight cars had to pass through the barn from State Street in order to reach the freight station. The R&S and RL&B cars were spotted along the north side of the brick freight house building while the New York State Railways Rochester & Eastern and Rochester & Sodus Bay cars worked off the south side.

The Electric Freight Terminal in Syracuse was located on West Belden Avenue. Built about 1911 by the Syracuse, Lake Shore & Northern, it was also used by the RS&E and the South Bay line.

There never was a common freight terminal in Syracuse for all the electric lines that entered the city. The New York State Railways Oneida Line, the third-rail line from Utica, and the Auburn & Syracuse shared a freight house at 344 West Fayette Street, near the New York Central passenger station. The Syracuse & Eastern, an 18.5-mile suburban line reaching Jamesville, Fayetteville, Manlius and Edwards Falls, had its own quarters at East Fayette and Pine streets, a mile or more from the others. The West Fayette Street station had been used by all of the Beebe lines during the first few years of their freight and express operations. The West Belden Avenue yard was frequently used to store passenger cars as well as freight equipment since they were the only off-street tracks available for the Lake Shore, the South Bay and the Rochester roads.

A 1906 view of the original car shops of the RS&E at Newark, New York. Car 113 is standing on the fifth track. Offices are seen in the left background adjacent to the main line. The machine shop section was on the right-hand side in this picture. Each track could hold three of the 53-foot interurban cars under cover. The building, of wood construction, was destroyed by fire on April 1, 1912. No cars were lost in the fire although two were severely damaged.

Newark Shops

The original car barn on the Rochester, Syracuse & Eastern Railroad was located on Grace Avenue at the southwestern edge of Newark, just two blocks west of the point where the cars entered or left the village streets. Of one-story frame shed-type construction, the building contained 5 tracks with a total capacity of 15 cars. On April 1, 1912, this building was destroyed by fire caused by a short circuit in the paint shop. A freight motor and a passenger car were badly damaged but so far as is known, no cars were destroyed.

A temporary tarpapered frame building was erected over a shop area and two of the three tracks with pits so cars could be serviced, but work was immediately begun on a new shop of fireproof construction. The new shops built around the temporary building were patterned after the Lakeland shops of the Beebe Syndicate. These latter buildings were located at Lake Shore Junction on the Syracuse, Lake Shore & Northern and served as the heavy repair headquarters for all the Beebe lines operating out of Syracuse.

The Newark shops were completed in August 1913 and were considered to be the most modern plant yet constructed at the time. Built on the site of the original shops, the main building was a one-story brick and steel shop containing three tracks. Attached to its north wall was a two-track brick and steel storage barn 240 feet long. It was originally planned to have a six-track storage barn with 3 two-

Courtesy of New York Museum of Transportation

The original 5-car wood frame car barn of the RS&E at Newark, New York, burned to the ground on April 1, 1912. This July 1912 picture shows the temporary frame and tar paper building that was erected over two of the tracks having inspection pits. Car servicing continued while the replacement facilities were being built.

Construction of the Newark shops of the RS&E was begun immediately after the April 1, 1912 fire. Here can be seen the bricks and mortar of the new building completely surrounding the temporary tar paper inspection shed. This view is looking northeasterly across the main line. A new 2-story brick office building is just out of view on the right.

Another view of the RS&E shops at Newark under construction.The main machine shop will occupy the area where car 98 and its mate are standing. The bricked in spaces will be auxiliary rooms for storage of various materials. Construction is indeed substantial. The main line showing at left is looking toward Port Gibson and points west.

track bays, however, only the one bay was built. Its capacity was 8 interurban cars. Track 5 (in the storage barn) ran over a 125-foot long inspection pit.

The car shop measured roughly 95 x 180 feet. It was fitted out with the usual assortment of lathes, drill presses, a forge, an 18-foot truck turntable, a truck transfer table between two tracks and an overhead trolley hoist for carrying trucks, motors and other heavy material from one part of the shop to another. The capacity of the three shop tracks was 9 interurban cars. Each track ran over concrete inspection pits (25 feet under track 1 and 125 feet under tracks 2 and 3). The floors on each side of the two long pits were depressed 18 inches below the

The new RS&E car shops at Newark were completed in August 1913, just 16 months after the original facility burned. Its general design and layout were patterned after the extensive Syracuse, Lake Shore & Northern shops at Lakeland, four miles north of Syracuse. Comparison of before and after views shows a complete redesign of the yard track layout. The two tracks in the foreground were leads to four outdoor storage tracks numbered 6,7,8 and 9. The working shop portion of the building was located to the left of line car 50 shown standing on track 1.

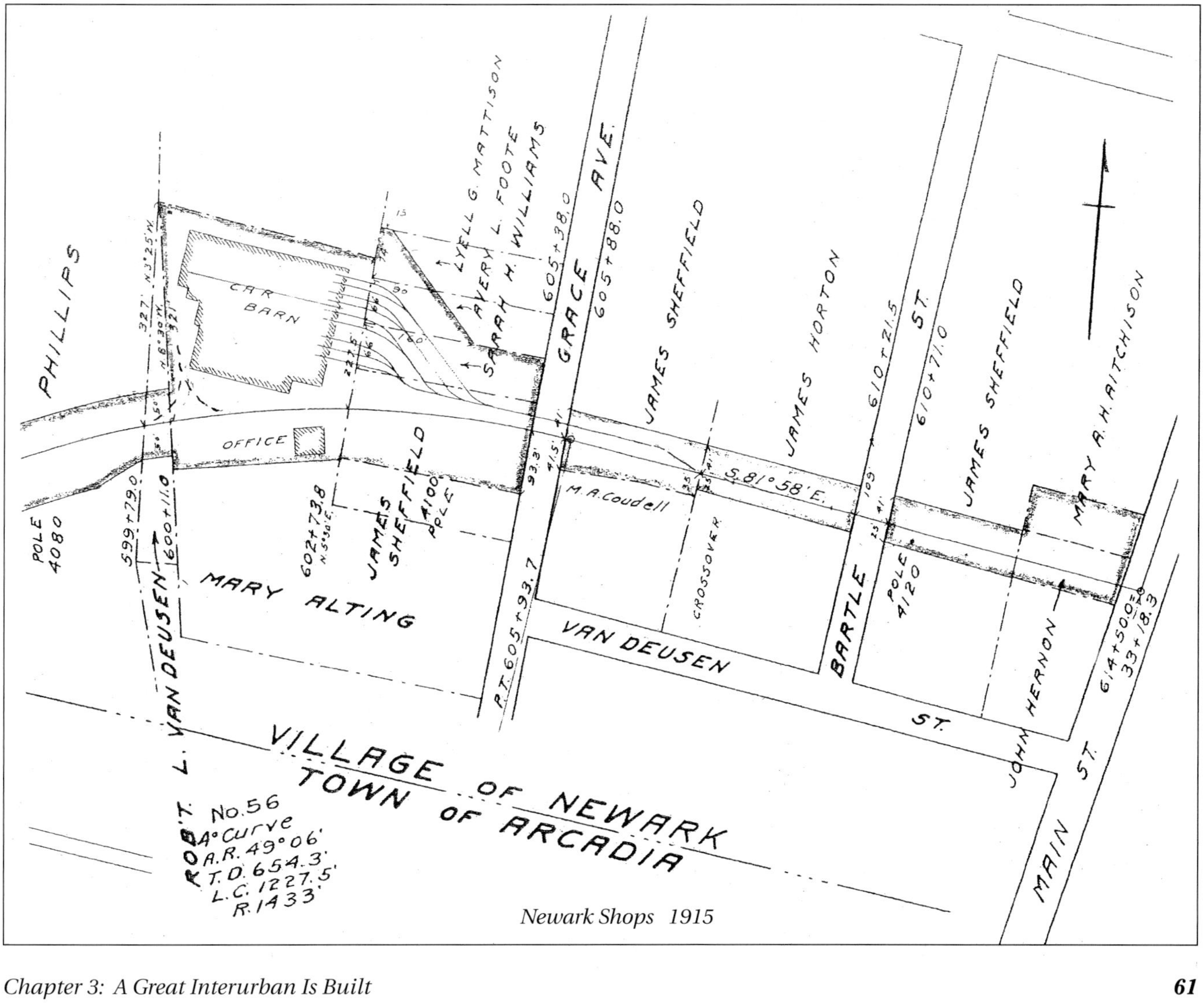

Newark Shops 1915

Rochester & Syracuse Railroad car 114 standing on track 2 at the Newark car shops on August 3, 1920.

Courtesy of New York Department of Transportation

Westbound car is passing RS&E general office building at the Newark car shops in 1913. This building provided quarters for the superintendent, train dispatcher and car crews. Virtually all of the trainmen's runs originated and terminated at Newark shops.

main floor level. This depression enabled workmen to more easily inspect and maintain trucks and underbody parts. Floors in the shop were wood laid directly on concrete in the repair section and just concrete elsewhere. Small rooms built onto the main line or south side of the shop and across the back or west side of the building contained store rooms, line, carpenter and electric shops, paint storage, sand and boiler rooms and coal storage space. The Newark car shops were quite capable of doing almost every kind of repair work to interurban rolling stock.

A two-story brick office building was located directly across the main line from the car shop. The office building measured 30 x 50 feet and contained space for the Superintendent and his staff, the Train Dispatcher, trainmen's headquarters and a large fireproof vault. A recreation room in the building was equipped with pool and billiard tables.

A section house, a tool house and a crossing shelter completed the list of buildings in the Newark shop area. The Newark shop and office building are still in use today. The Village of Newark Department of Public Works owns the car barn. The old office building is home to the Newark Grange.

This section foreman, his four men plus two summer extras are shown where the RS&E tracks left Clinton Street, Jordan, for points west. Two grain elevators adjacent to the Erie Canal are seen in the background.

Maintenance of Way and Structures

For many years, the RS&E maintenance standards were on a par with those of first-class steam roads. For track and roadway maintenance, the electric line was divided into eight sections, each approximately ten miles in length. When originally built, there were fourteen sections but economics soon dictated a reduction to eight. Each section had a foreman and four men with two seasonal men being added for summer work. The track was walked twice daily and a bonus of $1 was given for the discovery of any broken rails. As time went on, the sections were lengthened and the number of section men reduced until, by 1928, 34 men and their foremen handled all the track and roadway maintenance on the R&S.

For some years, the company's tie program included a generous portion of creosoted cross ties since their life was considered to be much longer than the untreated ones. Later on, most replacements were of the latter variety so that by

Courtesy of Wayne County Historical Society

Here is the RS&E substation in a rural setting three quarters of a mile west of Savannah. Note the well kept grounds with flower gardens surrounding the building and the white washed cattle return fences at the country road crossing. These would date the picture in 1908 or1909 when hopes for the new interurbans were high and when the employees had time to take especial care of their property.

Left: *RS&E line car 50 is seen at Warners, 10 miles west of Syracuse. Apparently the care of station grounds was one of the duties of this crew. This real photo postcard is dated about 1910.*

Facing page: *Here is the RS&E right-of-way looking east from Amboy station, Stop 95, 7.5 miles west of Syracuse terminal. Note the groups of snow fences piled along each fence line. This classic 1912 picture was handed down from a relative of Thomas H. Mather, first chief engineer of the RS&E.*

Right: *Bridge 6 - A 1906 company picture of "Blue Cut" bridge and viaduct located mid-way between Newark and Lyons. The structures crossed over the double-track West Shore Railroad (in the foreground) and the four-track New York Central main line and a local road just beyond. The entire structure was 648 feet long. As an integral part of State Highway Route 31 between Newark and Lyons, this bridge and viaduct outlasted the electric line by 53 years. It was finally replaced in 1983.*

1931 only a quarter of the ties in track were treated. This state of affairs contributed heavily to the road's rough riding qualities experienced in the last years of operation.

The first Track Supervisor on the RS&E was Helmer Snow. He started with the Beebe lines in Skaneateles in 1901, the day after President McKinley was shot. After supervising the grading of the Auburn & Syracuse line, he moved to Clyde. He was in charge during construction of the RS&E between Clyde and Syracuse. This job of supervisor was no easy one, for Snow walked many miles inspecting track and roadway after the line was completed. For instance, he often rode to Fairport and walked back to Newark. Also he might ride to Clyde, walk to Savannah and ride home to Newark, a solid 18 hour day with 27 miles of it on foot. In 1911, Snow moved to the Buffalo, Lockport & Rochester Railway as its Road Master. He remained with that company until it stopped running in 1931.

Overhead maintenance work on the RS&E was handled by one foreman, four linemen (later three) and a helper together with their line car 50. Winters were hard on the railroad in general and on the overhead in particular. Snow packed in the flange-ways at grade crossings caused many derailments which sometimes took out the overhead. A February 1910 incident at Warners necessitated the crew walking the five miles from Lakeland to the stranded car and repairing enough of the line so a work car could be brought in. In time, the company found that the maintenance costs of the steel bridge and catenary construction was less than half that of the wood pole and span construction.

By 1929, the R&S Power Department was being handled by 11 substation operators and 2 electricians. There were very few changes in this department throughout the life of the company beyond the installation of automatic equipment at the Macedon substation in 1923.

The loss of power one night started a chain of events that ended in the tragic death of motorman Bart DeHond. For years, a night freight run was called "The Three AM." It left the Newark shops eastbound every night except Sunday at 3 o'clock in the morning. On January 22, 1922, car 63 left Newark with C.W. Croucher conductor, and Earl Botcher TFA (traveling freight agent), on board. Stops were made at Lyons and then Clyde at which point they phoned the dispatcher and reported themselves ready to go. As the car passed under the circuit breakers opposite the Savannah substation, the lights went out and the motors went dead. The car drifted to a stop in a few hundred feet. The conductor walked back to the substation and for some reason the motorman did not get out and flag his train.

In the meantime, a milk car had left the Newark barns with orders to run to Port Byron and pick up milk from there to Rochester. This car was number 68 in charge of conductor Charles Soper. Bart DeHond was motorman. At fifty miles an hour they breezed past the Savannah sub and, in the early morning fog, crashed into the rear end of car 63, crushing Bart in his cab.

The maintenance of the bridges was handled by a foreman and two bridge men. Initially, RS&E Bridge Supervisors inspected each bridge at least every two months. This routine was later changed when a firm of bridge engineers was hired to periodically inspect the large steel bridges. These structures must have received excellent care from the day they were built for two of them remained in service at least 50 years after the R&S folded. Bridge number 1A at Allen Creek was built in 1905 as a two-span concrete arch. Although enlarged since that time, it still does its share of supporting Interstate Highway I-490 near Rochester. Bridge number 6 was a 254-foot pin-connected through-truss over the New York Central and West Shore railroads at "Blue Cut" a few miles east of Newark. After the R&S quit in 1931, its roadway and Bridge 6 became part of State Highway Route 31 between Newark and Lyons. This bridge was replaced in 1983. So far as is known, there were never any serious accidents on the electric road in connection with its bridges.

The entire Maintenance-of-Way Department as well as Equipment and Power Departments were under the supervision of the Chief Engineer. There were three Chiefs during the company's lifetime. The first was Thomas Mather. He supervised the RS&E's location, layout and construction, and he was in charge of maintaining it until September 1914 when he moved on to other endeavors. The second Chief Engineer was W. B. Voth who came to the Empire United from the Sheboygan (Wisconsin) Railway & Electric Company. It was under his direction that the complete sets of right-of-way maps of both the Rochester-Syracuse (72 sheets) and Syracuse-Oswego (37 sheets) Divisions were prepared. Each plan, revised to October 1, 1915, bears the signature of the company's Assistant Engineer J. C. McGonagle. Scaled 1" equals 200', these plans contain a wealth of information on the two companies' rights-of-way. Fortunately, one complete set is still in existence. They have been of considerable value in the preparation of this history.

In August 1917, David E. Crouse resigned his position as Chief Engineer of the Auburn & Syracuse line to become Chief Engineer of the RS&E. Crouse continued with the company in that capacity until it was finally dismantled in the early 1930s. He also became Chief Engineer of the Empire State Railroad and the Syracuse Northern Electric Railway. Crouse had come to the Auburn & Syracuse in March of 1916 from the Maryland Electric Railways (Annapolis Short Line) where he had been Electrical Engineer for a number of years. He came to the A&S as part of the Allen & Peck management team.

Cars on the RS&E 4

Passenger Cars

The standard interurban passenger car on the Rochester, Syracuse & Eastern Railroad was really a beautiful piece of equipment. The first eight cars built for the road (97-99, 100, 101, 110-112) had bodies constructed entirely of wood while those built thereafter carried a ½-inch steel plate 30 inches wide in their sides for the full length of the body. This added considerably to the strength of the car and allowed for wider seats inside.

The car exteriors were finished in the familiar vertical wood siding and they had double plate glass windows capped with arched leaded glass panes. The cars had clerestory roofs with arched ventilating

Above: *A 1906 portrait of Niles built car 110, taken at the Newark car shops. A beautiful car indeed.*

Right: *Interior view of RS&E car 110, built by Niles in 1906.*

Facing page: *Chair Car 112 standing on the Empire State Railroad main line opposite the Lakeland shops in December 1926. ES block signal 12 in the foreground was one of six that protected southbound moves on the 3 miles between Lake Shore Junction and Syracuse city streets. (See additional photos of Chair Car 112 on pages 83-85.)*

Niles-built car 100 was one of two combination cars in the RS&E original 1906 order. In this early view, 100, westbound has just left Main Street, Macedon. A picture at this location taken after 1911 would show block signal 18, being described in a companion view (page 49, top).

Here are two of the three 45-foot cars (97, 98 and 99) used primarily in the R&S 8-mile commuter service between Fairport and Rochester city line at Culver Road and University Avenue. The green flags on car 99 suggest this pair has just been moved from points west as the first section of a regular train and has been backed into the Newark shops area on track 2. The view dates from 1919 or 1920.

The original Syracuse, Lakeside & Baldwinsville barn and car shop at Lakeland, 4.5 miles north of Syracuse, was later used as a storehouse for all the Beebe Syndicate lines. Here, just outside the shop, is a brand new Brill-MCB truck of the type seen on the RS&E Niles-built cars 97-99, 100-102 and 110-112.

R&S car 119 was built by G. C. Kuhlman Company. It was delivered to the Beebe lines as Auburn & Northern Electric Railroad number 10 in June 1908. The car was officially taken into the RS&E fleet in 1910 and was renumbered 119. According to Kuhlman shop order listings, A&N 10 was an exact duplicate of RS&E cars 117 and 118.

Wilbourne B. Cox collection

This is a G. C. Kuhlman Car Company's builder's view representing cars 113 and 114 (shop order 285). They were delivered to the RS&E in January 1906, nearly six months before the road opened in June 1906. In the period 1906-1909, the railroad purchased nine cars, 113-118, 120, 121 and A&N 10, all of the same design, at the rate of two cars per year.

windows. The interiors were finished in Philippine mahogany and the ceilings were three-ply wood, painted. All seats were the high-back interurban style reversible type, those in the main compartment being covered in genuine leather while those in the smoking compartment were finished in cane. A toilet room was located at the platform end of the main compartment. The cars were usually operated with the smoking compartment ahead.

The cars were originally painted Pullman Green. They all came from the car builders with THE ELECTRIC SHORT LINE emblazoned in two places on each car side. Later on, the standard car color was dark blue and in the last days, all cars were a light orange with Pennsylvania Red trim and black roofs. They were indeed a handsome sight streaking through the green countryside on a warm summer afternoon.

All cars were double-ended and after 1910 they were equipped for multiple-unit operation. Except for cars 97, 98 and 99 which were 45 feet long, all were 53' 6" in length and weighed around 42 tons equipped. They cost an average of $13,500 each. Six of the straight passenger cars and the three combines were built by the Niles Car and Manufacturing Company of Niles, Ohio. The rest of the cars, straight passenger, (113-129) were products of the G. C. Kuhlman Car Company of Cleveland, Ohio.

The three combination cars were 100, 101 and 68. As the numbers might suggest, 100 and 101 were mostly passenger and 68 was mostly express. Cars 100 and 101 each had a small baggage compartment at one end with wide baggage doors on each side. Each car seated 46 passengers, the same as the short cars (97-99) and twelve less than the straight passenger cars (110-129). In the spring of 1917, car 101 was leased to the Syracuse & South Bay road becoming its number 22. Upon its return to the R&S in 1922, it was assigned number 102.

Wilbourne B. Cox collection

A Kuhlman builder's view of cars 115 and 116. They arrived on the property in May 1907. They were the same design as cars 113, 114, 117, 118, 120, 121 and A&N 10.

This 1910 view at Weedsport station, is the only known picture of RS&E car 101. In 1917, it was leased to the Syracuse & South Bay line and renumbered 22. Five years later, it was returned to the Rochester & Syracuse and was given the number 102. From time to time, a colored postcard of this same scene shows up where the artist had converted it to a summer view. Bushes and paved sidewalks replaced the piles of snow. We know that the original picture was taken in winter, not summer, because the artist didn't clean off all the snow in the car's pilot, the forward truck and the trolley pole retriever.

Wilbourne B. Cox collection

A Kuhlman builder's view of cars 117 and 118. They arrived on the property in May 1908. They were the same design as cars 113, 114, 115, 116, 120, 121 and A&N 10.

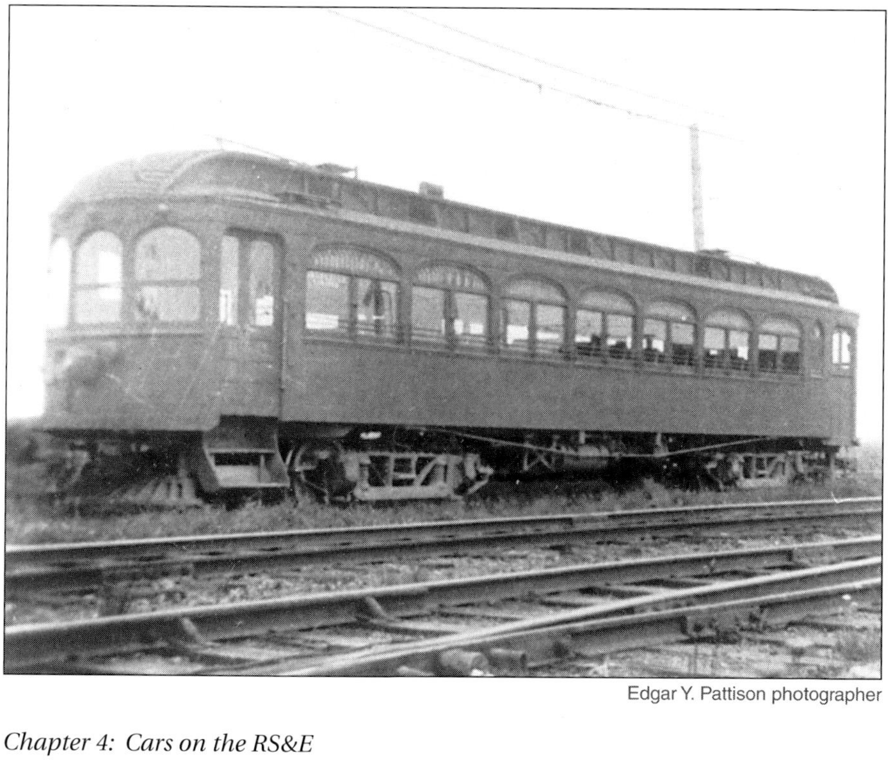

Edgar Y. Pattison photographer

An R&S car of the 113-121 series was photographed on a siding at the Empire State Railroad's Lakeland shops in July 1922.

An accident photo of R&S Chair Car 110 Lyons at the Newark car shops December 7, 1927. Damage appears to be limited to the pilot on one end.

An R&S two-car train, cars 114 and one of the 122-129 series, is seen in the yard at Lakeland shops in the late 1920s.

James I. Barstow collection

Rochester & Syracuse car 100 westbound on East Union Street, Newark, NY, opposite the railroad's passenger station. In 1922, this combination car was reconfigured. The sliding baggage doors at one end were removed. Controls were moved to the right-hand side of each vestibule opposite the two passenger entry doors.

Wilbourne B. Cox collection

A Kuhlman builder's view of cars 120 and 121. They arrived on the property in January 1909. They were the same design as cars 113, 114, 115, 116, 117, 118 and A&N 10.

The other combine, car 68, seated only 5 passengers in one end. It was used principally as a milk car and for many years had the run from Port Byron to the Brighton Dairy at Culver Road in Rochester. In 1920, the passenger compartment was removed from this car and it was assigned to regular express duties.

On at least one occasion, car 100 was chartered as a funeral car. When General Robert B. Ward, founder and president of Ward Baking Company in Rochester, passed away in October 1915, his body was transported to Oswego for burial. The funeral party left Rochester about 10 A.M. Upon arrival at Lake Shore Junction, the crew took on a pilot and the car was turned on the Lakeland shops loop so as to be properly pointed for the trip to Oswego and its cemetery. After the ceremonies, the group and car 100 returned to Rochester.

No new passenger cars were acquired by the RS&E after 1910. The two business cars, *Marcella* and *999*, were rebuilt for passenger service in 1915 and one additional car was purchased in 1918 from the Syracuse Northern Electric Railway. The two ex-business cars became freight cars after World War I so the company wound up its operation in 1931with nearly the same number of passenger cars it had in 1910.

When purchased, the interurban cars were delivered to the property on railroad flat cars and were unloaded at the West Shore Railroad track connection east of Newark. They were equipped for operation at the Newark shops, the electrical equipment having been supplied separately.

As the years rolled by, minor differences began to crop up in the passenger cars. For instance, the earlier cars with controls in the center of the platforms were converted to right-hand drive. By the latter part of 1919, all controls had been changed to Westinghouse HL (multiple-unit) type. It was found that rectangular windows in the car ends were less

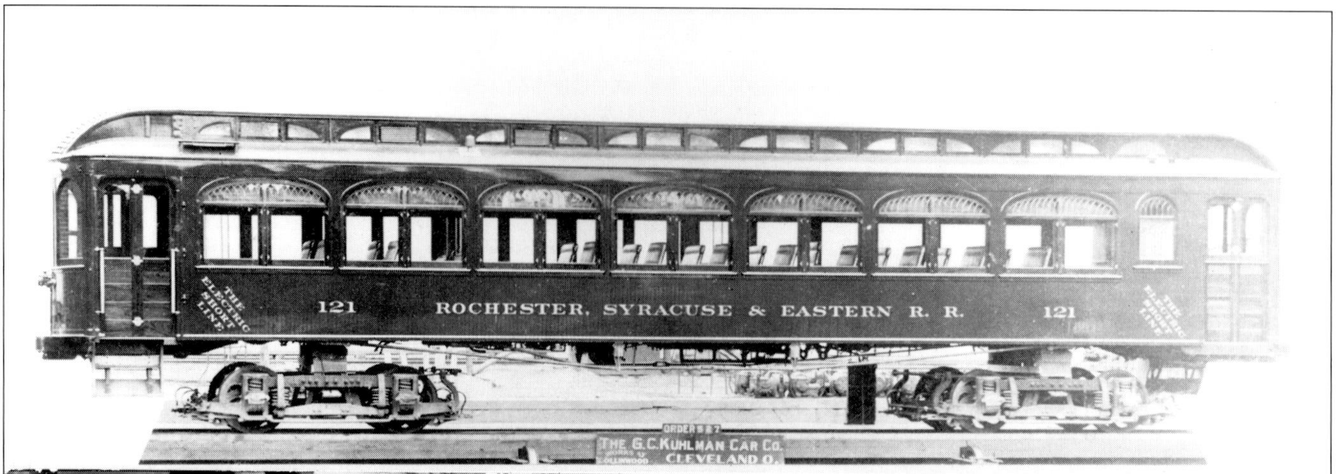

Wilbourne B. Cox collection

RS&E car 121, originally delivered by Kuhlman in 1909, was returned to its manufacturer in the spring of 1912 for rebuilding. The end vestibules were restructured. The right-hand entry doors were permanently closed off to become fake-looking doors with windows and the car's operating controls were moved from the center to the right-hand side. The RS&E subsequently applied these same alterations to all its operating fleet (cars 97-99 and 110-120) that initially came with center controls and four entry doors.

costly to maintain than the ones with rounded tops as originally built. Such changes were made as the occasion arose. A few of the cars, such as 125, had rounded windows at one end and rectangular at the other. When the controls were moved over to the right-hand side, the corresponding entrance doors were closed in and the steps removed. These changes mimicked car 121 which had been rebuilt by Kuhlman in 1912 and returned to the RS&E with this strange looking door panel. These cars never did look as handsome as the 122-129 series that were built for right-hand controls with only two entrances in opposite corners of the car.

After WWI, the R&S installed roller destination signs in its cars. These replaced the large painted metal signs that slid into frames mounted on the car sides next to the doors. The roller signs were mounted in the last window on each side next to the doors.

There is no evidence that the Rochester & Syracuse management ever seriously considered replacing its heavy-weight passenger car fleet with modern light-weight interurbans. Money for such an investment was simply not available even in the early to mid-1920s. Besides, the technology timing was off. The light-weight inter-city cars that prolonged the life of some of the long-distance midwest interurban lines were just being developed about the same time the R&S was being torn up. Such cars on the R&S would certainly have saved money - reduced cost of repairing the aging fleet, lowered power bills and reduced track maintenance charges.

But the company struggled on. It was always faithful in maintenance of its rolling stock. Most, if not all, of the passenger cars were in serviceable condition right through the last day of operation.

Wilbourne B. Cox collection

The eight passenger cars, 122-129, purchased from Kuhlman were the final additions to the RS&E fleet. Delivered in 1910, they were the same general design as the rebuilt car 121 except they presented a more finished appearance. These cars were handsome examples of the heavy interurban cars in the final days of wood construction with some steel reinforcing.

Parlor Cars

On two occasions, attempts were made to provide plush service between Rochester and Syracuse on the "The Electric Short Line." The first was in 1915 by the Empire United Railways and the second was in 1927 by the Rochester & Syracuse Railroad. In the first instance, two former business cars, the *999* and the *Marcella*, were converted into parlor cars and on the second try, seven standard passenger cars were rebuilt into chair cars.

In-as-much as the two private cars were considered to be the finest on wheels when new, it might be interesting to see what they were like. The *Marcella* was originally bought for Mr. Beebe by the Auburn & Syracuse Electric Railroad early in 1903. Built by Kuhlman in 1902, it was first exhibited at the Detroit convention of the American Street Railway Association that fall. The car, as exhibited, was divided into three compartments: an observation room with motorman's cab in the front right-hand corner, a stateroom with a three-quarter bed, toilet facilities and a shower stall, and at the rear end another lounge complete with built-in refrigerator and buffet. The interior finish of the car was Mexican mahogany. Equipment included wicker chairs and a green plush carpet. There was a built-in mahogany writing desk in the front room. In place of a rear vestibule, the *Marcella* had an open observation platform complete with heavy wrought iron grill work and a railing. This platform served as the main entrance to the car.

Even before the arrival of its replacement, the *Marcella* was released from private car duty and was converted into a parlor car by simply removing the stateroom, relocating the lavatory and installing a carpet and 24 wicker chairs. It was assigned to extra fare service between Syracuse, Skaneateles and Au-

The Kuhlman Car Company builder's photo (shop order 154) of Beebe's first private car Marcella, *acquired in 1903.*

burn on the Auburn & Syracuse line on August 22, 1909. This was mostly a summer run and as such was not financially successful. After a few seasons, this service was discontinued and thereafter the car was used only on charter runs and special occasions.

One such occasion occurred soon after the formation of the Empire United Railways and just before the car was assigned to a regular parlor car run on the Rochester-Syracuse Division of the EUR. It seems that the *Marcella* had carried a group of newspaper men over the line on a railroad publicity tour. After the trip, the car was stored for the night at the Newark shops. The rest of the tale is best related by an unknown poet whose effort was recorded as:

"The Marcella's Visit."

The best old car on the E.U.R
They sent on a trial trip.
She ran all day with her cargo gay,
Without e'er a hitch or slip.

She lay all night 'neath the fair stars bright
In the yard at the Newark barn,
And Woe is me;
What a sight was she, at eight o'clock next morn.

For reports went 'round that booze could be found
Within that dear old car.
Some unknown men right there and then
Tried her every bolt and bar.

They forced each door, and what is more
They entered with their dirty shoes.
And oh how sad these bold men bad
Drank up all the excellent booze.

That was stored away on the previous day
By officials of the grand old pike,
That pushers of the pen might recommend
This car to the ones who hike.

When the car went home with the booze all gone,
That was not drunk the day before,
The men higher up asked to know what "pup"
Had unlocked "Marcella's" door.

This mystery cloud, like a mighty shroud
Is wrapped 'round all concerned.
They tried inquiry set in language fiery,
But nothing at all could be learned.

Unhappy situation this,
A one 'twere better far to miss.
Another instant, sad but true
That shows what evil booze can do.

SMOKING ROOM OF THE *MARCELLA* SHOWING BUFFET

OBSERVATION ROOM OF THE *MARCELLA*

These interior views of Marcella *appeared in a G. C. Kuhlman Car Company 1902 advertising piece. They were reproduced in a May 1919 issue of* Electric Railway Journal *and then in volume 9 number 3 May 1976 issue of* Traction Heritage.

Late in 1910, the Rochester, Syracuse & Eastern, together with all the other Beebe roads, purchased from Kuhlman Car Company a private car the equal of which would have been hard to find. In fact, the *999* was one of the most luxurious pieces of interurban equipment ever built. The car was a 56-footer and weighed 45 tons. It was equipped for double-end operation, there being a motorman's cab in the left-hand corner at each end. The car wiring was arranged for both overhead and third-rail current collection. In one surviving photo of the car, its trucks appear to have been outfitted with third-rail shoes, so it could have operated over the New York State Railways Oneida Line between Syracuse and Utica. However, no records have been found that any such trips were ever made.

The car was divided into six rooms. At one end was a parlor compartment finished in African mahogany, fitted with a plush carpet and a number of wicker chairs. Next came a bedroom with an adjoining two-piece lavatory, then a dining room finished in African mahogany and equipped to serve eight people, followed by a kitchen complete with hot water heater and tank, stove, ice refrigerator, copper sink and storage areas for food, etc. The smoking or lounge room was the last room and at the opposite end of the car from the parlor. It was finished in Mission oak, had a writing desk in one corner and was furnished with leather covered chairs. All floors were covered with a thick carpet except for the marble in the lavatory and rubber tile in the kitchen and motorman's compartments. The car's end windows were the large observation type with low sills, two windows per end. Both end rooms and the dining room occupied the full width of the car. Passageways were provided along one side to get around the bedroom, lavatory and kitchen.

Financial records of the Auburn & Northern indicate that the "Directors' private car *999* was owned jointly by the Auburn & Northern, the Syracuse & South Bay, the Buffalo, Lockport & Rochester, the Auburn & Syracuse, the Rochester, Syracuse & Eastern and the Syracuse, Lake Shore & Northern Railroads." In 1911, the A&N share of the cost of the car was shown as $740.22. There are no records showing the original cost of the *999*. By extrapolating from the known cost to the Auburn & Northern and based on route miles of line owned by each company, the *999* cost in the neighborhood of $21,300.

Incidentally, the *999* should not be confused with the *Northern* built by the Niles Car Company in 1909 for the Northern Ohio Traction & Light Company. While the two cars were principally alike, a cursory inspection of plans and pictures would reveal many differences.

In the spring of 1915, the Empire United Railways inaugurated an extra fare Parlor Car service on weekdays between Rochester and Syracuse. The company's two business cars were chosen for this service as management saw that such equipment was a luxury they could not afford to reserve for just a few people. The *999* was converted by simply removing the bedroom and dining room equipment and installing 26 wicker chairs. The car was renamed *Rochester*. The *Marcella* was also put to work and it was renamed *Syracuse*. By this time, it had been stripped of its motors and was being used as a trailer. The parlor car service was short-lived and ended in the fall of 1916 due to the financial failure of the EUR. The two ex-business cars were rebuilt into freight cars (80 and 64).

Here are eight Kuhlman Car Company builder's views of the Beebe Syndicate Business Car 999. Descriptions of the individual compartments will be found in the text of travElectric. *Floor plan of 999 is from* Brill Magazine *V4 N10 1910.*

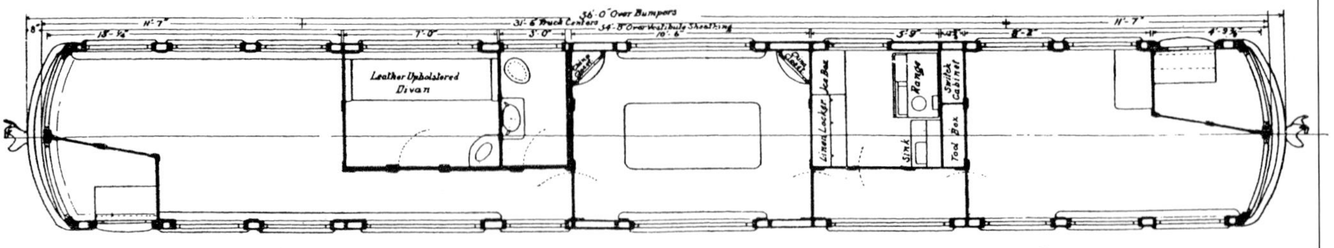

Parlor — Retiring room — Dining room — Kitchen — Smoking or Lounging room

Beebe Syndicate Business Car 999
Built by G.C.Kuhlman Car Company 1910
Folio of six interior views

Car 999 - Smoking or Lounging Room

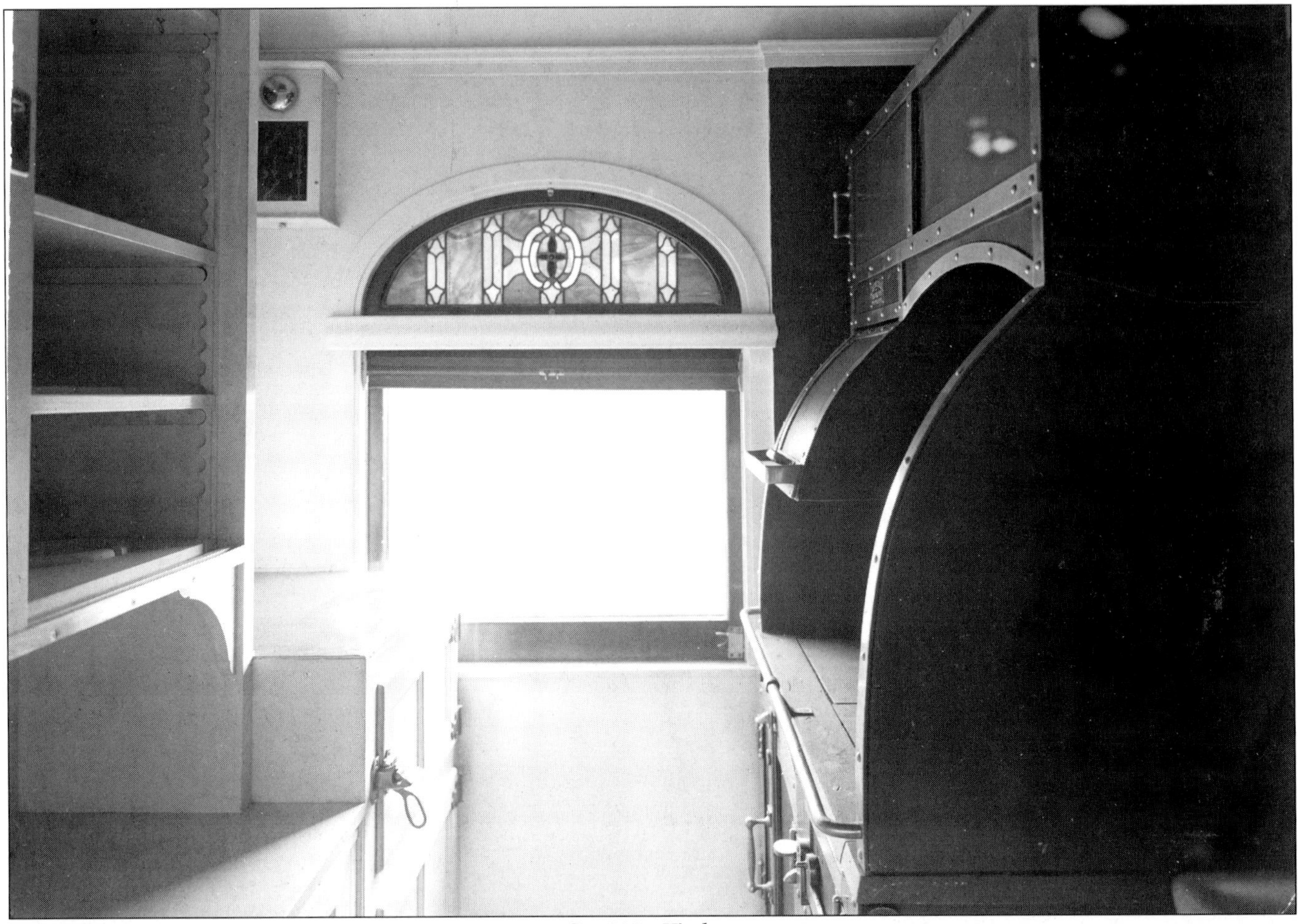
Car 999 - Kitchen

Car 999 - Dining Room

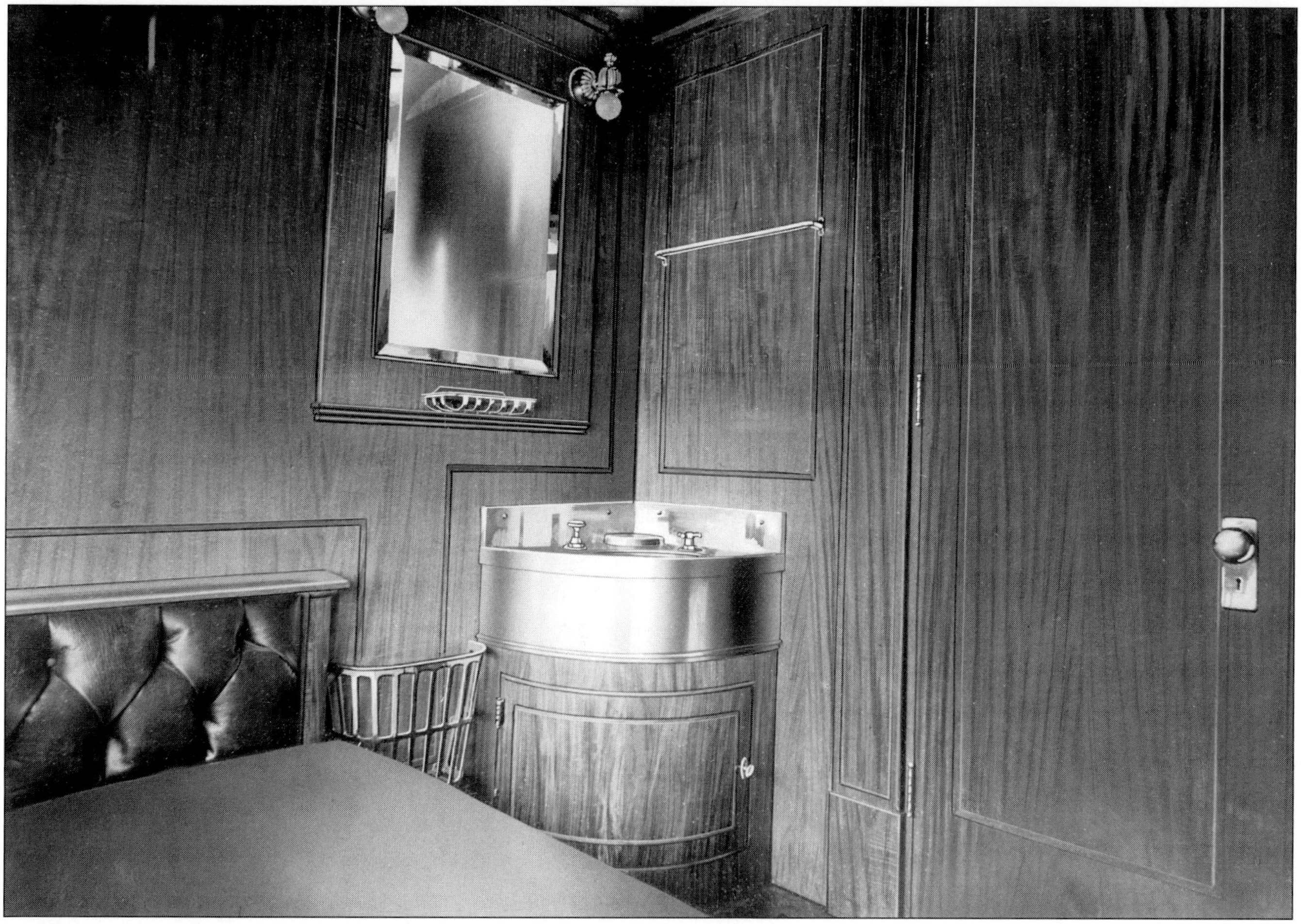

Car 999 - Retiring Room

Car 999 - Parlor

Courtesy of New York Museum of Transportation

The Beebe Syndicate business car 999 *is seen on track 1 at the Lakeland car shops c1910. This was the longest passenger car on the system, 56 feet, and weighed in at 45 tons. In 1915, the car was converted into an extra fare parlor car by removing its kitchen, dining room and bedroom facilities and filling the spaces with wicker chairs. After World War I,* 999 *was further converted. This time it became a freight trailer numbered 80.*

Chair Cars

The Company's second attempt to spruce up passenger service by car rebuilding occurred in 1926 and 1927. One by one, seven of the standard passenger cars were withdrawn from service and put through an extensive rebuilding and general overhaul program at the Lakeland shops. The cars emerged strengthened with steel siding where needed. The center posts of the double windows were removed to create large picture windows and each was fitted with storm sash for added winter comfort. The regular cross seats were replaced with individual double cushion bucket-type chairs fastened to the floor. The seats in the main compartment were wider than usual so only three across the car were possible. They were arranged two on the left side of the aisle and one on the right side. All were covered with maroon striped plush. The seats in the smoking compartment were more conventional in width, with two on each side of the aisle. They were covered with gray leather. The lavatory was located in the left rear corner of the main compartment. Each car had 40 chairs, 14 in the smoker and 26 in the main section. With the addition of 5 bench seats tucked in the corners, the car's seating capacity became 45. The interiors of the cars were painted in soft colors. Interlocking rubber tile floors served to deaden road noises. Extra-large overhead baggage racks and modern lighting fixtures were added for the comfort and convenience of the passengers. The cars' exteriors were painted light orange with tuscan red trim and gray roofs.

Although the cars retained their double-end operating equipment for turning purposes, the chairs were not movable, so the cars were operated in only one direction when in service with the smoking compartment always ahead. The cars could be turned on the loop at Lakeland, on the wye at the Newark shops and on the wye at West Belden Avenue freight terminal in Syracuse. When the Rochester Subway was opened, there was a loop at Oak Street and a storage track near City Hall Station to accommodate R&S cars.

The first car rebuilt was 112 and was named *Newark.* It entered service late in February 1927. The other six cars converted were 110 *Lyons,* 111 *Palmyra,* 122 *Rochester,* 123 *Syracuse,* 126 *Clyde* and 129 *Weedsport.* These cars all continued in chair car service as long as the road operated.

Here are seven company views of Rochester & Syracuse Railroad Chair Car 112 Newark *at the Lakeland shops. Car 112 was the first of seven standard R&S passenger cars gutted and rehabilitated in 1926 in what turned out to be a valiant but futile attempt to win back its rapidly dwindling passenger business. All work was done at the system's Lakeland shops located on the Empire State Railroad just 4 miles north of Syracuse.*

In the above view, 112 has just been rolled out of the paint shop for its first photo - December 1926. *Car 112 is also shown on page 66.*

Chair Car 112 Newark *made its first appearance on a main line in December 1926. With its winter storm windows in place, it was a gorgeous example of a 42-ton interurban car. The 112 would be placed in service in April 1927 when more of the rehabilitated cars were available to make up a suitable chair car service.*

In the very early spring of 1927, R&S Chair Car 112 Newark *was posed for a series of five portraits to advertise the new chair car service between Syracuse and Rochester. Later pictures of the other six cars created for this service suggest that 112 probably received the most extensive remodeling of the lot.*

A flat side view of Newark *standing on the loop track at Lakeland shops.*

This interior of Chair Car 112 shows 14 gray leather covered seats in the forward smoking section. Interlocking tile covered the floor.

The main sections of each chair car were fitted with 26 bucket-type seats covered with maroon striped plush. Two corner seats immediately beside the photographer were out of sight in this view.

This view of the main passenger compartment from the rear shows the two extra seats tucked in the front corners. None of the seats were reversible so the chair cars were always operated with the smoking compartment ahead.

CHAIR CAR SCHEDULE

In Effect April 17, 1927

WESTBOUND

Miles from Syracuse	STATIONS	TRAIN NUMBERS						
		A.M.	A.M.	A.M.	P.M.	P.M.	P.M.	P.M.
0	Lv. Syracuse Terminal	7 10	9 10	11 10	1 10	3 10	4 10	7 15
5	Lake Shore Junction	7 25	9 25	11 25	1 25	3 25	4 25	7 30
10	Warner	7 33	9 33	11 33	1 33	3 33	4 33	7 38
13	Memphis	7 37	9 37	11 37	1 37	3 37	4 37	7 42
18	Jordan	7 45	9 45	11 45	1 45	3 45	4 45	7 50
23	Weedsport	7 53	9 53	11 53	1 53	3 53	4 53	7 58
26	Ar. Port Byron	7 58	9 58	11 58	1 58	3 58	4 58	8.03
0	Lv. Auburn (E. S. R. R.)	7 30	9 30	11 25	1 25	3 25	4 25	7 35
26	Lv. Port Byron	7 58	9 58	11 58	1 58	3 58	4 58	8 03
34	Savannah	8 09	10 09	12 09	2 09	4 09	5 09	8 14
41	Clyde	8 18	10 18	12 18	2 18	4 18	5 18	8 23
48	Lyons	8 30	10 30	12 30	2 30	4 30	5 30	8 35
54	Newark	8 42	10 42	12 42	2 42	4 42	5 42	8 47
63	Palmyra	8 59	10 59	12 59	2 59	4 59	5 59	9 04
67	Macedon	9 06	11 06	1 06	3 06	5 06	6 06	9 11
76	Fairport	Stops to discharge passengers only.						
78	East Rochester	Stops to discharge passengers only.						
84	Culver Road	9 38	11 38	1 38	3 38	5 38	6 38	9 43
87	Ar. Rochester (Erie Station)	9 57	11 57	1 57	3 57	5 57	6 55	10.00
		A.M.	A.M.	P.M.	P.M.	P.M.	P.M.	P.M.

EASTBOUND

Miles from Rochester	STATIONS	TRAIN NUMBERS						
		A.M.	A.M.	A.M.	P.M.	P.M.	P.M.	P.M.
0	Lv. Rochester (Erie Station)	7 00	9 00	11 00	1 00	3 00	4 00	7 15
3	Culver Road	7 19	9 19	11 19	1 19	3 19	4 19	7 32
9	East Rochester	A	A	A	A	A	A	A
11	Fairport	B	B	B	B	B	B	B
20	Macedon	7 51	9 51	11 51	1 51	3 51	4 51	8 04
24	Palmyra	7 58	9 58	11 58	1 58	3.58	4 58	8 11
33	Newark	8 15	10 15	12 15	2 15	4 15	5 15	8 28
39	Lyons	8 27	10 27	12 27	2 27	4 27	5 27	8 40
46	Clyde	8 39	10 39	12 39	2 39	4 39	5 39	8 52
53	Savannah	8 48	10 48	12 48	2 48	4 48	5 48	9 01
61	Ar. Port Byron	8 59	10 59	12 59	2 59	4 59	5 59	9 12
9	Ar. Auburn (E. S. R. R.)	9 25	11 25	1 25	3 25	5 25	6 25	9 50
61	Lv. Port Byron	8 59	10 59	12 59	2 59	4 59	5 59	9 12
64	Weedsport	9 04	11 04	1 04	3 04	5 04	6 04	9 17
69	Jordan	9 12	11 12	1 12	3 12	5 12	6 12	9 25
74	Memphis	9 20	11 20	1 20	3 20	5 20	6 20	9 33
77	Warner	9 24	11 24	1 24	3 24	5 24	6 24	9 37
82	Lake Shore Junction	9 32	11 32	1 32	3 32	5 32	6 32	9 45
87	Ar. Syracuse Terminal	9 47	11 47	1 47	3 47	5 47	6 47	10 00
		A.M.	A.M.	P.M.	P.M.	P.M.	P.M.	P.M.

(A) Will stop at East Rochester when signalled by Agent, to receive passengers for all limited stops east of Fairport.

(B) Will stop at Fairport when signalled by Agent, to receive passengers for all limited stops.

ROUTE OF CARS IN THE CITY OF ROCHESTER DAILY EXCEPT SUNDAY—INBOUND—Via University Ave., East Main, Franklin, Andrews, St. Paul, South Ave., Court to Erie R. R. Passenger Station. OUTBOUND—From Erie R. R. Passenger Station, via Exchange, East Main and University Ave.

ROUTE OF CARS IN CITY OF ROCHESTER SUNDAYS—INBOUND—Via University Ave., East Main, N. Clinton, Andrews, St. Paul, South Ave., Court to Erie R. R. Passenger Station. OUTBOUND—Via Exchange, East Main and University Ave.

Wide Windows for Vision

Rochester and Syracuse Railroad

THE ELECTRIC LINE

Chair Car Service

1. Lowest fare between Rochester and Syracuse.
2. 87 Miles of high speed double track.
3. Maximum passenger comfort without extra fare.
4. Clean ride, no cinders - no smoke.
5. Elimination of automobilist's worries.
6. Stations in center of cities and villages.
7. Courteous trainmen.
8. Safest form of transportation: not a passenger fatality in the twenty years' history of the road.

THE Rochester and Syracuse Railroad has always been one of the foremost electric railroads of this country, and it is still the policy of this Company to maintain its supremacy in the electric railway transportation field.

For the past two years the officers of this Company have been working on a design of a car which would embody all of the beauty and easy riding qualities contained in the private automobile, steam road chair car and the deluxe bus.

The new chair cars are operated in limited service between Rochester, Syracuse and intermediate villages.

The cars, weighing 45 tons and equipped with 500 horsepower motors, have individual double cushion chairs of the most comfortable type, extra large windows give an unobstructed view, rubber floor to deaden noise, modern lighting fixtures and wide racks for suitcases and coats.

The interior of the car is finished in a soft color and with the gray leather and rich maroon striped chair covering and restful lighting, a pleasing effect is secured. These refinements with the comfort, spaciousness and courteous attention, all contribute to make your chair car journey most enjoyable.

This Company offers without extra fare this unexcelled chair car service.

Main Compartment

The Rochester and Syracuse Railroad is a high speed double track Electric Line, directly connecting the Cities of Rochester and Syracuse, a distance of eighty-seven miles. As the line traverses the main streets of numerous villages, the traveler will find it convenient to alight near the Hotel, Bank, Store or Residence, while through passengers find terminals in the heart of the principal cities. Connection with various Electric, Steam and Bus lines afford unusual facilities for safe and rapid travel, thus bringing into close touch the great population of Central New York.

Limiteds make direct connection with Auburn cars at Port Byron. At Lake Shore Junction travelers make connections to and from Baldwinsville, Phoenix, Fulton, Minetto and Oswego.

An Interior View of New Chair Car

FARE

Between Rochester and Syracuse

$2.50 ONE WAY — $4.00 ROUND TRIP TEN DAY LIMIT

WEEK END TICKET

Between Rochester and Auburn or Syracuse

$3.40 ROUND TRIP

Good Saturdays and Sundays Only

TICKETS ON SALE AT TICKET OFFICES ONLY

For further information telephone Local Agent or address

TRAFFIC DEPARTMENT
500 Syracuse Savings Bank Building
Syracuse, New York

This nice 4" x 7" 6-panel slick paper folder announced the new Chair Car service on the R&S between Syracuse and Rochester beginning April 17, 1927.

R&S Chair Car 126 Clyde *and car 125 are seen on track 2 in the Lakeland car shop on June 25, 1931. The 126 required less structural rehabilitation work than the 112. 126 did not need steel plating on its sides and the end windows retained their arched tops.*

Freight and Service Cars

When the Rochester, Syracuse & Eastern Railroad was first opened, its freight equipment consisted of three 53' 6" motor express cars of all-wood construction (61, 67 and 68). As business increased, additional cars of the same general type were purchased. Details will be found in the Roster section of this book. Most of the express cars were equipped with two sliding doors on each side. One car had meat hooks installed along one side during a period when calves were being delivered in Rochester. All cars were double-ended and were equipped for multiple-unit operation.

This is an early view of RS&E car 68. The occasion for this picture is unknown although it is thought to have been the first express car delivered to the property in 1906. Builder was Niles Car and Manufacturing Company of Niles, Ohio.
James I. Barstow collection

This is a "last day" picture of Rochester & Syracuse express car 63 taken on Main Street, Palmyra June 27, 1931. Note the plank hanging from the car side between the two sliding doors. This plank was a personnel bridge between the car floor and an adjacent loading dock.

From Brill Magazine V9 N5, May 1915

In 1914, the Empire United Railways purchased from G. C. Kuhlman Car Company five 53-foot steel express cars numbered 62-66, for its flourishing freight business between Rochester, Syracuse and Oswego. Three of the cars, 62,65 and 66, were assigned to the Rochester - Syracuse Division and the other two, 63 and 64, were assigned to the Syracuse - Oswego Division. These last two cars were renumbered 33 and 34. The 3-car train seen here was standing on Belden Avenue in front of the Syracuse freight house. Note each car had end doors for personnel and to accommodate long loads that couldn't fit through the sliding side doors.

Wilbourne B. Cox collection

These 1914 builder's views represent a group of five 53-foot freight and express cars purchased by the Empire United Railways. Numbered 62-66, cars 62, 65 and 66 were assigned to its Rochester - Syracuse Division and 63 and 64 worked the Syracuse - Oswego Division. They were renumbered 33 and 34 respectively. In the 1920s, these five cars saw through freight train service between Syracuse and Buffalo over the neighboring Rochester, Lockport & Buffalo and the International Railway Company.

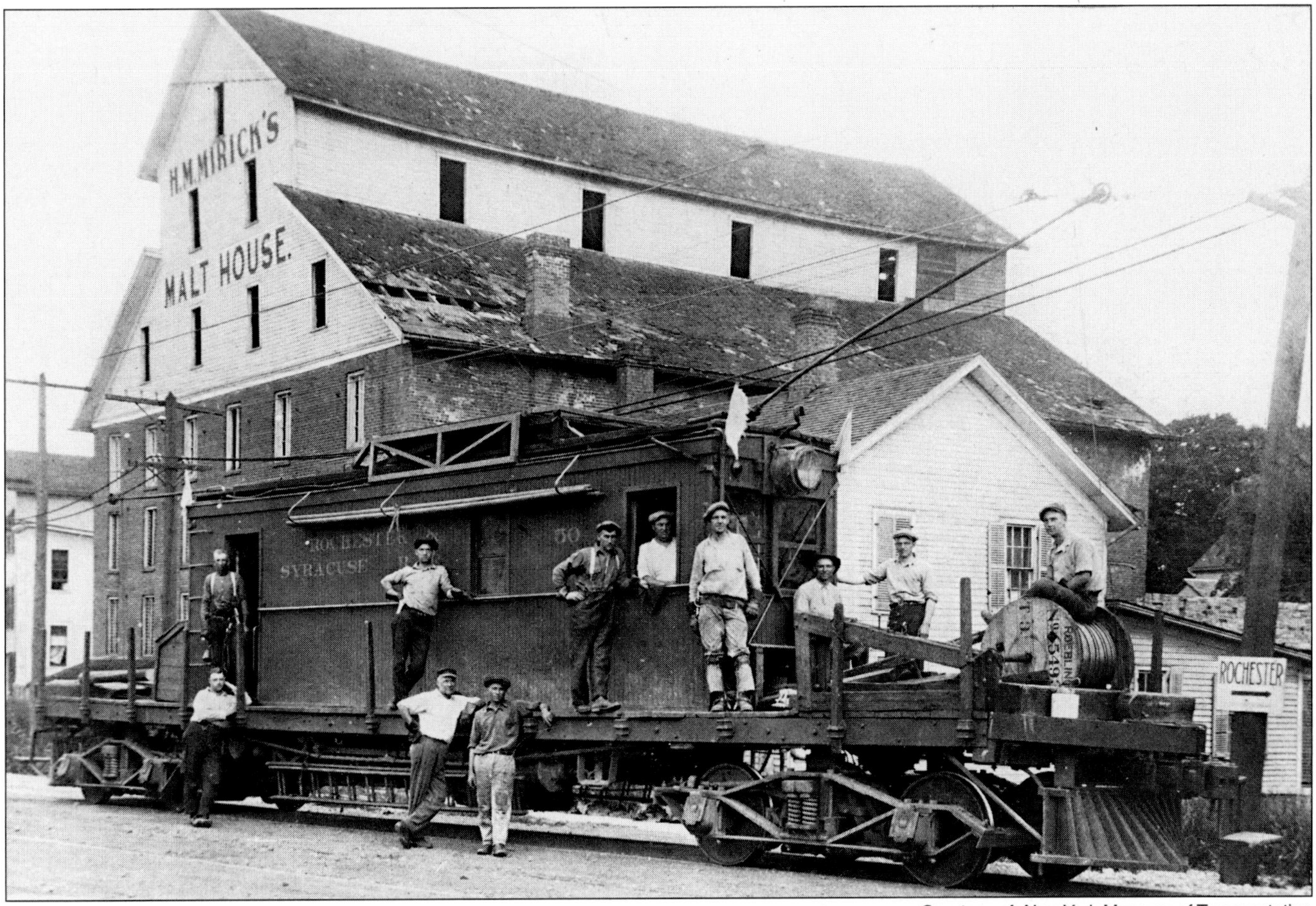

Courtesy of New York Museum of Transportation

Niles Car and Manufacturing Company produced this RS&E line car, number 50, in 1906. It was there to build the railroad and was still there, going strong, when the road closed in 1931. This view, taken at the east end of Main Street, Palmyra, is dated about 1928.

In 1914, the Empire United Railways purchased five 53-foot freight motors of standard design from J. G. Brill Car Company for a total of $48,750. After the EUR was broken up, three of these cars were assigned to the Rochester & Syracuse (62, 65 and 66) and the other two went over to the Empire State Railroad (33 and 34).

Line car 50 was a veteran of the road from first to last. It assisted in the construction of the RS&E and was still in use in 1932 when the property was dismantled. Work car 64 was a freight motor with a fixed platform added to its roof so it was also capable of handling overhead wire work.

Central New York state was a region of generous snowfalls so the rosters included a considerable amount of snow fighting equipment. The RS&E list

Richard Pearson collection

Central New York state winters worked hardships on the RS&E. One of its snow plows is seen adjacent to the station, perhaps preparing for a trip over the Auburn & Northern to Auburn. Date unknown. Pick most any winter.

Richard Pearson collection

RS&E express car 63 eastbound at Port Byron. This amount of winter snow was not uncommon. c1912.

Earl W. Fletcher, photographer

Some of the R&S equipment is lined up on the scrap track at Lakeland shops in the summer of 1931. Snow plow 1002 was the first double-end electric snow plow ever built by Russell. The year was 1906. The sign on car 97 reads: "Culver Road Limited."

Both photos, Robert O. Waters collection

R&S Russell snow plow 1003 at Lakeland scrap track in the summer of 1931.

R&S rotary snow plow at Lakeland shops for scrapping in the summer of 1931.

at the time of the road's opening in 1906 included a Russell rotary snow plow and a Russell double-end snow plow with wing attachments. The latter was the first double-end plow that Russell ever built for an electric line. In 1918, a snow sweeper was purchased. Two more snow plows had been added by 1909. All equipment was of wood construction, all were built for double-end use and all were available for use as long as the road existed. The cars in this freight and service class were painted red. The sweeper (1000) outlived the R&S for it was sold in 1931 to the New York State Railways for use on its Syracuse lines.

Even with all this snow-fighting equipment, the line still had its share of winter troubles. Sleet was the electric railways' worst enemy but drifting snow caused much grief as well. There were some winters when the cuts near Macedon drifted in so tight that neither the Russells nor the rotary could keep the line open. When cars got stuck under those conditions, it was necessary for the section forces to dig them out. More than once, passengers spent

Onondaga Historical Association Museum & Research Center, Syracuse, NY.

This winter scene is looking westerly at Memphis, Stop 91, about 12 miles west of Syracuse. Memphis was really an open agency station. For years, the agent was John Patterson who owned Patterson's general store on the right in this view. No doubt, RS&E tickets were sold in the store rather than in the shelter. The hamlet of Memphis (population 190 in 1910) lay a half-mile to the left from this view, across the tracks of the West Shore and New York Central railroads. Note the little-used crossover partially buried in the snow just beyond the near catenary bridge. At many of these crossovers along the line, the company felt it unnecessary to have accompanying crossover trolley wires.

Both photos, J. J. McCarthy, R&S Engineering, photographer

These two pictures show some of the weed spraying operation on the R&S in 1920. Seven nozzles mounted on the end of the flat car sprayed the weed killer, two on each side of the rails and three between the rails. The right view was looking east at Stop 82, one mile east of Weedsport. Parts of the spray nozzle mechanism can be seen at the bottom of the picture. Note the two sets of cattle guards to discourage wayward cattle on the public roads from entering the railroad's right-of-way.

the night on the road. Once or twice when the line west of Newark was plugged for any length of time, the company borrowed Buffalo, Lockport & Rochester passenger cars to provide service into Rochester.

Two non-powered flat cars on the roster, 10 and 11, were carryovers from the construction days. In the summer of 1920, a herbicide weed killer outfit was mounted on one of these cars. Product was sprayed onto the track area through seven nozzles arranged across the end of the car as it was pushed along the line. Surviving pictures indicate that this was pretty much a home-made arrangement for weed control.

A third flat car, number 12, was acquired in 1922 when the Lyons cut-off was built. Four 80,000-pound hopper cars were purchased second-hand in 1922 for hauling cinders on the Lyons track relocation job and they remained on the property for general ballast work until the windup. In order to widen the fill at Lyons for two tracks, four side-dump ballast cars were rented from the Goodwin Car Company near Chicago.

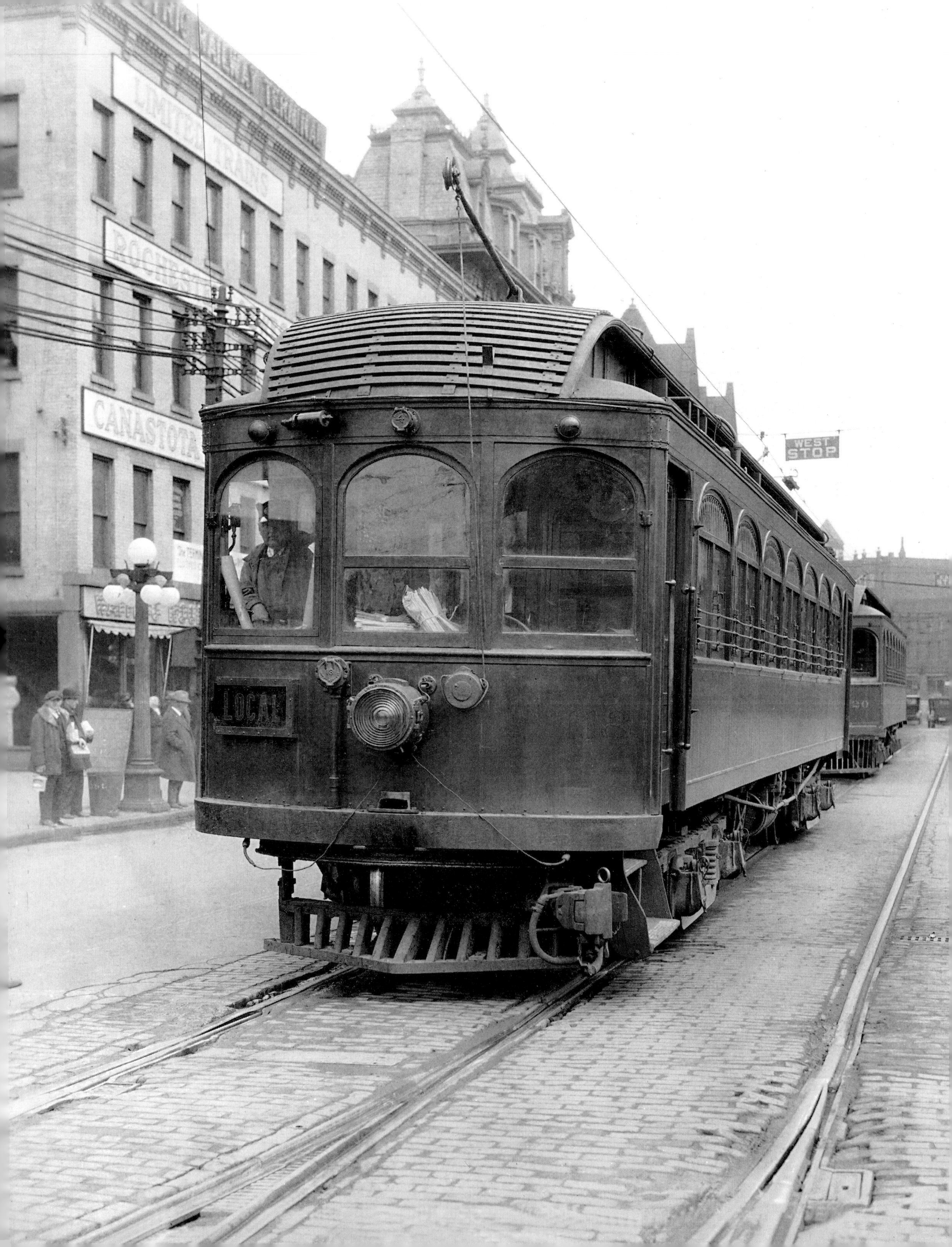
RAILWAY TERMINAL
LIMITED TRAINS
CANASTOTA
WEST STOP
LOCAL

5

RS&E in Operation

All train operation on the Rochester, Syracuse & Eastern Railroad was under the control of the Trainmaster whose office was located in Newark. Since the line was double-track, there were no meets under ordinary conditions so train orders were seldom needed. Regular passenger trains were first-class and regular freight trains were second-class. Both were listed in the working timetables. Eastbound trains were given even numbers while odd numbers were applied to westbound trains. Local cars were required to clear Limited cars by 5 minutes. Second-class cleared first class by 5 minutes and all extra trains (which carried white flags) cleared scheduled trains by 10 minutes.

In the early days, the spacing of cars traveling in the same direction was controlled by train registers located at Culver Road (Rochester), Fairport, Palmyra, Newark Car Barn, Clyde, Port Byron, Jordan and Lake Shore Junction. At each of these stations, the car's conductor was required to register his train, car number and his time of arrival at the station. Each conductor had to check the time of arrival of the next train ahead of him. No train could leave a register station with less than 10 minutes on the car ahead except between Fairport and Culver Road where a 5-minute headway was allowed. The train registers were discontinued in 1916. Standard flagging rules were spelled out in the company rule book. These rules continued to give rear end protection to any train falling back on another's time between stations.

Facing page: *This is a publicity view of Crouse-Hinds Company in Syracuse to advertise its "Interurban Trolley Car Luminus Arc Headlight Installation." The subject car is R&S 118 at the Electric Railway Terminal on Clinton Square, Syracuse. Syracuse Northern Electric car 20 is seen in the background, date early 1920s.*

There were only two rulebooks in use during the lifetime of "The Electric Short Line." The first was issued by the Rochester, Syracuse & Eastern Railroad and was effective January 1, 1907. It was a little red leather covered 26-page book patterned after one of several styles in use on interurban lines of that period. A supplement issued in 1911 covered operations in the signal territory between Macedon and Culver Road. The second "Book of Rules and Regulations for the Government of Employees" was issued by the Rochester & Syracuse Railroad on February 1, 1918. It had a dark blue cloth cover and its content and layout was patterned after the "Standard Code of Rules for Interurban Operation" as adopted by the American Street and Interurban Railway Association at their 1909 Denver convention.

Instruction books on Electrical Equipment and

This is one of the few views of a three-car train on the RS&E. Here cars 128-126-125 are seen standing on the yard lead at the Newark car shops. The third car is standing on one of the very few facing point switches on the railroad's double-track main line. In the far distance, the tracks turn to the left or northerly into South Main Street for a run of 1.5 miles of street running through Newark village.

This has to be one of the earliest pictures of an RS&E car (110, 111 or 112) on the streets of Newark, NY. The car was westbound on the eastbound track turning from East Union Street onto South Main Street. No destination sign showing suggests that the car, on the wrong track, was not yet in service. The card was postmarked August 22, 1906, less than 60 days from the road's opening, July 2, 1906. At the postcard date, the RS&E was in operation from Lyons, 6 miles to the east, to Fairport, 21 miles to the west.

Air Brakes were issued on two occasions, the first jointly by the RS&E and the Syracuse, Lake Shore & Northern Railroad in April 1911, and the second by the Empire United Railways in April 1914. These books were written in the "question and answer" format.

In addition to the Special Instructions carried in the employees' timetables, bulletins were issued from time to time covering special operating conditions.

The first superintendent of the RS&E was Paul E. Emerson. He remained in that capacity until 1914 when he left the railroad to join the Comstock Canning Company in Newark. He was succeeded by J. M. Delaney. W. H. Sheehan followed Delaney in the latter part of 1916 and was in turn succeeded by R. E. A. Pitman in January 1917. Five months later, Alan P. Norris was appointed superintendent and held that position till the end of operations in 1931.

Norris brought many years of railroad experience to the R&S. He began in the Baltimore office of the Atlantic Coast Line. In 1908, he joined the Washington, Baltimore & Annapolis Electric Railroad where he worked his way up to trainmaster. His next move, in 1913, was to the Maryland Electric Railways (Annapolis Short Line) where he became associated with the Allen & Peck electric railroad management firm. Norris became purchasing agent for the Short Line. At that time, Talmadge C. Cherry was its general manager. In 1916, Allen & Peck moved both Cherry and Norris to another of their properties, the Auburn & Syracuse Electric Railroad. Here, Norris became purchasing agent. A year later he went over to the Rochester & Syracuse as superintendent. In 1927, Norris became superintendent of the Empire State Railroad and the Syracuse Northern Electric Railway as well.

During much of the company's lifetime, its operating men were members of the Amalgamated Association of Street Railway Employees. Beginning June 1, 1913, the motormen and conductors of the Empire United Railways were organized under the Brotherhood of Locomotive Engineers and the Order of Railway Conductors. As such, they enjoyed the privileges of free transportation on the neighboring New York Central between Rochester and Newark. This was very convenient if the beginning or end of their runs were in Rochester and they lived in Newark.

The only work stoppage that ever occurred on the Rochester & Syracuse was a 10-day jurisdictional strike in 1919. According to the *Lyons Republican* for May 16th of that year, "the Amalgamated Association objected to having the Rochester & Syracuse cars run into either Syracuse, Rochester or Auburn by members of the Brotherhood of Locomotive Engineers. This made it necessary to change employees when entering Rochester at Culver Road. A demand was then made for the same arrangement on entering Syracuse. This would cost the company about $60,000 annually." The outcome was that the R&S men joined the Amalgamated and this arrange-

This 1907 real postcard view of Newark's commercial district was later copied and sold as a tinted card. In the newer cards, the large telephone pole in the foreground had been carefully removed but the artist left the man in the white shirt and straw hat leaning with no pole to support him. Anyone with a tinted card can check this out.

ment continued as long as the cars operated.

In later years, the Amalgamated was expanded to include freight and express car messengers, ticket and freight agents, shop and barn men, bridge men, substation operators, substation electrical repairmen and bonders. The linemen were members of Local 300 of the International Brotherhood of Electrical Workers.

The labor-management relations on this railway were always carried out on a very high plane. Very few difficulties ever arose and the working conditions, wages and hours generally improved throughout the life of the company. For example, by 1926, the wages of motormen and conductors had increased more than 75% over the 1913 rates.

In October 1906, the employees of the RS&E organized the Employees Mutual Aid Society to promote fellowship and mutual assistance among its members in times of distress. Nominal monthly dues were charged and modest sick benefits were available to members. The first club rooms were in the DuBois Block on Main Street in Newark. They contained a pool room, reading room, etc. A similar organization known as the Lake Shore & South Bay Mutual Benefit Association cared for employees of the Syracuse, Lake Shore & Northern and the Syracuse & South Bay roads.

In the summer of 1910, the men developed a baseball league between the railroads. The Auburn & Syracuse was included. Under the schedule set up, each team played each of the others three times in a season. The records of the first season showed that the A&S got off to the best start for they won the first game from the RS&E by 21-0 and then beat the SLS&N by 3-0. Games were played in Newark, Syracuse and Auburn. It is not known how many seasons the league lasted.

The men who operated the cars were a great bunch. They were patient too. Conductor Pollock was in charge of the last car into Rochester from Fairport on Saturday nights. There was generally one man from the local canning factory on board. He was always armed with a $10 bill and no change to pay for the 25-cent fare. This sort of thing got tiresome after a while so Pollock was ready one night. When the usual $10 bill was offered, Pollock broke open a roll of quarters and gave the young man his change, $9.75 all in quarters. The man was so mad that he threw his hands in the air, scattering the quarters to the four corners of the car. He soon cooled off and spent the rest of the trip scooping up quarters with the rest of the passengers.

As with many of the country's electric interurban railroads, the RS&E did not come under the jurisdiction of the U. S. Railroad Administration during the first World War. If these electrics had been more active in handling carload freight at the time, their story might have been different. Even so, they did exchange electric express cars with each other, offering through service between major upstate points, and so were able to assist the war effort in that way.

RS&E car 98 in the Fairport - Culver Road stub service is seen discharging and loading passengers at East Rochester.

Car 110 was pointed west on the eastbound track at Fairport station, having just arrived from Culver Road, Rochester. If spot time for this commuter run was short, the car, after loading, would pass through a crossover just west of the station on its way back to Culver Road and University Avenue.

Passenger Service

The Rochester, Syracuse & Eastern Railroad was designed and built to provide fast and frequent passenger service for the people of Syracuse, Rochester and all intermediate points. As soon as the first section of the RS&E was opened, local passenger service was offered on an hourly basis. When construction was completed westward to Culver Road, Rochester, in September 1906, the company began running Limited cars making three round trips daily between that point and Lyons, 45.6 miles. The running time for these cars was 1:15 while the locals, operating every 50 minutes throughout the day, made the trip in 1:40. All passengers for Rochester changed at Culver Road to cars of the Rochester Railway's University Avenue line for the 15-minute ride into downtown Main Street. At this time the company also inaugurated half-hourly commuter service between Fairport and Culver Road, an 8-mile trip. As many as 1,000 tickets a day were sold over this portion of the road when it was first opened. Many just went for the ride. This commuter service was always popular even after the novelty wore off. The half-hourly service continued right up to the end in 1931. This service was never extended west of Culver Road onto street railway tracks although, in 1931, there was some talk of extending street railway service to Fairport.

The first revenue movement over the RS&E was actually operated 10 days before the road was officially opened. On Saturday June 23, 1906, the Garlock Packing Company of Palmyra wound up its three-day annual convention of office managers with a banquet at the Hotel Gardenier in Newark. Two separate cars were used to transport the group to Newark and back. The eastbound trip left Palmyra at 7 P.M. and made a 17-minute non-stop run. The party broke up about midnight and the trip back to Palmyra was made without incident. No one present ever dreamed that the very last revenue car would roll into the Newark barn very close to 25 years from the day these first cars turned in for the night.

On June 1, 1907, the Company opened its new waiting room and ticket office at Culver Road and University Avenue, Rochester. Limited cars began operating into the center of Rochester as far as East Main and Franklin streets on June 17, 1907. Timetable 14, effective that date, listed four Limited cars in each direction. They made only five intermediate village stops to Lyons. Two local cars in each direction also ran into the city as far as Main and Franklin

Onondaga Historical Association Museum & Research Center, Syracuse, NY.

On June 23, 1906, the office managers of the Garlock Packing Company wound up a three day convention in Palmyra with a round trip on the brand new Rochester, Syracuse & Eastern electric railway to Newark. A banquet in Newark was part of the trip. This was the initial revenue run for the electric cars as the line did not officially open for business between Newark and Macedon until July 2nd.

RS&E car of the 122-129 series, signed "Limited Car for Syracuse" is eastbound on East Main Street, Rochester. The date is about 1909 and the time is 11 AM according to the street clock in the background.

One of the RS&E "short cars" (97-99 series) signed "Culver Road-Fairport" is eastbound on University Avenue, Rochester. Lack of street traffic suggests a date in the 1908-1910 period.

Westbound RS&E car 110 making a station stop at Port Gibson. The substation and ticket office were over the photographer's left shoulder. "The Electric Short Line" is painted diagonally at each end of each side panel.

streets. All other trips terminated at Culver Road.

Timetable 22, issued August 10, 1908, showed the first through service between Rochester and Auburn via Port Byron and the Auburn & Northern Electric Railroad. At Auburn, close connections were made with Auburn & Syracuse cars for their 1:25 run into Syracuse. By this time, all RS&E cars (except the Fairport-Culver Road stub) were running into Main and Exchange streets, Rochester, known as "Four Corners." Amsden's Tourist Agency on the southeast corner of the intersection became the line's downtown ticket office at that time.

With the opening of the direct line to Syracuse via Weedsport and Jordan on December 18, 1909, the through service between Rochester and Auburn was discontinued. At the Syracuse end, the RS&E cars operated over the tracks of the Syracuse, Lake Shore & Northern Railroad from Lake Shore Junction 4.40 miles into the heart of Syracuse. The ticket office and waiting room was located on the north side of Clinton Square, within a few blocks of downtown Syracuse. The Terminal had been opened by the Syracuse, Lake Shore & Northern in the summer of 1909 and was used as long as the interurbans operated.

By the following summer, the RS&E was in top condition and its schedules were altered to meet the traffic requirements. Here is how a local guide *Trolley Talk* described the schedule that was dated June first of 1910:

> The new running time provides for making the run between the Electric Railway Terminal in Syracuse and the Four Corners in Rochester by the Limited trains in two hours and thirty-seven minutes, a distance of eighty-seven miles. Exactly thirty minutes of this time is consumed in getting out of one terminal city and into the other so that the actual running time between the two city lines is but two hours and seven minutes including the time used in making twelve station stops.
>
> To make this schedule on time the motorman must drive the Limited trains at a speed of a mile a minute on the private right-of-way between the villages. That this can be accomplished day in and out without difficulty has been demonstrated frequently during the

Port Byron was the point of interchange for passengers from the RS&E bound for Auburn. In this view, Auburn & Northern car 51 was boarding passengers for the 8-mile 30-minute trip south to Auburn. Car 51 had a long history. Built in 1901 by Stephenson Car Company for the Auburn Inter-Urban Electric Railroad, it became Auburn & Syracuse 51 in 1903 and was sold to A&N in 1910. The track connection between the A&N and RS&E was an extension of the RS&E freight house track passing the station bay window and then turning south onto Main Street, Port Byron. RS&E car 120 on the right was eastbound. The photo is dated about 1910.

On occasion, Auburn & Syracuse car 60 was pressed into service on the Auburn & Northern line for runs between Auburn and Port Byron. The RS&E car in the background was eastbound, and was headed for Weedsport, Jordan and Syracuse. The picture dates about 1910.

past two months when regular Limited trains have made runs during which a speed of practically sixty-five miles per hour was maintained for stretches of several miles.

No other electric railroad in the United States has attempted to approach this speed even in test runs not to mention applying it to regular daily schedules, thus making the Rochester, Syracuse & Eastern schedule the fastest in the United States.

A feature of the new schedule is the suburban 'stub' service inaugurated between Syracuse and Weedsport. The new schedule eliminates the stopping of Limited runs at Memphis and Warner, but provides this special suburban service. All of the local stops are afforded an hourly local service in and out of Syracuse during the day and early evening.

In addition, for a year or so, local cars followed the Limiteds out of Rochester as far as Lyons with some variations. These were the golden years of interurban travel.

Although the above statements of speed in *Trolley Talk* were somewhat enthusiastic, the RS&E and later the R&S did maintain reasonably high speeds throughout the life of the railway. Between 1924 and 1933, an electric railway trade journal *Electric Traction* conducted an annual "Big Speed Contest" ranking two dozen of the country's interurban lines for elapsed time in miles per hour (MPH) when including stops. In 1929, the R&S ranked tenth by elapsed time, with the following statistics: 87 miles of road, 18 regular stops, 2:35 running time and 33.7 MPH including stops. Excluding stops, the R&S placed sixth with a speed of 43.9 MPH. The neighboring 48.57-mile New York State Railways, Oneida

An RS&E local car westbound had just left Warners station, 10 miles west of Syracuse. An eastbound car can be seen approaching from the distance.

This real photo postcard shows the layout of a typical stop at local crossroads on the RS&E. Montezuma, Stop 70, was a non-agency station and served a hamlet of about 400 persons in the 1910 era. Waiting passengers could flag local cars using one of the signal boxes mounted on poles closest to the shelter. The picture was taken in 1909 or 1910, judging from the immaculate condition of the building and grounds.

Louis C. Hennick collection

Westbound RS&E car 119 had just left Stop 71 and was about to pass under one of the few country side roads that were carried over the tracks in a cut. The location was three miles west of Port Byron station. The time was July 1914.

Line, ranked eleventh by elapsed time with 2 stops, 1:28 running time and 33.1 MPH including stops. Excluding stops, the Oneida Line placed tenth with a speed of 34.7 MPH. The number one contest entry in 1929 was the 89.8-mile Chicago, South Shore & South Bend Railroad. They had 6 stops, took 2 hours for the trip, averaged 44.9 MPH including stops and 49.9 MPH excluding stops. All information was compiled from actual timetables submitted by each contestant. The speed contests arbitrarily allowed 2 minutes per stop.

RS&E cars stopped near the Northern Central underpass on Union Street, Newark, for passenger connections with the Northern Central and the Newark & Marion railroads. Cars stopped at Brutus and Willow streets in Weedsport for passenger connections with the Lehigh Valley Railroad.

The New York Central announced, on April 10, 1910, that it was withdrawing six local trains between Syracuse and Rochester due to the decrease in traffic. At the same time, Beebe was announcing that some of his trains would be expanded to two

The RS&E passenger and freight station was in a prime location in Jordan. It occupied the entire southeast quadrant of the village main "four corners." Car 127 is westbound for Lyons, Newark and Rochester. Photo dates to the summer of 1910.

The RS&E was brand new in this summer 1910 view at Jordan station. Car 129 is eastbound. Its terminal will be Syracuse, 18 miles and 35 minutes away if on a Limited schedule. Note the switch-back track arrangement for express cars to reach the freight platform. A one- or two-track tail track was necessary to avoid a facing point switch in the westbound main line. Company policy was to avoid facing point switches in the main line if at all possible.

cars to handle the increase in business. He said the shops at Newark were equipping cars for multiple-unit operation as rapidly as possible.

The early years were busy ones for the Rochester, Syracuse & Eastern. After the cars were equipped with multiple-unit controls (1910), two-car trains were a common sight and three-car trains were not unheard of. Through the week of the New York State Fair each fall, the company had all its cars in service and sometimes had to lease several from the Buffalo, Lockport & Rochester. Also, during State Fair Week, the BL&R ran its 500-series cars in two-car trains from Lockport to Syracuse, stopping at the Rochester depot only long enough to change crews to RS&E men. In the late afternoon, cars would leave the Fair Grounds near Syracuse and run to Rochester as close together as possible with safety. On such occasions, "spacers" were placed at certain points along the line. These men kept in touch with the dispatcher by phone to keep the cars properly spaced.

During Fair Week 1910, conductor Charlie Soper reported a crowd of 138 on the lead car and

Louis C. Hennick collection

This westbound local car was at Memphis, about 12 miles west of Syracuse. The car was built by Kuhlman in 1908 as Auburn & Northern Electric Railroad car 10. It was acquired by the RS&E in 1910 and renumbered 119. The irregular quality of the car number painted on the car's end suggests a quick shop job of changing a 10 to a 119. This real photo postcard dates to 1910.

136 on the rear car of a two-car train leaving Rochester. At least another carload was left standing on the platform so a Fairport stub car was pressed into service making it a three-car train. There were 128 packed into the short car and still people were left behind. Only 6 got off at points short of the Fair Grounds.People were left waiting at every stop. Some of them waited all morning and part of the afternoon before a car came along with room for them.

In the heyday of the road, normal weekend traffic was so heavy that a fourth man was often added to the car crew of a two-car train. He was usually a high school boy and was called a "Bell Boy." He stood on the back platform of the first car and signaled the motorman when the passengers were all on or all off both cars. Because of the packed cars, the conductors were often unable to get to the back platforms and still collect the fares. Many local boys depended on this sort of job for their summer work.

Raymond Murphy of the *Lyons Republican* and a friend, Clyde Tims, were bell boys at the age of seventeen. They each wore a snappy visor cap with "Bell Boy" lettered across the front. Their uniforms were dark to match the conductors. They were paid 20 cents an hour and days were often 12 hours long. Lunch was grabbed during a 30-minute layover at the end of the line. Such tips as they received usually consisted of candy bars or cookies.

On April 10, 1911, RS&E cars began operating to and from the Electric Railway Terminal Station on the northeast corner of Court and Exchange streets in Rochester. This was also the terminal for cars of the Rochester & Eastern and Sodus Bay lines of the New York State Railways as well as those of the Buffalo, Lockport & Rochester Railway. RS&E cars continued to operate through the "Four Corners" and the time at that point was carried in their timetables. BL&R and RS&E cars laid over between runs on Exchange Street opposite the #1 Precinct Station. Two crossovers were provided to enable Exchange Street local cars to run around the interurbans. There was also a short storage track near the Erie Railroad freight house where two cars could be stored.

On April 20, 1914, the Rochester terminal for passenger cars of the RS&E (now Empire United)

An Interurban neighbor of the RS&E at Rochester.

The New York State Railways, Rochester & Eastern Line was a near neighbor of the RS&E. This 41-mile line from Rochester to Canandaigua and Geneva on Seneca Lake was opened as the Rochester & Eastern Rapid Railway June 15, 1904. The R&E became a tenant of the Rochester Subway December 1, 1927 and continued until the last car was run July 31, 1930. R&E car 162 is seen standing on Castle Street, Geneva, in 1922.

An Interurban neighbor of the RS&E at Rochester.

The New York State Railways, Rochester & Sodus Bay Line, was a 39-mile side-of-the-road trolley serving a string of villages along the south shore of Lake Ontario between Rochester and Sodus Point. Perhaps anticipating heavier passenger traffic on a continuing basis, four of these beauties were purchased from Kuhlman in 1909. They were numbered 115-118. The flag on this car indicates that a second car is following on the same schedule, c1910. The RS&E and Sodus Bay cars shared the same Rochester terminal on Exchange Street from April 1911 until April 1914 when the RS&E moved to the Erie Railroad station on Court Street.

Charles R. Lowe collection

An Interurban neighbor of the RS&E at Rochester.

In 1907, the Erie Railroad electrified its 34-mile Rochester-Mount Morris branch. Unlike the other interurbans in central and western New York state, the Erie electrification used an 11,000 volt alternating current system. Pantographs replaced trolley poles on the cars. While the RS&E/R&S were tenants at the Erie station, virtual across-platform transfers between the two electric lines were possible. The R&S cars moved to the Rochester Subway April 15, 1928 and the Erie gave up electric car service November 29, 1934.

RS&E car 112 on Court Street, Rochester, about 1914. The Erie Railroad passenger station and train-shed appears in the background.

RS&E car 119 on Court Street, Rochester, standing in front of the Erie Railroad passenger station. The man on the extreme right was a traveling freight agent (TFA) for the RS&E. He was the third man on local freight runs between Syracuse and Rochester, handling all the paper work, billing, routing and sorting of the less than carload shipments. Car 119 was originally lettered Auburn & Northern Electric Railroad 10.

A Rochester & Syracuse car of the 122-129 series on a layover track at the Erie Railroad station yard, Rochester. The time was September 1922. This car has received the new roller destination sign. These signs were mounted in the windows nearest the passenger entry doors.

G. A. Doeright, photographer

After descending the 4% grade from bridge number 1, westbound car 127 is approaching Winton Road, Rochester and is less than a mile from the end of RS&E track at Culver Road and University Avenue.

Views of Empire United Railways parlor car Rochester *(ex-999) are rare. Here,* Rochester *is leading a two-car train eastbound on University Avenue, Rochester. The second car is 97, 98 or 99, one of the shorter cars used in the Fairport-Culver Road (Rochester) service. This view is dated 1915 or 1916 because the Empire United Parlor Car service only lasted these two years.*

and BL&R was again moved, this time to the Erie Railroad passenger station on Court Street. Cars would wye off Court Street and were stored on two stub tracks laid along the west side of the Erie station. There was a crossover in the middle of these tracks to move cars by each other. An express office was located in the rear of this little yard. This was the last move of terminals until the R&S began using the Rochester Subway April 15, 1928.

In 1915, the Empire United began rerouting their cars through the streets of Rochester to avoid the downtown traffic congestion. Inbound cars were routed via University Avenue, East Main Street, Franklin, Andrews, St. Paul and Court streets to the Erie Terminal. Outbound cars were routed via Exchange Street to Main Street, thence east to University Avenue, except the 5 P.M. and 6 P.M. cars which left the Terminal via Court to Clinton to Main streets, thence east to University Avenue. On Sundays all inbound cars came west on Main Street to Clinton to Court Street and the Erie Terminal. By these routings, EUR traffic through "Four Corners" was reduced by 50%.

On March 7, 1915, the Empire United Railways inaugurated a plush extra-fare Parlor Car service between Rochester and Syracuse. The ads read:

$25 Worth of Luxury for 25 cents
GET THE ELECTRIC PARLOR CAR HABIT

At first, only the two ex-private cars were used. They were generally in two-car trains consisting of a regular passenger car and a parlor car. The *Rochester* (formerly *999*) was a motor car and was the

These two colored postcards were produced for the Empire United Railways in 1915 to promote its Extra Fare Parlor Car Service between Rochester and Syracuse. Parlor car Rochester *was former Beebe Syndicate business car* 999. *Car* Syracuse,*"used as a trailer, was the former parlor car* Marcella *on Auburn - Skaneateles - Syracuse route. The new EUR service was not financially successful. The cars were taken off in the fall of 1916.*

leading unit of its two-car train. The parlor car *Syracuse* (ex-*Marcella*) was a trailer by this time so it was the rear car on its two-car train. This would have been a pleasant sight for the *Syracuse* had retained its wrought-iron-railed observation platform. One parlor car seated 26 and the other 24. The extra fare of 25 cents per seat was charged, regardless of the distance traveled. All seats could be reserved in advance.

Business was so good for a while that a third parlor car was added to the fleet on February 3, 1916. This car, named *Newark*, was converted from a standard car and seated 26. Records fail to indicate the converted car's number. With the three cars, it was possible to operate a parlor car service on a two-hour headway throughout the day. The service was extensively advertised. Colored post cards showed both interior and exterior views of one of the parlor cars. Business was attracted by offering special taxi service (at a nominal rate) making direct connections with the cars at the Syracuse terminal. Special round-trip fares were offered between Rochester and Syracuse: $2.50 for a 30-day return limit ticket; $2.00 for a ticket going one day and returning the next; and $1.65 for a Sunday round-trip.

The March 7, 1915 timetable also showed the inauguration of a number of Limited through cars

A close-up of RS&E car 110 taking passengers at Clyde station about 1910.

This westbound two-car train was posing for a picture at the R&S Clyde station in the early 1920s. When the motorman, Corry Heald, gave me this glass plate negative many years ago, he did not know why the 124 was missing its front pilot. Note the hinged cover on the old style headlight, used to reduce the light's glare when operating on village and city streets.

between Rochester and Auburn. Limited cars left Rochester every hour on the hour throughout the day. Those leaving on the even hour ran to Syracuse and those on the odd hour ran to Auburn.

All these efforts were insufficient to put the Empire United on its feet so the parlor car service did not last. In September 1916, the RS&E was taken out of the Empire United receivership for a separate reorganization at which time the parlor car service was discontinued.

Timetable 47 dated September 25, 1916 was the first one issued by the RS&E shortly after it was taken out of the Empire United system. Even in receivership, the new management really stepped up the passenger service in an effort to attract business. Limited cars were being scheduled every hour in both directions with locals following the Limiteds out of each terminal every other hour. In all, there were 22 Limited trains and 18 through locals plus stub runs between Fairport and Culver Road every 20 minutes. Cars on the Auburn-Port Byron Branch ran every hour and connected with main-line cars at Port Byron. All this approximated taxi service rather than interurban service but the new management was determined to offer the very best. Gradually the under-patronized runs were eliminated but all through the 1920s virtually hourly service was maintained. Limited and local cars alternated throughout the day.

One of the biggest specials operated in the 1920s was on July 23, 1927 when Mr. D. M. Edwards, president of E. W. Edwards Stores (department stores in Buffalo, Rochester and Syracuse) entertained his employees at Sea Breeze Park on the shore of Lake Ontario, Rochester. The people from Buffalo came by New York Central train. The Rochester employees were already close at hand. There were 300 people from Syracuse who boarded three 2-car trains of the Rochester & Syracuse Electric for a fast run to Culver Road. Possible problems with the large interurban wheels negotiating unfamiliar city line tracks and switches were avoided by transferring all

Onondaga Historical Association Museum & Research Center, Syracuse, NY.

Three 2-car trains of R&S cars were lined up to accommodate a September 14, 1919 excursion sponsored by the Syracuse Rubber Company. All cars are shown standing on the southbound track of North Clinton Street, Syracuse. The four cars in the distance were properly headed south according to the extra flags and trolley poles showing. The two closest cars, 113 and one other appear, by flags and pole, to be pointed north against the two rear trains. If the two nearest cars were to reverse positions of trolley pole and flags, then all six cars would be properly oriented to go around the double-track downtown loop in a counter-clockwise direction and head for their destination. Car 113 would then be at the head of the procession.

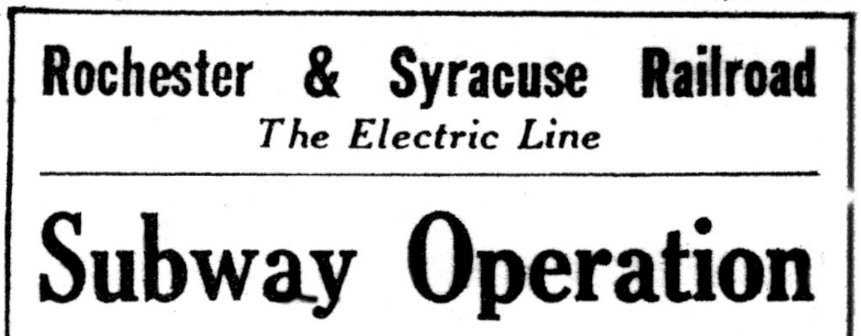

Rochester & Syracuse Railroad
The Electric Line

Subway Operation
IN
ROCHESTER

Cars of the Rochester & Syracuse Railroad will start operation in the Rochester Subway

Sunday, April 15th, 1928

Cars now operating to and from Erie Terminal will be routed via the Subway to City Hall Station, Exchange St. near Main, at which point a terminal and ticket office will be maintained.

Consult any Agent for additional information.

The tripper service to and from Culver Road at University Ave. will be continued as at present.

TELEPHONE—MAIN 4200

RIDE THE CHAIR CARS TO SYRACUSE—No Extra Fare

Rochester Democrat & Chronicle

passengers to the green and cream colored city cars of the New York State Railways at Culver Road.

In February 1927, the R&S began operating chair cars on their main line. Rebuilt from standard passenger cars as more fully described in the "Chair Cars" section, they were the latest word in heavy interurban electric cars of the luxury class. As fast as these cars were put through the shops, they were placed in service. By April 1927, seven round trips per day were being operated, leaving each terminal as Limiteds approximately on the odd hour. This was the company's last valiant attempt to retain some of the patronage that was rapidly being lost to the private automobile and the paved roads. How better could a person travel between Syracuse and Rochester, see all the countryside while riding in comfort and all for $4.00 round trip? Business was good for a time but deteriorating track conditions due to reduced maintenance and the continual

R&S car 111, Chair Car Palmyra *is awaiting its mid-morning departure from the Erie Railroad terminal, Rochester on a Limited run to Syracuse. The picture is dated between 1927 when chair car service was introduced, and April 15, 1928 when the Rochester Subway was opened for R&S cars. The bundles of newspapers will no doubt be loaded on the next local car.*

An undated newspaper half-tone shows an R&S car in the Rochester Subway. This operation began April 15, 1928 and ended June 27, 1931 when the R&S was abandoned.

pounding of 42-ton cars made the ride less desirable as the last years went by.

Beginning April 15, 1928, the R&S passenger cars were taken off the streets of Rochester and reached the center of town via the city's new Subway. The terminal for R&S cars was City Hall station, 3.83 miles from Rockwood Street (City Line). The R&S issued transfers to the local lines that intersected the subway at intermediate stations (Winton N, Colby, Monroe, Meigs-Goodman, Court Street and City Hall). Interurban cars of the Rochester, Lockport & Buffalo Railroad and the Rochester & Eastern Line of New York State Railways also used the new subway so connections at City Hall Station for through passengers were convenient. Starting on July 27, 1928, R&S cars spent 20 minutes of their layover times in Rochester by operating an additional 2.92 miles through to Driving Park loop at the western end of the subway. Transfers were available to R&S passengers who alighted at the four intermediate stations beyond City Hall.

Onondaga Historical Association Museum & Research Center, Syracuse, NY.

This eastbound R&S car had crossed the Genesee River under Broad Street and was turning to parallel South Avenue, Rochester on the last Sunday of operation, June 21, 1931. The site is now occupied by the Rundel Library.

This extended service ended July 31, 1930, when all R&S car runs terminated at the City Hall station. It turned out that a new Service-At-Cost contract between the City and the New York State Railways, Rochester Lines, effective August 1, 1930, did not include any arrangements for operating R&S cars in revenue service beyond City Hall.

T. H. Schuelke, photographer

Eastbound Rochester & Syracuse car 122, Chair Car Rochester, *was passing Stop 81 the afternoon of June 7, 1931. Stop 81 was two miles east of Weedsport and about 21 miles west of Syracuse. The east portal of Bridge 15 can be seen in the far distance.*

Courtesy Liverpool (NY) Public Library, T. H. Schuelke, photographer

One of the R&S chair cars is seen passing Stop 81 westbound. Running on a Limited schedule, its next stop was Weedsport. This picture was taken June 7, 1931, just 20 days before the end of all service on the Rochester & Syracuse Railroad.

The R&S Fairport-Culver Road stub cars did not enter the subway but continued to operate over their original route from the signaled Rockwood Street junction to Culver Road and University Avenue.

On April 15, 1930, the neighboring Auburn & Syracuse electric line discontinued all interurban service so, on August 3rd of that same year, the R&S inaugurated a through service between Syracuse and Auburn via Port Byron and the Auburn & Northern line of the Empire State Railroad. Five round trips a day were offered. Chair cars were normally assigned to these runs. It is interesting to note that although the distance between Syracuse and Auburn via Port Byron was 7 miles longer than the 27 miles on the A&S, the 1:15 running time of the R&S cars was 10 minutes less than via the old A&S. It should also be noted that the 8-mile Auburn-Port Byron line (owned by ESRR but operated in its final two years by the R&S) scheduled 18 round trips daily

Onondaga Historical Association Museum & Research Center, Syracuse, NY.

In the late afternoon, this westbound R&S car was fast approaching Newark from Lyons, the next stop east. The car was less than two miles east of the R&S Newark station. Date of the picture is c1930. The negative has suffered damage but this is a great view of the R&S in action during its closing years.

G. A. Doeright, photographer

A September 1922 view of R&S 2-car train (100 and 114) at the Syracuse Electric Railway Terminal on Clinton Square in Syracuse. Possibly a Labor Day crowd, judging from the decorations on the adjacent Board of Education Building.

between its terminals including the five chair car round trips. Two daily-except-Sunday freight trips were also listed. It was a busy single-track line, complete with block signals.

As the end drew nigh, the timetables reflected the drop in business. The last one issued, number 64 dated September 28, 1930, listed only 10 through trips each way each day between Rochester and Syracuse. They were mostly Limited runs stopping only at village stations. Chair cars were generally used. Running time was still 2:45. The cars undoubtedly made many an unscheduled stop at the intermediate road crossings where the faithful still waited for their electric cars to take them to town or bring them home. A number of local trips were scheduled between Rochester and Port Byron where connections could be made with the cars of the Auburn-Port Byron branch.

The R&S was already in receivership when its Syracuse-Auburn through car service began, so the end was plainly in sight. Some people always felt that the line might have survived longer if lightweight equipment and a single-track operation had been tried. However, there were no funds available to buy new cars and, in addition, there would have been too much track and signal work required to

William M Hayes, photographer

R&S Chair Car 110 Lyons *is seen at the Syracuse Electric Railway Terminal. The picture is dated 1931. The apparent lack of passengers points toward the end of R&S service June 27, 1931.*

Courtesy Liverpool (NY) Public Library, T. H. Schuelke, photographer

The bank clock and shadows on the sidewalk indicate that R&S Chair Car 122 Rochester *is about to leave for a local trip to Auburn via Port Byron on June 11, 1931. The last R&S timetable, dated September 28, 1930, listed chair car service on all Syracuse - Auburn runs and most Syracuse - Rochester trips.*

R&S Chair Car 111 Palmyra *was loading at the Syracuse Electric Railway Terminal on June 25, 1931 for a trip to Rochester. The destination sign in the last window next to the passenger entry door read "Rochester Local - Limited." This 4:10 PM departure made local stops as far west as Fairport, then ran Limited into Rochester. Tom Beston was the conductor and Andrew Vande Voorde was the motorman.*

safely carry the light weights at the high speeds for which they were designed. Then, too, it was quite evident that for an interurban railroad to survive in depression times, it had to have more than passenger service to sell. Although it was known that freight is the life-blood of any railroad, be it steam or electric, the Rochester & Syracuse Railroad was just not laid out properly to make the necessary transition.

Early in 1931, the R&S was granted an injunction by the courts against the United Arrow Lines, Inc., operators of a bus line between Syracuse and Rochester. The bus company used a Pierce Arrow 25-passenger bus and made two round trips daily. Greyhound was ultimately granted the rights to operate after the R&S cars stopped running.

People just wouldn't ride the electrics in preference to the family car or that of a neighbor. A story told by Receiver T. C. Cherry illustrates the point vividly. Shortly before the R&S closed down, the newspapers were full of accounts of the last ditch efforts to save the line. This one particular story, however, did not get into print. It seems that a number of men from a village on the R&S near Syracuse wrote Cherry for an appointment to discuss the future of electric passenger service. They wished to strongly protest the forthcoming abandonment as an act of faithlessness on the part of the railroad's management.

The meeting was set for 9 o'clock on a mid-week morning in Mr. Cherry's office at the Syracuse terminal. The men arrived primed with questions, petitions, etc. and were soon seated around Cherry's desk.

"Now, gentlemen", Mr. Cherry began, "Before you begin your questions, may I ask just one?"

They nodded their assent.

"Would each of you mind telling me just how you got to Syracuse this morning?"

The spokesman for the group began, "Why, all six of us came in Ed's car. What makes you ask?" The other members of the delegation were not so slow-witted and they saw the light very quickly.

Mr. Cherry then said, "Are there any further questions?"

The group got up and silently filed out. Not one of them had the nerve to say that he was sincerely interested in the future of the electric line. None had even considered riding train 20, a chair car, into Syracuse that morning. It had passed through their village at a convenient time and had arrived at the Syracuse terminal at 8:45 A.M., on time as usual.

The last cars on the Rochester & Syracuse left

R&S car 123, Chair Car Syracuse, *entering Lyons on the new cut off route on Saturday June 27, 1931, the last day of the railroad's operation. This is the only view of Chair Car* Syracuse *that has turned up so far.*

David Ennis, MD, Lyons, NY, photographer

Here is the Newark yard of the R&S on July 15, 1931. At this time, the company was still hoping to sell some of its cars, particularly the seven chair cars. But in the middle of the Depression, nobody was interested in 25-year old 42-ton wooden interurban cars.

The fleet of R&S cars was stored at the Newark shops after the road was discontinued, June 27, 1931. All the cars were moved to Lakeland on the Empire State Railroad for burning and recovery of metals. None were saved except for Russell snow sweeper 1000 that was purchased by the New York State Railways, Syracuse Lines.

W. C. Felton, Lyons, NY, photographer

their terminals for the Newark shops on the night of Saturday June 27, 1931 after a full day of operation. Motorman Corry Heald and conductor LeRoy Gaston left Auburn with car 121 at 11:30 P.M. for their final run to Port Byron and Newark, arriving at the shops at 12:49 A.M. Sunday.

Next in was car 125 from Syracuse in charge of motorman Elmer Barclay and conductor Coles Holland. They left Syracuse as local train 67 with 12 passengers aboard and pulled into Newark barn at 1:39 A.M. Two of the passengers getting off at Clyde were Mr. & Mrs. Thomas Mehan. Tom worked at the Newark shops.

The last car out of Rochester was 122, Chair Car *Rochester,* with motorman Eugene Terbush and conductor Thomas Slater of Newark. Vince Kennelly, a spare conductor, was along too. He was deadheading home to Fairport. They left City Hall Station at 12:35 A.M. as local train 78. It was a lonesome trip. At 1:45 A.M., car 122 arrived at the shops, ending for all time electric railway service between Rochester and Syracuse. Remember, it was almost exactly 25 years earlier that the first RS&E passenger cars in revenue service had returned to the Newark shops from their first evening's work.

One of the RS&E Niles-built express cars (61, 67 or 68) was eastbound on a milk run at Warners. Note one extra panel on opposite sides has been added to the standard octagonal shelter. Either heavy eastbound passenger traffic was expected or extra space was required for the agent. Warners was an open agency station, 10 miles west of Syracuse.

Freight Service

Freight and express service on the Rochester, Syracuse & Eastern Railroad was handled from the beginning by the company's three freight motor cars (61, 67 and 68) of about 20-ton capacity each. One of the cars was a combination type that could accommodate 5 passengers. Prior to 1911, the City of Rochester had imposed severe restrictions on the movement of freight cars through its streets. Local freight and express business grew slowly.

The RS&E was not designed to handle carload freight. Much street running and short radius curves in three of the intermediate villages (East Rochester, Newark and Lyons) precluded operation of standard steam railroad cars. Thus the company was never in a position to attract industries to its rails which would produce business in carload lots. About the only standard steam road freight cars ever hauled on the electric line were carloads of coal received at the West Shore Railroad interchange connection east of Newark. The coal was hauled to the Newark shops. Even these movements were not without complications. It was necessary to adjust the coal car's brake rigging and to use extension couplers in order to negotiate the 75-foot radius curve at Main and Union streets in downtown Newark. Coal for the company's Lyons power house was delivered to its elevated trestle by the adjacent New York Central Railroad.

On August 1, 1911, Wells-Fargo Express Company signed a contract with the RS&E for handling express between Rochester and Syracuse. Three years later W-F contracted with the Buffalo, Lockport & Rochester Railway to operate through express business between Rochester and Buffalo. W-F also contracted with the Erie Railroad in Rochester for use of space in their freight house as a gathering point for local business and that to or from the RS&E. It is not known whether sufficient traffic was generated to require through W-F cars at Rochester.

At Syracuse, Wells-Fargo maintained an office for its agent and messengers in the West Belden Avenue freight house of the SLS&N. Beginning sometime in 1915, a special Wells-Fargo express car, train 305, was added to the Empire United freight timetable. It left Syracuse at 5:30 P.M. daily except Sunday and made a 2 hour and 45 minute non-stop run to Rochester. The car left just ahead of the regular passenger local. This special Wells-Fargo schedule apparently lasted until December 31, 1918 when the Wells-Fargo Company was consolidated into the American Railway Express Company. In this same time period, the Buffalo, Lockport & Rochester scheduled a Wells-Fargo express car, train 105, leaving Erie freight house at 10 or 11 at night making a non-stop run between Rochester and Buffalo daily except Sunday. Presumably this was an extension of the Empire United express train 305.

The man most active in the freight and express business on the Beebe lines was Harry Stanton, General Freight Agent. Beginning in the days of the Empire United, Stanton was directly responsible for all the freight and later the passenger promotional activities of the company until late 1927 when he resigned to enter the local real estate business in Syracuse.

The RS&E and its successors gradually developed a very creditable less–than–carload–lot (LCL) freight business. In 1914, the Empire United Railways added three 53-foot motor express cars to the fleet to handle the increasing express and LCL freight business. The average capacity of these new cars (62, 65 and 66) was 20 tons. Ward Baking Com-

SHIPELECTRIC

2282-A

EMPIRE UNITED RAILWAYS

NO. 3 TIME SHOWN IS LEAVING TIME

EFFECTIVE SEPTEMBER 25, 1916

EMPIRE UNITED RAILWAYS

TIME TABLE

EMPIRE UNITED RAILWAYS, INC.

Rochester, Syracuse & Eastern R. R. Co. Syracuse, Lakeshore & Northern R. R. Co.

Fast and Frequent Electric Freight Service

BETWEEN

Adams Basin	Eagle Harbor	Knowlesville	Middleport	Port Byron	Warner
Albion	Fairport	Lyons	Memphis	Rochester	Weedsport
Auburn	Fulton	Lockport	Newark	Savannah	
Baldwinsville	Gasport	Macedon	Oswego	Skaneateles	
Brockport	Holley	Marcellus	Palmyra	Syracuse	
Clyde	Hulberton	Medina	Phoenix	Spencerport	
EastRochester	Jordan	Minetto	Port Gibson	Split Rock	

Also Marion via Newark and Cato, Ira, Martville, Sterling, Fair Haven and North Fair Haven via Weedsport

Rates Between Above Points Are Strictly Competitive with the Slower Steam Routes

EASTBOUND	*300	302-306	304-308	310
Lv. Rochester	10.30 P.M.	12.15 A.M.	2.00 A.M.	12.00 P.M.
" E. Blvd. Road	11.00 "	12.45 "	2.15 "	12.30 "
" E. Rochester	.....	.....	.....	12.40 "
" Fairport	.....	.....	2.50 "	1.00 "
" Egypt	.....	.....	.....	1.06 "
" Macedon	.....	.....	.....	1.20 "
" Palmyra	.....	.....	3.45 "	1.40 "
" Port Gibson	.....	.....	3.53 "	1.48 "
Ar. Newark	.....	1.39 A.M.	4.02 "	2.00 "
Lv. Newark	.....	6.10 A.M.	1.40 P.M.	2.20 "
" Lyons	.....	6.30 "	2.05 "	2.40 "
" Locke Berlin	.....	6.38 "	2.11 "	2.47 "
" Clyde	.....	7.15 "	2.45 "	3.05 "
" Savannah	.....	7.45 "	2.55 "	3.20 "
" Montezuma	.....	7.52 "	3.02 "	3.27 "
Ar. Port Byron	12.38 A.M.	8.00 "	3.10 "	3.35 "
Lv. Port Byron	.....	8.00 A.M.	4.00 P.M.	4.00 "
Ar. Auburn	.....	8.25 "	4.25 "	4.25 "
Lv. Auburn	.....	9.15 A.M.	.....	5.35 "
Ar. Port Byron	.....	9.37 "	.....	6.00 "
Lv. Port Byron	12.53 A.M.	10.05 A.M.	3.15 P.M.	
" Weedsport	1.13 "	10.15 "	3.25 "	
" Jordan	1.36 "	10.30 "	3.40 "	
" Memphis	1.43 "	10.37 "	3.47 "	
" Warner	1.48 "	10.42 "	3.52 "	
Ar. Syracuse	2.13 "	11.05 "	4.15 "	

WESTBOUND	301	303	305	307
Lv. Syracuse		12.10 P.M.	5.30 P.M.	6.50 P.M.
" Warner		12.45 "	.....	7.17 "
" Memphis		1.00 "	.....	7.27 "
" Jordan		1.29 "	.....	7.47 "
" Weedsport		1.57 "	.....	8.05 "
Ar. Port Byron		2.02 "	.....	8.10 "
Lv. Port Byron		4.00 P.M.	.....	8.00 A.M.
Ar. Auburn		4.25 "	.....	8.25 "
Lv. Auburn		9.15 A.M.	.....	5.35 P.M.
Ar. Port Byron		9.37 "		6.00 "
Lv. Port Byron	7.07 A.M.	2.27 P.M.		8.20 "
" Montezuma	7.16 "	2.35 "		.....
" Savannah	7.28 "	2.57 "		8.43 "
" Clyde	7.45 "	3.27 "		9.12 "
" Locke Berlin	7.51 "	3.33 "		.....
" Lyons	8.02 "	4.13 "	.....	9.48 "
Ar. Newark	8.15 "	4.29 "	.....	10.03 "
Lv. Newark	8.20 "	5.15 "	.....	10.23 "
" Port Gibson	8.32 "	5.30 "	.....	10.32 "
" Palmyra	9.08 "	6.05 "	.....	10.55 "
" Macedon	9.17 "	6.20 "	.....	.....
" Egypt	9.25 "	6.28 "	.....	.....
" Fairport	9.40 "	7.30 "	.....	11.40 "
" E. Rochester	9.50 "	.....	.....	.....
" E. Blvd. Road	10.00 "	8.00 "	.....	12.00 "
Ar. Rochester	10.15 "	8.15 "	8.15 "	12.20 "

305: WELLS FARGO & CO. EXPRESS and ROCHESTER THROUGH FREIGHT

Train 300 daily except Sunday and Holidays.
Train 302-306 daily except Sunday. On Holidays Newark to Syracuse only.
Train 304-308 daily except Sunday and holidays.
Train 310 daily except Sunday and holidays.
Train 301 daily. Runs to East Boulevard road only on Sunday.
Train 303 daily except Sunday. On holidays Syracuse to Newark only.
Train 305-307 daily except Sunday and holidays.
* Train 300 will stop at stations not scheduled above upon request at the General Freight Agent's office.

NORTHBOUND	1-3	41-45-49-53-55
Lv. Syracuse	* 4.20 A.M.	* 12.40 P.M.
" Long Branch	.....	1.05 "
" Baldwinsville	.....	1.55 "
" Phoenix	.....	2.30 "
" Fulton	5.55 "	3.16 "
" Minettto	.....	3.40 "
Ar. Oswego	6.25 "	3.55 "

* Will stop at stations not scheduled to deliver perishable shipments only. Carries trailer, Syracuse to Fulton.

SOUTHBOUND	24-26-30-34-38	76-80
Lv. Oswego	8.23 A.M.	* 6.03 P.M.
" Minetto	8.50 "	6.18 "
" Fulton	9.29 "	6.54 "
" Phoenix	10.14 "	7.18 "
" Baldwinsville	10.50 "	7.32 "
" Long Branch	11.04 "	7.44 "
Ar. Syracuse	11.28 "	8.07 "

* Carries trailer, Fulton to Syracuse.

Close connections are made with the Syracuse and South Bay Electric R. R. Co., and Syracuse, Watertown and St. Lawrence River R. R. Co., at Syracuse, for North Syracuse, Cicero, Brewerton and South Bay.

Auburn & Syracuse Electric R. R. at Auburn for Skaneateles, Marcellus and Split Rock.

New York State Railways (Oneida Lines) at Syracuse for Utica, Rome, Little Falls and all intermediate points.

Buffalo, Lockport and Rochester Railways at Rochester for all points between Rochester and Lockport.

INSTRUCTIONS TO SHIPPERS.

Freight houses are open for the receipt and delivery of freight daily except Sundays and holidays as follows:

Auburn ....7.00 A.M. to 6.00 P.M.
Rochester ....7.00 A.M. to 5.00 P.M.
Syracuse ....7.00 A.M. to 5.30 P.M.
All other stations....7.00 A.M. to 6.00 P.M.

On the foregoing time tables are shown the leaving times of all freight cars. Freight shipments must be delivered to freight houses between the hours mentioned above and at terminal stations at least 30 minutes and at all other points 15 minutes before the leaving time as shown on schedule.

The Company reserves the right to change schedule without notice to the public, and does not guarantee to forward shipments upon any particular train.

An experienced man will call upon you at your request and explain our service and just how it is best adapted to your needs.

For rates, maps and further information apply to

LOCAL AGENTS, or
H. C. Stanton, General Freight Agent
S. W. Bullock, Commercial Freight Agent
Syracuse, N. Y. (Telephone Warren 4980)

SHIPELECTRIC

pany in Syracuse was a heavy shipper along "The Electric Short Line." Fresh vegetables were hauled to the cannery in Egypt (the only industrial siding on the line). Freight service on the R&S varied from four to seven trains daily except Sunday in each direction. Some trains ran through from terminal to terminal while others were scheduled as short turns in order to meet the needs of traffic.

An early attempt was made to establish a merchandise traffic connection with a neighboring steam road. On March 1, 1915, the Empire United Railways inaugurated a fast freight service via Rochester to over 50 points in western New York state served by the Erie Railroad. Merchandise was transferred at the jointly occupied Erie freight house in Rochester. A 1922 freight tariff dealt with LCL shipments from points on the R&S to Newark for transfer to the Marion Railway, and to Weedsport for transfer to the Lehigh Valley Railroad, only for their points north of Weedsport.

On November 3, 1919, through electric freight runs were inaugurated between Syracuse and Buffalo. The operation of a through car made possible overnight delivery between these two stations. Generally, all freight received at Syracuse before 5 P.M. was available in Buffalo for next morning delivery. In later years, it was not uncommon to see 4- and 5-car freight trains leave Belden Avenue freight house in Syracuse for Rochester, Buffalo, Dunkirk and Erie, Pa. made up of cars owned by all of the participating carriers. The companies together advertised "High Speed Electric Freight Service at Slow Freight Rates." Store-to-door delivery by local trucking firms from the Rochester and Syracuse terminals was inaugurated in August 1925.

Surviving Joint Freight Tariffs of the early 1920s to 1929 for LCL traffic reveal some extensive joint arrangements that existed between the Empire State/R&S/RL&B group and other electric lines in central and western New York state:

Auburn & Syracuse – Local LCL including carload rates in A&S cars and in foreign equipment

Buffalo & Lake Erie Traction Co. - LCL including Auburn & Syracuse, N.Y. State Railways, Rochester Lines, and Northwestern Electric Service Co. of Pennsylvania. This tariff included a stick map of the territory covered showing all interurban electric lines between Meadsville, Pa. and Oneonta, N.Y.

Empire State Railroad – LCL window shades from Minetto and Oswego to points on the R&S

R&S - Local LCL including "carloads in trailer cars" and "carloads in chartered electric freight cars."

R&S - LCL with A&S, ES, RL&B and NY State Railways, Rochester Lines

R&S - LCL with points on International Rail way, Lockport – Olcott Division.

There are no known Joint LCL Freight Tariffs for traffic to and from the electric lines east of Syracuse.

In the mid-1920s, there were LCL tariffs written with the Detroit & Cleveland Navigation Company for Detroit traffic via the port of Buffalo and with the Cleveland & Buffalo Transit Company for Cleveland traffic via the port of Buffalo. Until the season of 1926, through rates were in effect from points on the R&S and Empire State Railroad to Chicago and Milwaukee, via the Rutland-Lake Michigan Transit Co. This boat line made connections with the electric cars at the port of Oswego on Lake Ontario. A nice business in perishable fruit from the Oswego River valley was built up. The company advertised first morning delivery in Buffalo via the Rochester, Lockport & Buffalo and International Railway.

In 1926, the Buffalo & Erie Railway (successor to the B&LET) set up LCL service to a few electric railway points in Ohio. This service required trucking between Erie and Cleveland because the chain of connecting electric lines had been broken in 1922. It is not known if any amount of LCL from the Syracuse ever moved on this route.

There was an interesting 1920 Buffalo & Lake Erie Traction Local Freight Tariff "For Transportation of Electric Railway Cars (Passenger or Freight) On Own Wheels Over Tracks of Issuing Carrier." The charge was 63 cents per car mile using B&LET crews, so moving one electric car 91.2 miles from Erie, Pa. to Buffalo cost $57.46.

One of the more unusual freight movements over the Rochester & Syracuse was made on a Saturday night in February 1918. The New York State Railways shipped a dozen of its 300-series double-truck city cars from Rochester to Utica. The cars were lined up on University Avenue at Culver Road. After being coupled and chained together and with trolley poles hooked down, an R&S express motor towed the string to Syracuse. There an express motor of the New York State Railways Oneida Line took over for the trip over its third-rail line to Utica. The cars were used there and in Rome for some time. A reverse exchange of cars from Utica to Rochester was made in late 1927 when 10 cars from the Utica city line went west on the R&S under their own power for service in the new Rochester Subway. After alterations in the local St. Paul Street car shops, they were renumbered 2000-2018, even numbers only.

Traveling Freight Agents were employed on the RS&E for some years. Nicknamed TFAs, they were generally young lads in their late teens who traveled on each freight train taking care of freight bills and other paper work. Since these trains very often included through cars from lines west of Buffalo destined for Syracuse as well as local way cars, the TFAs usually had their hands full.

TRAVELECTRIC

THE Safe way to Go
Fast way to Go
Clean way to Go
Comfortable way to Go
Convenient way to Go

Rochester & Syracuse Railroad

the

Center to Center

Double Track Electric Route

For information relative to special cars or extra service for excursions, outings, theatre, lodge, parties or funerals, address General Passenger Agent, Syracuse, N. Y., or inquire of any local agent. Such service may be quickly and reasonably arranged.

SHIPELECTRIC

DAILY EXCEPT SUNDAYS

BETWEEN

Syracuse Rochester
Oswego Auburn
Lockport Buffalo

and intermediate points

Freight Service that is
Fast and Convenient

Consult agents about our rates and service or address General Freight Agent, Syracuse, N. Y.

The Onondaga Printing Co., Syracuse, N. Y.

March 3, 1918

TRAVELECTRIC

The
Center to Center
Double Track Electric Route

Fast Limited Trains of the
ROCHESTER & SYRACUSE R. R.

Lands You in the Business Centers of the Villages and Cities.

Special 10-Day Round Trip Ticket Rate
Between
$4.00—Syracuse and Rochester—$4.00

Good Either Direction—On Sale Every Day

The Best Passenger Service
Between Syracuse and Rochester

Special Cars for Excursions, Outings, Theatre, Lodge, Parties or Funerals, may be quickly and conveniently arranged for by consulting Agents or address General Passenger Agent, Syracuse, N. Y.

SHIPELECTRIC

Have You Used

The Electric Freight Service

For Frequent and Speedy Dispatch of Shipments Between

Adams Basin	Hulberton	No. Tonawanda
Albion	Ira	Oswego
Auburn	Jordan	Olcott
Baldwinsville	Knowlesville	Palmyra
Brockport	Lyons	Phoenix
Buffalo	Lockport	Port Byron
Burt	Macedon	Port Gibson
Cato	Marcellus	Rochester
Clyde	Marion	Savannah
*Corwin	Martville	Sterling
East Rochester	Medina	Skaneateles
*Eagle Harbor	Minetto	Syracuse
Fairport	Middleport	Spencerport
Fulton	Memphis	*Split Rock
Fair Haven	Newark	*Tonawanda
Gasport	New Fane	Warner
Holley	No. Fair Haven	Weedsport
		*Wrights

*Prepaid Points.

IF NOT, WHY NOT?

CONNECTIONS

AT SYRACUSE—New York State Railways (Oneida and Utica Lines) and Syracuse Northern Electric Railway.

AT ROCHESTER—Erie R. R. and New York State Railways (Sodus Bay & R. & E. Lines).

AT BUFFALO—Buffalo & Lake Erie Traction Co., to Detroit and Cleveland via steam lines and boat lines during navigation season.

Consult agents about our service and rates or address General Freight Agent, Syracuse, N. Y.

The Onondaga Printing Co., [Syracuse, N. Y.

January 11, 1920

SHIPELECTRIC

Increased business in our freight traffic shows that once a shipper uses our line he continues. By using our line you make more prompt deliveries and handle your freight with greater convenience to your customer and yourself.

MAKE NEW CUSTOMERS

AND PLEASE OLD ONES BY QUICKER DELIVERIES VIA FAST

Electric Freight Service

BETWEEN

ROCHESTER

Clyde East Rochester
Savannah Fairport
Port Byron Macedon
Weedsport Palmyra
Jordan Port Gibson
Memphis Newark
Warner Lyons

SYRACUSE

Costs you no more than the steam lines to get this superior

FAST FREIGHT SERVICE

Joint freight rates slightly higher than the steam lines are in effect between points on the line of this company and Auburn, Adams Basin, Albion, Baldwinsville, Brockport, Buffalo, Burt, Corwin, Eagle Harbor, Fulton, Gasport, Holley, Hulberton, Knowlesville, Long Branch, Lockport, Marcellus, Medina, Minetto, Middleport, Newfane, North Tonawanda, Oswego, Phoenix, Olcott, Skaneateles, Spencerport, Split Rock, Tonwanda, Troopsville and Wrights.

Also Marion via Newark, and Cato, Ira, Martville, Sterling, Fair Haven and North Fair Haven, via Weedsport.

THIS SERVICE WILL ALWAYS SAVE YOU HOURS AND MANY TIMES DAYS.

Agents will render every assistance in giving information by calling on the phone or call Traffic Department, Syracuse, N. Y. Telephone Warren, 4700.

June 13, 1921

Advertising freight service on the Rochester & Syracuse public timetables

The R&S freight cars never ran in the Rochester Subway. Their route to the Frank Street freight house, at the rear of the State Street barns, was via University Avenue from Culver Road to East Main Street, then to Franklin Street, Andrews Street and State Street to the Union Freight Terminal at the rear of the State Street barn. The connecting track from State Street actually passed through the car barn itself. The R&S route from Culver Road was 2.73 miles long.

Freight business held up pretty well until the end of all service on the R&S. The company's annual report for 1928 reveals that although passenger revenues for that year were 12% under those for 1927, the freight income was down only 1.4%. In 1928, the freight revenues represented over 19% of the company's total revenue from transportation. The last employees' timetable, issued September 28, 1930, listed two round trips daily except Sunday between Rochester and Syracuse, one round trip between Auburn and Rochester and a local round trip between Newark and Rochester. The noon freight out of Syracuse made a side trip into Auburn and right back out to Port Byron before proceeding on to Rochester.

Fares

The Rochester, Syracuse & Eastern Railroad maintained ticket offices in its terminal cities and in each of the villages and towns through which it passed. Most of the agents handled both passenger and freight business, although in Syracuse and Rochester there was sufficient business to warrant both a freight agent and a passenger agent.

The RS&E sold the usual assortment of tickets and cash fares good for passage over the line. Tickets were printed for single and round trips. Reduced fare books were available for school children and commuters. Mileage books good for everyone and interline tickets were also available. Generally, an excess fare of 10 cents was charged by the conductor when a passenger boarded a car at an open agency station and had not bought his or her ticket in advance. Then, a cash fare receipt was issued and the excess fare punched. In order to get the 10 cents back, the passenger had to send the receipt in to the general office for refund. This rule tended to encourage the use of ticket offices.

Sample one-way ticket fares from Syracuse in 1910 were:

25 cents to Memphis	$1.00 to Newark
50 cents to Port Byron	1.25 to Macedon
75 cents to Clyde	1.50 to Rochester (Four Corners)

At that time, a round-trip fare to Rochester was $2.50 with a 30-day return limit. Strip mileage books were offered at $10.00 worth of transportation for $8.00 or $5.00 for $4.75.

Even before "The Electric Short Line" was entirely completed, it had entered into an agreement with the other leading electric lines in the area whereby they issued an "Interchangeable Coupon Ticket". This book of 240 coupons, each worth 5 cents, provided $12.00 worth of travel for $10.00. This made electric railway transportation particularly attractive to the traveling salesmen who made many calls in the various small towns around the

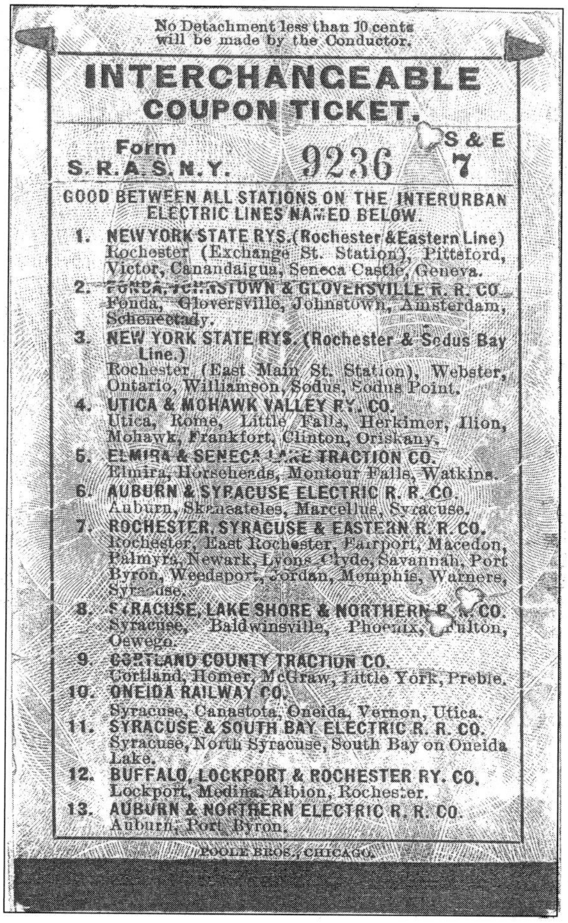
No Detachment less than 10 cents will be made by the Conductor.

INTERCHANGEABLE COUPON TICKET.

Form S.R.A.S.N.Y. 9236 S & E 7

GOOD BETWEEN ALL STATIONS ON THE INTERURBAN ELECTRIC LINES NAMED BELOW.

1. NEW YORK STATE RYS. (Rochester & Eastern Line) Rochester (Exchange St. Station), Pittsford, Victor, Canandaigua, Seneca Castle, Geneva.
2. FONDA, JOHNSTOWN & GLOVERSVILLE R. R. CO. Fonda, Gloversville, Johnstown, Amsterdam, Schenectady.
3. NEW YORK STATE RYS. (Rochester & Sodus Bay Line.) Rochester (East Main St. Station), Webster, Ontario, Williamson, Sodus, Sodus Point.
4. UTICA & MOHAWK VALLEY RY. CO. Utica, Rome, Little Falls, Herkimer, Ilion, Mohawk, Frankfort, Clinton, Oriskany.
5. ELMIRA & SENECA LAKE TRACTION CO. Elmira, Horseheads, Montour Falls, Watkins.
6. AUBURN & SYRACUSE ELECTRIC R. R. CO. Auburn, Skaneateles, Marcellus, Syracuse.
7. ROCHESTER, SYRACUSE & EASTERN R. R. CO. Rochester, East Rochester, Fairport, Macedon, Palmyra, Newark, Lyons, Clyde, Savannah, Port Byron, Weedsport, Jordan, Memphis, Warners, Syracuse.
8. SYRACUSE, LAKE SHORE & NORTHERN R. R. CO. Syracuse, Baldwinsville, Phoenix, Fulton, Oswego.
9. CORTLAND COUNTY TRACTION CO. Cortland, Homer, McGraw, Little York, Preble.
10. ONEIDA RAILWAY CO. Syracuse, Canastota, Oneida, Vernon, Utica.
11. SYRACUSE & SOUTH BAY ELECTRIC R. R. CO. Syracuse, North Syracuse, South Bay on Oneida Lake.
12. BUFFALO, LOCKPORT & ROCHESTER RY. CO. Lockport, Medina, Albion, Rochester.
13. AUBURN & NORTHERN ELECTRIC R. R. CO. Auburn, Port Byron.

POOLE BROS., CHICAGO.

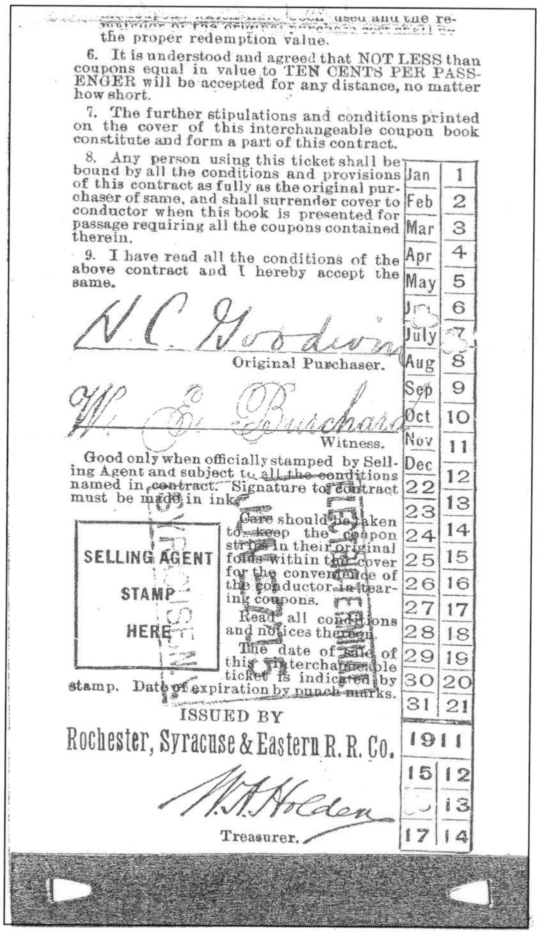
the proper redemption value.

6. It is understood and agreed that NOT LESS than coupons equal in value to TEN CENTS PER PASSENGER will be accepted for any distance, no matter how short.

7. The further stipulations and conditions printed on the cover of this interchangeable coupon book constitute and form a part of this contract.

8. Any person using this ticket shall be bound by all the conditions and provisions of this contract as fully as the original purchaser of same, and shall surrender cover to conductor when this book is presented for passage requiring all the coupons contained therein.

9. I have read all the conditions of the above contract and I hereby accept the same.

Original Purchaser.

Witness.

Good only when officially stamped by Selling Agent and subject to all the conditions named in contract. Signature to contract must be made in ink.

SELLING AGENT STAMP HERE

Care should be taken to keep the coupon strips in their original folds within the cover for the convenience of the conductor in tearing coupons.

Read all conditions and notices thereon.

The date of sale of this interchangeable ticket is indicated by stamp. Date of expiration by punch marks.

ISSUED BY

Rochester, Syracuse & Eastern R. R. Co.

Treasurer.

Jan	1
Feb	2
Mar	3
Apr	4
May	5
June	6
July	7
Aug	8
Sep	9
Oct	10
Nov	11
Dec	12
22	13
23	14
24	15
25	16
26	17
27	18
28	19
29	20
30	21
31	
1911	
15	12
	13
17	14

This book of Interchangeable Tickets was purchased June 7, 1915 at the Syracuse Terminal. Its cover listed a wide variety of interurban stations in central and western New York state, located between Lockport on the west and Schenectady on the east.

state. For years the following electric lines honored these coupon tickets:

New York State Railways (Rochester Lines)
Buffalo, Lockport & Rochester Railway
Auburn & Syracuse Electric Railroad
Empire United Railways, Inc.
New York State Railways (Oneida Line)
Syracuse & South Bay Electric Railroad

With the arrival of the automobile, this type of ticket fell into disuse. On February 1, 1918, the Rochester & Syracuse along with the Buffalo, Lockport & Rochester, the Auburn & Syracuse and the New York State Railways discontinued their participation in the joint mileage book. Thereafter the only interline tickets sold by the R&S were in connection with the New York State Railways, Rochester City Lines (over which it operated into Rochester) and the Empire State Railroad, both the Syracuse-Oswego and Auburn-Port Byron divisions.

Sample one-way ticket fares offered by the R&S to Empire State Railroad points in 1927 were: Rochester to Auburn via Port Byron $2.44; Rochester to Oswego via Lake Shore Junction $3.50.

In the mid-twenties, the company offered one-day-round-trip fares good on Sundays and Wednesdays in an effort to keep people on the rails. One could go from Culver Road Rochester to Syracuse and back for $2.50 on Sundays and for $3.34 on Wednesdays.

Passenger fares were raised from time to time until the final tariff of the R&S issued September 1, 1925, under which the one-way fares were based on $0.036 per mile with a 5-cent minimum. A special 10-day round trip fare of $4.00 applied between Rochester terminal and Syracuse terminal. The per-car charter rate was based on 50 passengers at $0.036 per mile. One way Rochester to Syracuse was $145.00 and round trip was $290.00. A year later these prices were shaded to $125.00 and $250.00. Transfers were issued by the R&S and its predecessors good on the Rochester local city lines upon payment of a fare from some R&S point to Rochester terminal. Likewise, street car transfers issued on Rochester city cars were valid for transportation on R&S cars as far east as Culver Road. There were no transfer privileges with the Syracuse local lines as the Rochester and Oswego interurbans entered the city on their own tracks.

Advertising

The Rochester, Syracuse & Eastern Railroad advertised extensively in its early days. Colored post card views of many of the stations and the Newark car shops could be purchased in drug stores along the line. In 1909 and again in 1911, the Beebe lines produced a high-class booklet of standard railroad timetable size entitled *Trolley Trips in Central New York*. It opened into a 16-page illustrated affair, "designed to furnish a short description of these roads, the territory through which each operates and some facts concerning points of general interest along the several routes." Copies could be had for the asking. It was an expensive piece of advertising at that time, for the cost to the company was 25 cents a copy.

In addition to the regular timetables issued by each line separately, all of the Beebe lines' schedules were combined into a very attractive standard size folder entitled *Interurban Electric Railroad*

Guide. These system timetables appeared in 1911 and continued through 1914. During the navigation season, the timetables included schedules of the company-owned boat lines on Oneida and Skaneateles lakes, and the steamer across Lake Ontario between Olcott, (on the International Railway) and Toronto. These folders carried no paid advertising. Their covers told the traveler that the Company offered "Fast Service between Buffalo, Lockport, Rochester, Syracuse, Auburn, Oswego and Intermediate Points."

Every attorney in Syracuse received a letter dated January 13, 1910 from J. Stanley Moore, General Passenger Agent of the RS&E. The letter pointed out the fast service to Rochester every hour from 6 A.M. to 9 P.M. The 7 A.M. Limited stopped in front of the Monroe County Court House (Rochester) at 9:50 A.M. Round trip fare was only $2.50 with no excise tax. There was no smoke or cinders, and the fare was 70 cents cheaper than on the steam road. Besides, passengers were let off at the Court House and not a mile away on Central Avenue. Letters were often sent to traveling men inviting them to ride "The Electric Short Line" between Syracuse and Rochester.

The Empire United Railways also advertised extensively during its short lifetime. Division timetables were issued, of course. Beginning in January 1915, a monthly system timetable was made available to the public. Entitled *TRAVELECTRIC*, it was replete with illustrations, fancy covers in color and a map of the system. It was at least partly self-sustaining for it carried paid advertising. *TRAVELECTRIC* was later expanded. The colored covers were dropped but the schedules of neighboring electric lines were added. It was widely distributed and became well known among traveling salesmen. The issue for January 1916 stated that 175,000 people read it every month. Short articles were included. For example, "Jack's Reef is a retreat for fishermen on the Seneca River about a mile's walk north from stop 89 on the Rochester–Syracuse Division of the Empire United Railways. Stop 89 is about 14 miles west of Syracuse and can be reached in about 30 minutes on local cars from the Electric Railway Terminal on Clinton Square."

Two very interesting booklets were issued by the Empire United and associated lines: *Summer Trips from Syracuse* in 1914 and *The Solution of the Summer Trip Problem* in 1915. Each of these publications pointed out the many one-, two- or three-day excursions that were available over the electric lines and associated boat lines on Oneida and Skaneateles lakes. "Every Sunday evening, the steamer 'City of Syracuse' (capacity 600 passengers) sails from Skaneateles for a three hour search light trip to the head of the lake and return, making but one stop at Glen Haven." This excursion was operated in connection with the Auburn & Syracuse line and the round-trip fare from Syracuse was 75 cents. Patrons were advised of the advantages of such places as Lakeside Park in Auburn, Otisco Lake, Glen Haven and Ten Mile Point on Skaneateles Lake, and Frenchman's Island and Sylvan Beach on Oneida Lake. Suggested trips to more distant places included one from Oswego to the Thousand Islands, also the combination trolley and boat trip to Toronto via cars of the Buffalo, Lockport & Rochester Rail-

way to Olcott Beach and the steamer *Olcott* across Lake Ontario. For the latter trips, the BL&R ran through cars between Rochester and Olcott Beach.

The timetables of all the Beebe lines appeared in *Trolley Talk*, a standard railroad size booklet of 24 pages or so, independently published by W.C. and F. D. Burgess of Newark. Issued monthly from February 1908 until August 1917, *Trolley Talk* was distributed free of charge in the cars, in stations and shelters of the electric roads, in hotels and in the business places of the advertisers. By 1911, this interesting pamphlet was carrying short articles of progress being made on Beebe's electrics, of construction, new cars, etc. Individuals could subscribe to *Trolley Talk* for 50 cents a year.

Other efforts in the field of railway guides included the *New York State Electric Railway Guide* edited by R. M. Colt, General Passenger Agent for the Fonda, Johnstown & Gloversville Railroad. It included detailed timetables of all the major electric

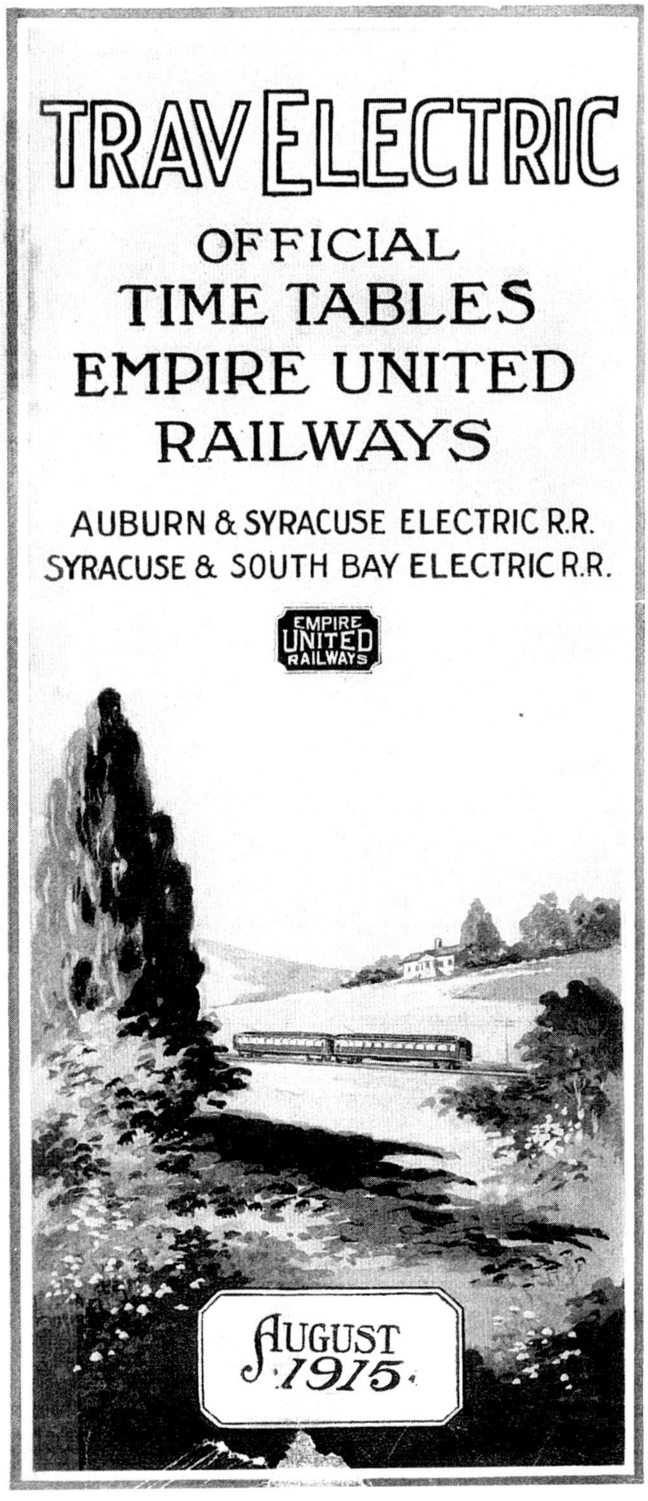

lines between Lake Erie and the Hudson River. Mr. Colt's guides ended about 1917. In later years, the R&S schedules were carried in *The People's Railway & Motor Bus Guide* which covered most every rail line in New York state. Timetables of the Beebe roads never appeared in the *Official Guide of the Railways.*

In 1915, the Empire United announced a photo contest designed to stimulate interest in their line. Suitable prizes were to be awarded for the best view of points on the EUR. The winning photo appears to have been lost to the ages.

The EUR participated in the Syracuse Electric Show held November 29 through December 4, 1915. Their booth, as pictured here, was replete with posters, pictures, timetables, a pair of railroad lanterns and a group of wicker chairs intended for their third parlor car *Newark*. This booth would, indeed, have been a spot of heaven for the modern-day railfan.

Car cards were used from time to time to pro-

mote the R&S. These 21" by 11" colored posters were made to fit in slots in the curves of street car ceilings for advertising purposes.The R&S produced one such card advertising the comfort and economy of its new chair car service. The particular card illustrated here would have appeared in Syracuse and Rochester street cars in the 1927-31 period. For several years after the interurbans stopped running, it was possible to observe two large signs painted on brick walls of buildings in Syracuse advertising "The Electric Line to Rochester, $4.00 round trip." One of the neatest bits of advertising was a wallet size celluloid calendar with a colored map of the Beebe system on the reverse side. So far as is known, this calendar was only issued in one year, 1912.

The last piece of "handout" advertising done by the R&S was the two-fold leaflet "Chair Car Service" prepared in 1927, announcing with words, pictures and timetables the advantages of riding on its new chair cars. No extra fare was charged for this extra comfort.

The Empire United Railways had a booth at the Syracuse Electric Show November 29 - December 4, 1915. The panel on the left advertised the Auburn & Syracuse and Lakeside Park on Owasco Lake near Auburn. The right-hand panel covered Niagara Falls and scenes on the Syracuse & South Bay line. A sign on the back wall offers information and invites people to come in and rest. What a great spot for 20th century railfans to visit. Piles of postcards, timetables and a couple of lanterns to check out. Note the mail box in the lower right-hand corner. Probably the 1c stamps were furnished.

Accidents

The Rochester & Syracuse Railroad was surprisingly free from accidents of a fatal nature. In all of its 25-year history, no passenger was ever killed. Unfortunately the same can not be said for the passengers of some of the automobiles that tried to beat the interurbans at grade crossings. One such accident occurred at the Hamilton-Clinton Streets crossing in Jordan in 1928 when an auto with three young children in it ran in front of car 125.

Except in towns and villages, the electrics op-

Beginning in 1927, the Rochester & Syracuse distributed these car cards for display in local street cars of the New York State Railways to advertise the new R&S Chair Car service. The original card measures 21" x 11".

erated at high speeds, a fact that many people never got used to. They always thought it was possible to beat the cars to the crossing but the auto seldom won. More often it was a tie. Even the horse and wagon tried to beat the trolley. A story was told of a farmer and his empty hay rack that were hit by a Limited car so hard that the wagon was completely shattered. After the motorman got his car stopped, he looked around in his front vestibule and found the farmer with a blanket wrapped around him sitting on the floor amongst a heap of glass. Then there was the time a two-car train hit a garbage wagon. The motorman couldn't get out of the way so he just ducked below the front window sill. The aisle of the first car was knee deep in garbage and some said that a little even got as far as the second car.

Some accidents were, of course, due to slippery highways. A case in point occurred at Stop 22, two miles west of Macedon. It was snowing and the highway was covered with ice. A roadster with two passengers had stopped a few feet from the crossing because of the approaching Limited car. Relatives of the couple in the roadster drove up behind them in a sedan. The roadster was hit in the rear with such force that it was shoved completely across the two tracks. The sedan, however, stalled in the middle of the westbound track and was struck by the trolley. It was pushed about 600 feet up the track. Both occupants of the sedan were killed. Probably the most tragic accident on the R&S occurred after the regular service was discontinued. Conductor Charles Soper was killed by a falling pole during the dismantling of the road near Fairport. He was the oldest conductor on the line, having been in charge of the first car out of Newark the day the line opened.

The R&S had its share of accidents due to heavy interurban cars operating through city streets. Generally, the wheels on interurban cars were larger with somewhat wider treads and deeper flanges than those of the average city streetcars. Girder rails of a lighter weight were found in many streets. Some of the city lines' switches were of the tongue and mate type which were not particularly attractive to the more massive interurban wheels. An example of wheel and switch mismatch occurred in Rochester on April 5, 1922. R&S car 114 left Rochester terminal at 8:05 P.M. as a local for Clyde.

About 8:15 P.M. on East Main Street, it stopped for a traffic light at Clinton Street. There was a string of automobiles waiting for the same traffic light. A large group of evening theatre goers were crowded between car 114 and the line of autos waiting for the 114 to pass so they could cross the street. When the light changed, car 114 moved forward but its rear trucks picked or mounted the switch points and the rear of the interurban plowed into the crowd of people. One person was killed and several were seriously injured. Very quickly the switch was examined by railway officials and was found to be in proper operating condition.

As a result of this accident the city fathers got pretty excited and passed an ordinance to prohibit interurbans from operating on the streets of

Rochester. Fortunately cooler heads prevailed and within one month's time, the Mayor of Rochester was seen throwing the first shovel full of dirt on the City's new subway project to be built in the old Erie Canal bed through town. It was about six years before the subway was complete and before the Rochester & Eastern, the Rochester & Syracuse and the Rochester, Lockport & Buffalo interurbans could leave the streets.

On June 11, 1929, excessive speed of an eastbound night freight while passing through a 55-foot radius curve caused this pileup. Note that the two eastbound freight cars wound up on the westbound track. In the top right picture, from the left: R&S work car 64 to the rescue, Rochester, Lockport & Buffalo trailer 403 (which remained upright) and the overturned R&S express motor 63. In the lower right picture, the RL&B trailer has been re-railed and moved. R&S 63 would soon be upright again.

The curve at Lyons leading off Water Street onto the bridges over the Barge Canal was a tough one to negotiate, especially for a freight car with trailers. The up-grade on Water Street for westbound moves was about 2% and the 55-foot radius curve off the street and onto the bridges was one of the sharpest on the road. Half of the up-grade on the viaduct approaching the bridges from the west was 2.5%. With too little power, the trains could stall and too much speed could result in the type of accident that occurred on June 11, 1929. An eastbound night freight with one trailer crossed the bridges and approached the curve onto the street moving much too fast. Both cars derailed on the curve and the motor, R&S car 63, overturned onto the westbound track. The trailer, RL&B 403, also ended up on the westbound track but remained upright. The crew was shaken up but only the conductor was injured. It was reported that the air brakes failed to work.

Occasionally there was an accident reported that in retrospect was very funny although at the time there was no humor in sight. The report of one such accident has survived the flames of the scrap heap. It carries the notation: "Culver Road, November 5, 1912. Feller got trimmed by an old lady with a cane who wanted to go into the city when the car turned at C.R." M. Alexander was the motorman of

Accident pictures by Mrs. L. C. Seymour, Hoboken, NY

car 116 and George Feller was the conductor. It was train 23 that left Newark at 8:45 A.M. and ran local to Culver Road arriving there at 10:15. There they changed ends and left at 10:20 A.M. for a local run to Syracuse.

Here is Feller's description of the "accident." "On our westbound trip due at Palmyra at 9:24 A.M. an old lady boarded the car and when I collected her fare, she gave me a ticket for Rochester. I called out at the station that the car only went to city line. And when we arrived at city line after all the other passengers had gotten off, she was still on the car. I went to her and tried to explain to her but she got mad and would not listen to me and even began to swear at me so I walked away and left her. Then she started to get off. I was on the ground and was going to help her off when she attacked me with a heavy cane which she carried. She said the agent at Palmyra told her that our car was a limited. (signed) Geo. R. Feller, Con."

SPECIAL
502

6 Looking West Toward Buffalo

Buffalo, Lockport & Rochester Railway
Rochester, Lockport & Buffalo Railroad

Buffalo, Lockport & Rochester Railway

The Buffalo, Lockport & Rochester Railway was the connecting link between the interurbans of central New York state and the lines operating in the Niagara Frontier area. It closely paralleled the Erie Canal and the Falls Road of the New York Central Railroad. The BL&R was extremely well built with easy grades and few curves. Some of its passenger cars when originally built were geared for 80 miles per hour so that many a race developed with the steam trains on the Falls Road.

The region through which the BL&R passed was a very prosperous fruit and vegetable producing district. Annual shipments from the area were in the neighborhood of several millions of dollars. The steam road was strongly opposed to the construction of an electric railway in the area for obvious reasons so several earlier attempts at such construction were in vain.

Facing page: *Buffalo, Lockport & Rochester car 502 is seen standing on the main road crossing at Knowlesville, 20.8 miles east of Lockport and 6 miles west of Albion station. These double-ended cars had a door only in the number 2 end so when operating in two-car trains, the cars were coupled back to back.*

Chartered June 23, 1905, the BL&R was a consolidation of three other companies, the Albion & Lockport Railway, the Albion & Rochester Railway and the Albion Electric Railway. Only the latter had succeeded in building any line, 1.7 miles of 85-pound rail extending through the village of Albion as far east as Mount Albion Cemetery.

The owners of the new company, many of whom were from Toronto, Buffalo and Rochester, lost no time in hiring the firm of J. G. White & Co. of New York to design and construct their railroad. When finished, they had a high-speed single-track line, completely graded for eventual double tracking. Even the bridges that were necessary were built to accommodate a second track but the rails were never put down. The 54-mile road connected on the west end with the East Avenue local line of the International Railway in Lockport and on the east end with the Lyell Avenue line of the Rochester Railway Company. The BL&R was double-tracked for 4.8 miles between the Rochester city line and Elmgrove Road, Greece, for 1.8 miles between East Lake and Hilers (as it passed the Monroe County Fairgrounds

Gasport, at mile 6.48, was the first BL&R agency station east of Lockport. This view, looking west, shows the single-end siding laid on the sub-grade of what could have supported a second main track.

There was single-track operation in Spencerport, Brockport and Albion but the location of BL&R car 205 in this picture is unknown, c1909. The conductor in this view was James Burns of Lockport. He later left the BL&R for service with the International Railway's Buffalo - Lockport - Olcott Division. Your author rode with him on the last day of IRC interurban operation between Buffalo and Lockport, October 30, 1937.

The BL&R closely paralleled the Falls Road of the New York Central for about half of the distance between Rochester and Lockport. Here is an eastbound car at Shelby siding #42, midway between Medina and Middleport.

at Brockport) and through the village of Medina. Track structure consisted of 70-pound-to-the-yard ASCE section T-rail on standard 8-foot ties, pine on the tangents and oak on the curves, all on crushed rock ballast from local quarries.

The BL&R was opened from Rochester to Lattin's siding, 1 mile west of Albion, on September 3, 1908. Construction continued westward and the first car rolled into Lockport on November 17th of the same year. The running time between Rochester city line and Lockport city line was 1:50 for Limited trains and 2:15 for locals. All cars were operated by written train orders issued by the dispatcher at the Greece car barn near Rochester. Later, the dispatcher's office was moved to Albion, then back to the car house and finally, according to the last employees' timetable, to Lockport.

At the Lyell Avenue connection, the BL&R laid about 1500 feet of double-track in the street, as far east as the Rochester city line (at Burrows Street), where it met the street railway rails. In 1923, the New York State Railways leased trackage rights from the Rochester, Lockport & Buffalo Railroad (successor

Car 201 is seen westbound at Spencerport station. Most of the BL&R local stations and waiting shelters were sited on the north side of the main line because the grading for a future second main track lay adjacent to and south of the existing main track. Thus, most of the sidings and passing tracks lay south of the main line.

Between 1910 and 1914, the BL&R terminal in downtown Rochester was at Court and Exchange streets. At that time, the terminal was also used by cars of the Rochester, Syracuse & Eastern and the New York State Railways Rochester & Eastern and Rochester & Sodus Bay lines. Layover time for the BL&R cars was spent on Exchange Street near the police station. Two crossovers in the street permitted city cars to be run around the interurbans. This view of 50(?) shows the train door in the car's #2 end.

to the BL&R in 1919) in order to reach a new loop at Glide Street. Street car service continued after the RL&B folded so one can say that the last section of Beebe Syndicate electric railway track in use was that 1500 feet on Lyell Avenue in Rochester. Last street cars ran to Glide Street loop on April 24, 1939.

When the BL&R first opened, its cars were unable to reach Rochester's downtown area because there was no street railway crossing over the New York Central's Charlotte Branch on Lyell Avenue, a gap of just 80 feet. The NYC did not favor the crossing and the New York State Public Service Commission was slow to act. Permission for the crossing was finally granted in April 1910. The matter was brought to a head with the arrival in Rochester of car 502 of the Oneida Railway (Syracuse-Utica third-rail line). In May of 1910, a party of 22 men from Utica chartered car 502 for a Chamber of Commerce Good Will trip to the mid west and the Kentucky Derby in Louisville. The car was run under its own power all the way across the states of New York, northwestern Pennsylvania, Ohio and half of Indiana. The track snag was reported in the *Utica Press* which said:

> To get from the Rochester City Lines owned by the New York State Railways to the tracks of the Buffalo, Lockport & Rochester Railway, it would be necessary to cross an interval of 80 feet at Otis Station on the Charlotte Division of the New York Central. For a long time the companies had been trying to get the permission of the Public Service Commission to fill in this gap, but as it was a grade crossing, it took a lot of "show me." The permission was finally granted and the work was to begin soon. But the coming of the Utica trolley party hastened the beginning. At 8 o'clock Tuesday night [May 10th] a New York Central train passed the spot. Just 25 minutes afterward, a temporary crossing had been built by a large gang of men, and the Utica car was the first piece of rolling stock to go over it. The Uticans were the first passengers carried over it [the following morning]. A permanent crossing will be installed before the Uticans return.

The permanent crossing was installed and on May 23, 1910, the BL&R cars began running to the Interurban Terminal at the corner of Exchange and Court streets in downtown Rochester. Three years later, on April 20, 1914, the terminal for both the BL&R and the Empire United Railway (RS&E) cars was moved to the nearby Erie Railroad station on Court Street. Cars laid over on tracks adjacent to the Erie's freight terminal.

On July 1, 1908, the company issued a Book of Rules for the Government of Employees in the Operating Department. The motormen were members of the Brotherhood of Locomotive Engineers and the conductors belonged to the Order of Railway Conductors. In 1919, a jurisdictional dispute arose among the unions. The Amalgamated Association of Street Railway Employees objected to having the Rochester, Lockport & Buffalo cars run into Rochester by members of the Brotherhood of Locomotive Engineers. This made it necessary to change employees when entering Rochester at the city line. The outcome was that the RL&B men joined the Amalgamated and this arrangement continued as long as the cars operated.

When the road was first built, there were 25 telephone booths located at the various passing sidings along the way. The telephone lines were connected to the dispatcher, the stations and substa-

BL&R car 214 has paused for a photo-op at a village non-agency station. The location is unknown but the probable lack of heat in the shelter is quite evident. There was no foundation under the building and no chimney was showing.

BL&R express car 302 was a 1908 product of Niles Car Company. The car is standing on the eastbound main opposite the Rochester car shops. Note the passenger shelter just beyond the front end of the car. Note, also, the signal light box mounted on the pole behind the car. The signal was actuated by passengers waiting at the shelter.

tions by two circuits, line 1 for power purposes and line 2 for dispatching. In 1915-16, the booth system was discontinued. Phone jacks were mounted on poles on each side of each switch close enough to the cars so they could be reached by the car crew without leaving the car. Each car was assigned two portable phones with long cords, one set for each end of each car.

There were no block signals on the BL&R. The major grade crossings had crossing bells as well as the standard cross-buck signs. There was a red signal at the dispatcher's office at Albion which was displayed when he wished to issue orders to a passing car.

The company began business with fifteen Niles-built passenger motor cars, numbered 201-215 and two Niles-built express motor cars numbered 301 and 302. A third express motor number 303 arrived from Brill in 1916. Snow fighting equipment included a Russell rotary plow number 400 (renumbered 103), a nose plow attachable to work car 100 and, in 1918, a sweeper numbered 102. The 200-series cars were designed for single-end operation with their baggage compartment ahead. However, they were equipped for double-end operation because there were no car turning facilities between the car barn near Rochester and the Lockport city line.

In 1909, the Cincinnati Car Company provided six more passenger cars numbered 500-505. These 51' 6" cars were the ones that could go 80 miles an hour before they were geared down. They were double-end left-side-drive cars, and they were capable of regularly leaving the parallel running steam trains in the dust. As built, each of the 500-series cars had a train door centered in the number 2 end. When coupled together back to back as a two-car train, trainmen could pass from one car to the other.

BL&R steel freight motor 303 came from Brill Car Company in 1916. Trailer 402 was one of five built in the company's shops in 1909. Freight business did well in the fruit belt area between Rochester and Lockport. Gradually, less-than-car-load traffic developed as well.

George Krambles collection

Walter A. Lucas, photographer, August 1919

The BL&R and the Rochester & Syracuse Railroads shared a portion of Erie Railroad's freight house off Court Street, Rochester until 1921 when a new Union Freight Terminal was built off State Street, Rochester, to serve all the electric lines entering the city. Tracks in the foreground were used by the two interurbans for passenger car storage.

In later years, these end doors were removed.

BL&R passenger cars were originally painted Pullman Green. Later they donned a coat of red and finally the general color scheme was brown and cream. In the late 1920s, three of the RL&B 500-series cars received special attention in the company paint shop. As an advertising stunt, one was painted red, one white and one blue. The 501 was painted completely white except for blue lettering. On the sides of the car below the windows were the words: "Ride The Electric Cars And Save The Difference." Car 502 was painted a rather light blue above and below the windows. The car sides surrounding the windows were painted white. No advertising lettering was applied to the blue and red cars but the railroad name and numbers were painted with dark outlines to make them appear in relief. "Handsome carriage" indeed.

The BL&R built five freight trailers in their own shops. They were numbered 400-404. Miscellaneous rolling stock included a line car, number 101, eight or nine high-side center-dump ballast cars (numbered in the 1200-series) and at least five flat cars (numbered 2000 and up). The dumps and flats were bought second-hand at the time the road was constructed. It is believed that all the freight cars were painted standard boxcar red.

Power for the operation of the line was purchased from the Niagara, Lockport & Ontario Power Company and was distributed through five substations spaced approximately 10 miles apart. Number 1 was a half-mile east of Gasport, number 2 was at Stop 27 between Medina and Knowlesville, number 3 was at East State Street in Albion, number 4 was 1.5 miles east of Brockport and number 5 was 0.25 miles west of South Greece. The transmission

This is one of two photos taken in connection with an accident case at Knowlesville, 20.8 miles east of Lockport. In this view looking west, BL&R express car 301 or 302 is seen standing at the Knowlesville station. Just beyond the car, there was a siding into a local pea cannery. Note the double trolley wires. At sidings where trains usually scheduled to meet, the second trolley wire was carried over the siding so no wire frogs were required.

voltage was 60,000-volt three-phase at 25-cycles, and trolley voltage was 600-volts dc. Each substation was equipped with two 400-kW rotary converters. Substations were of concrete block construction. The rotary room was one story high and the room for transformers was two stories high. The transformers were water-cooled, the water being circulated by electric pumps. A tank on the upper floor gave gravity cooling in case of pump breakdown.

The company's car barn, repair shops and general offices were all located in the Town of Gates, about half a mile from Lyell Avenue in Rochester and just west of the Buffalo, Rochester & Pittsburgh Railway (BR&P) overpass. All facilities were housed in one building, a 155' x 165' fireproof concrete block affair. There were nine tracks in the shops. Six were for inspection and storage, two ran into the carpenter shop and paint shop and one ran into the machine shop where truck and motor overhaul work was done. A unique feature of this machine shop was that the concrete floor was depressed 5 feet below track level and below the rest of the yard. Thus, no pit was necessary and the undersides of the cars were readily accessible. Total capacity of the building was 23 double-truck cars. A loop track encircled the car barn, off which there was a track connection with the BR&P. During construction of the line, there was also was a track connection with the adjacent New York Central's Falls Road at Campbell's Siding #44, just east of Middleport.

The BL&R got off to a rather shaky start. In August of 1909, the company defaulted on the bond interest due on $3,400,000 of 5% first mortgage gold bonds and was thrown into receivership. On January 1, 1911, the Beebe Syndicate acquired control of the company and it effected a reorganization without foreclosure. All past debts were either paid or cancelled and the BL&R was given a new lease on life.

BL&R car 501, eastbound on an inspection trip, is just entering the beginning of double-track at Greece substation, c1911.One might surmise that the operating official approaching the car, believed to be Acting General Manager W. E. Havens, has just reported the special move off the single-track main line west of this switch.

BL&R car 501, on an inspection trip, is westbound at one of the substations. Charles R. Barnes, Electric Railroad Inspector for the New York State Public Service Commission, Second District is seen on the left. Next to him is Delbert Sprague, BL&R Line Foreman. The man in the center is believed to be W. E. Havens, Acting General Manager of the BL&R. Next is believed to be John H. Cain, Superintendent and on the right Helmer Snow, BL&R Roadmaster. c1911.

One of the new management's first innovations to attract additional passenger business was the establishment of a combined rail and steamer line between Toronto and points on the Beebe system. The Buffalo, Lockport & Rochester Transit Company was formed in 1910 and the steamer *Olcott* was leased from the Peninsula Steamboat Company of Sandusky, Ohio. On June 10, 1911, the first BL&R "Toronto Special" left Rochester for Olcott Beach (located on the International Railway) and connection with the boat for Toronto. Limited trains leaving Rochester at 7:30 A.M. and 4 P.M. were operated through to Olcott with only change of crews at Lockport. Passengers from farther east made close connections at Rochester if they boarded the RS&E 1:00 P.M. Limited out of Syracuse or its 1:12 P.M. connection out of Auburn. The steamer *Olcott* made two round trips a day from Toronto, leaving there at 7:30 A.M. and 2:30 P.M. Patrons could leave Rochester aboard the morning "Toronto Special", enjoy a round trip across Lake Ontario, spend an hour in Toronto and be back home at 8:30 that evening. In the summer of 1912, the steamer *Chicora* replaced the *Olcott* and continued under Beebe system spon-

BL&R line car 101 was built by Smith & Wallace Car Company of Woburn, Massachusetts in 1908. It was rugged to say the least and was active as long as the railroad existed.

Electric power to operate the BL&R was distributed through five substations. Here is a postcard view of the one at Gasport, about five miles east of the Lockport city line. The rotary converters were located in the one-story portion of the concrete block building and the water-cooled transformers were in the rear two-story section.

sorship through the 1914 sailing season. No "Toronto Specials" were scheduled thereafter.

Arrangements were made with the International Railway Company for the operation of BL&R passenger cars directly into Buffalo. This service began January 12, 1914. Only the crews changed at Lockport. Through car operation was dropped in 1919 as there were not enough advantages to the service to compensate for the extra car expense.

Fares on the BL&R were comparable with those of the other interurbans in the area. Cash and ticket rates began at 2 cents a mile until the end of World War I when they began to creep up. The rate in 1929 was $.0325 per mile one-way and 2 cents round-trip. Passengers boarding cars at an open agency station who paid a cash fare on the car were charged an excess fare of 10 cents. Commutation books for 24 rides and 48 rides were available. Prior to World War I, the BL&R offered mileage books to individuals with 200 miles of transportation on its line for $5.00. These were good to all points between Rochester city line and Lockport city line. Also, during that period the company participated with most of the interurban lines in central New York state in of-

Wilbourne B. Cox collection

An early view of BL&R 207 lettered Buffalo, Lockport and Rochester at the Rochester car shops.

In this view, the conductor is polishing the back window of car 502, flagged for an extra move. Note one end of BL&R flat car 2000 seen on a back track at the Rochester car shops.

fering the "Interchangeable Coupon Ticket." The book contained 240 five-cent coupons giving $12.00 worth of travel for $10.00.

The BL&R gradually developed an important package freight and express business along its line. There were three canning companies located adjacent to railway sidings at Medina, Knowlesville and Albion. During canning season, it was customary to lease a few empty gondola cars from the neighboring steam roads and place them at certain BL&R sidings where farmers could load their corn for delivery to the canneries. Carloads of coal were picked up at the BR&P interchange at the rear of the Greece car barn and were delivered to the State School's side track in Albion. The BL&R also handled an increasing amount of through freight from Syracuse and vicinity destined for Buffalo and the west. By early 1914, the BL&R crews were operating their own freight cars into the Buffalo & Lake Erie Traction freight terminal on Swan Street in the heart of Buffalo. Their nightly freight trains included cars of many of the connecting lines. Through freight car service between Syracuse and Buffalo was inaugurated November 3, 1919.

One charter move of BL&R cars over foreign lines is noteworthy. According to Harry Harner, conductor, and Charles Havens, motorman, the car crew making the move, two 500-series passenger cars coupled up as a two-car train carried delegates to the Street Railway Association of New York convention at Cooperstown, NY on June 27, 1911. The special cars picked up delegates en route. They moved mostly under their own power over the RS&E, the Oneida Railway, the Utica & Mohawk Valley Railway and the Otsego & Herkimer Railroad to Cooperstown. The BL&R cars were towed over the Oneida Railway between Syracuse and Utica because they were not equipped for third-rail operation. Each host railway in turn furnished a pilot. The return trip was made the following day.

There is a record of at least one special move of an International Railway funeral car, *Elmlawn,* between Lockport and Albion. A copy of the train order dated October 30, 1918 has survived.

George Krambles Collection

BL&R cars 502 and 501 were standing at the crossover on the main line opposite the Rochester car shops, c1910. The train is pointing east.

In 1911, the Buffalo, Lockport & Rochester Transit Company leased the Great Lakes steamer Lakeside, *renamed it* Olcott *and placed it in summer service between Olcott, NY on the International Railway, and Toronto, Ontario, Canada. The* Olcott *was the connecting link for "Toronto Special" excursions operated by the BL&R between Rochester and Olcott Beach. The* Olcott *was replaced by a similar vessel* Chicora *the following season. Passenger travel patterns were changing by 1914 so no "Toronto Special" service was offered after that year.*

On October 30, 1919, the International Railway Company's funeral car Elmlawn *made a once-only round trip over the BL&R from Lockport to Albion, 27 miles. The motorman's (R. J. Gunnison) copy of the train order for the eastbound move has survived (right).* Elmlawn *was the second car with that name. Built by Brill in 1916, it was 44 feet long. The mourners compartment seated 40 and the pall bearers section seated 6.*

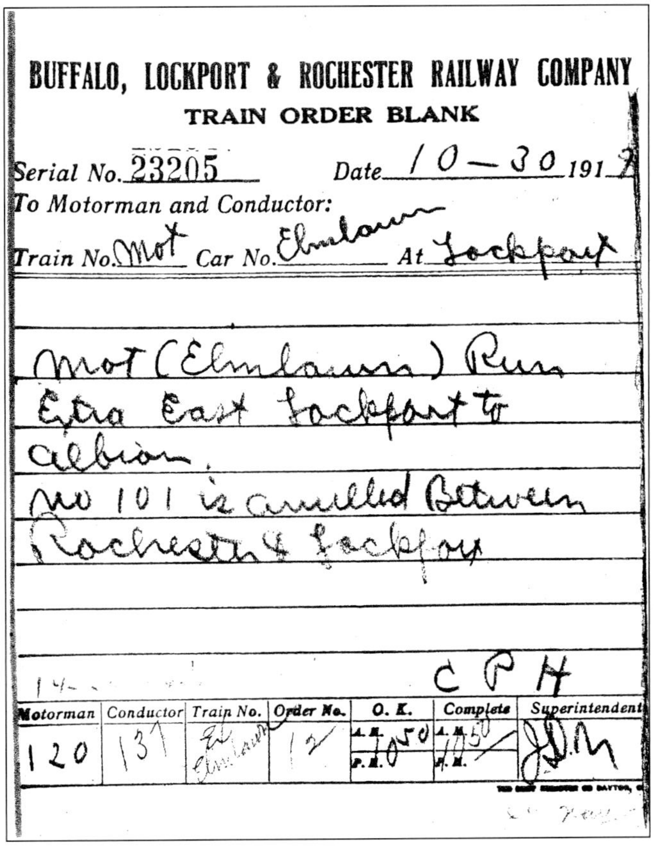

BUFFALO, LOCKPORT & ROCHESTER RAILWAY COMPANY

TRAIN ORDER BLANK

Serial No. 23205 *Date* 10 — 30 *191*9

To Motorman and Conductor:

Train No. Mot *Car No.* Elmlawn *At* Lockport

Mot (Elmlawn) Run Extra East Lockport to Albion.

No 101 is annulled Between Rochester & Lockport

14- CPH

Motorman	Conductor	Train No.	Order No.	O. K.	Complete	Superintendent
120	137	Ex Elmlawn	12	A.M. 1050 P.M.	A.M. 1050 P.M.	JDM

Another surviving artifact is the train order for motor 400 which covered the company's brand new rotary snow plow's first trip over the road on March 18, 1909. The plow was renumbered 103 into the work car series that same year when the five company-built freight car trailers (400-404) arrived on the scene.

During the fall of 1914, Wells-Fargo Express Company contracted with the BL&R to operate express service between Rochester and Buffalo. It was reported that BL&R train 105 was a Wells-Fargo through non-stop express car between Rochester and Buffalo on a daily-except-Sunday schedule. One can assume this car matched in with a similar through non-stop express run on the Empire United line between Syracuse and Rochester (its train 305). This great service was short-lived because the Wells-Fargo contracts with the various electric lines in New York state were terminated in December 1918 when the express company was consolidated into the American Railway Express Company.

The Rochester - Lockport interurbans terminated at the Erie Railroad station on Court Street between 1914 and 1928 when its cars were routed into the new Rochester Subway system. Two spare tracks near the Erie freight house were available for layover time. Here is 502 resplendent in its light blue and white advertising motif. Note the train door in the #2 end had been removed by the mid 1920s.

Rochester, Lockport & Buffalo Railroad

By the end of the First World War, the Buffalo, Lockport & Rochester Railway was again in financial trouble. Management of the company from its Syracuse offices was terminated December 1, 1917. This time the company went through the wringer in good shape, emerging April 4, 1919 as the Rochester, Lockport & Buffalo Railroad Corporation. It emerged from reorganization with 1.5 million dollars in 6% preferred stock and 2.2 million dollars in common stock. Its funded debt of nearly 3 million dollars was completely wiped out so the new company began operations with annual fixed charges of about $526 instead of $209,300. This was an unusual situation among electric railways as they were usually mortgaged up to their corporate ears. At any rate, it was a big help in keeping the RL&B above water for the next 10 years.

As a connecting link between the interurbans of central and western New York state, the RL&B was in a favorable position to increase its freight business. From interviews with interurban car crews held many years ago, it appears that there were several specific movements of freight over the RL&B that originated on connecting lines. In the 1920s the Locke Insulator Company in Victor on the Rochester & Eastern shipped parts in RL&B trailers to Niagara Falls. Pianos manufactured in East Rochester were shipped to Buffalo from time to time. The Brown-Lipe-Chapin Gear works in Syracuse consigned some of their products to points in the Buffalo area.

A surviving 1923 Rochester, Lockport & Buffalo Railroad "Joint Freight Tariff of Less Than Carload Class and Commodity Rates" included all points on the RL&B (Buffalo was an RL&B station in the tariff), the Rochester & Syracuse, the Auburn & Syracuse, the Empire State railroads and the New York State Railways, Rochester & Eastern and Rochester & Sodus Bay lines. The tariff indicated that these arrangements had been originated by the BL&R and were adopted by the RL&B after the company's 1919 reorganization.

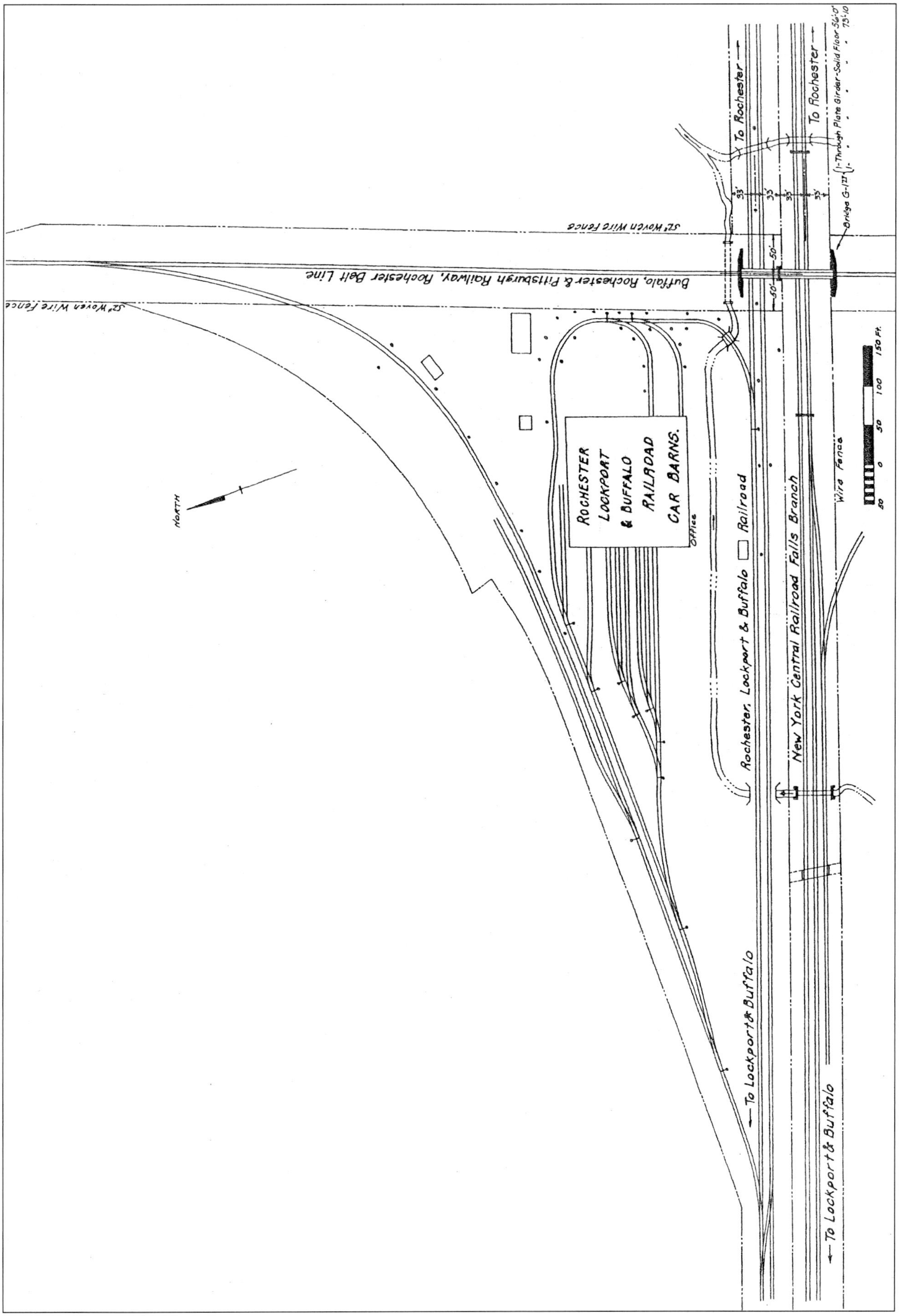

Art Work by Charles R. Lowe

In the mid 1920s, the RL&B repainted three 500-series cars for advertising purposes. The body of car 501 was white. With dark lettering, RIDE WITH US was painted above the car's end windows. RIDE THE ELECTRIC CARS AND SAVE THE DIFFERENCE appeared in dark letters on each side below the window sills. Car 502 was painted a powder blue but had no advertising messages. Car 503 was painted red. A view of this car has not turned up.

George Slyford collection

C.V. Hess, Rochester, NY, collection

In a winter setting, RL&B car 211 is seen in the yard at the Rochester car shops. The car's color scheme has gone from red to brown and cream. Indeed, a beautiful interurban car.

The most extensive interline less than carload freight movements on the upstate New York interurbans had been developed by the mid 1920s. A Buffalo & Lake Erie Traction Joint Tariff for 1924 and a Buffalo & Erie Railway (successor to B&LET) tariff for 1926 quoted through rates between Cleveland, Ohio and all points between Lockport, Rochester, Geneva, Sodus Point, Auburn, Syracuse and Oswego. Shipments west of Erie, Pa. were handled by truck because the chain of electric railways to Cleveland had been broken on September 16, 1922 when the Cleveland & Erie abandoned its Erie-Conneaut, Ohio line. By December of 1929, all such movements west of Buffalo had ceased.

An interesting Joint Passenger Tariff of the Rochester, Lockport & Buffalo Railroad and International Railway Company for 1928 has survived. It shows joint fares between agency stations on the RL&B with IRC stations Buffalo, Niagara Falls, North Tonawanda and Olcott, NY. There were special three-day-limit round-trip tickets available between Rochester city line and Buffalo or Niagara Falls for

George Slyford collection

Rochester, Lockport & Buffalo cars 207 and 210 were parked at the car shops just west of Rochester city line. Both cars were painted red. c1920.

Wilbourne B. Cox collection

Rochester, Lockport & Buffalo cars 215 and 504 standing on the eastbound main line opposite the Rochester car shops, c1920. Note the forward trolley pole of each car was hooked back over the car body.

$3.50. It also stated that passengers holding tickets to the center of Buffalo were entitled to transfers to Buffalo city car routes.

RL&B cars began using the Rochester Subway on February 4, 1928. The cars came into Rochester on Lyell Avenue as far as the subway where they turned south, descended on a single-track ramp to the tracks of the new rapid transit line. Their terminal station was "City Hall" but the empty cars continued a half-mile where, after climbing a ramp, they

Wilbourne B. Cox collection

RL&B car 214 at the Rochester car shops awaiting assignment. All service on the railroad was discontinued April 30, 1931.

G. A. Doeright, photographer

RL&B 209 and a 500-series car were awaiting assignment in the Lockport yard of the International Railway Company in September 1922. Between 1914 and 1919, these cars ran through from Rochester to Buffalo over IRC tracks, using IRC crews west of Lockport. BL&R cars also operated over IRC between Lockport and Olcott Beach for boat connections across Lake Ontario to Toronto.

turned on an elevated loop adjacent to South Avenue. There was a short spur off this loop where the Lockport cars could lay over. Passengers could make connections at City Hall station with cars of the Rochester & Eastern Line of New York State Railways for Canandaigua and Geneva as well as with cars of the Rochester & Syracuse Railroad for points east. The official mileage of the RL&B cars running over New York State Railways tracks was 3.05 miles, of which 1.10 miles were on Lyell Avenue and 1.95 miles were in the subway system.

The RL&B freight cars never ran in the Subway. Eastbound freights continued in Lyell Avenue to State Street, then south on State, first to the Erie freight house on Exchange Street and then, beginning in 1921, only as far as the State Street car barn of the New York State Railways. Here they turned west and passed right through the barns to the new Union Freight Terminal on Frank Street. They occupied the tracks on the north side of the freight

ROCHESTER SUBWAY SIGNAL SYSTEM

Sections on route of Rochester, Lockport & Buffalo RR cars

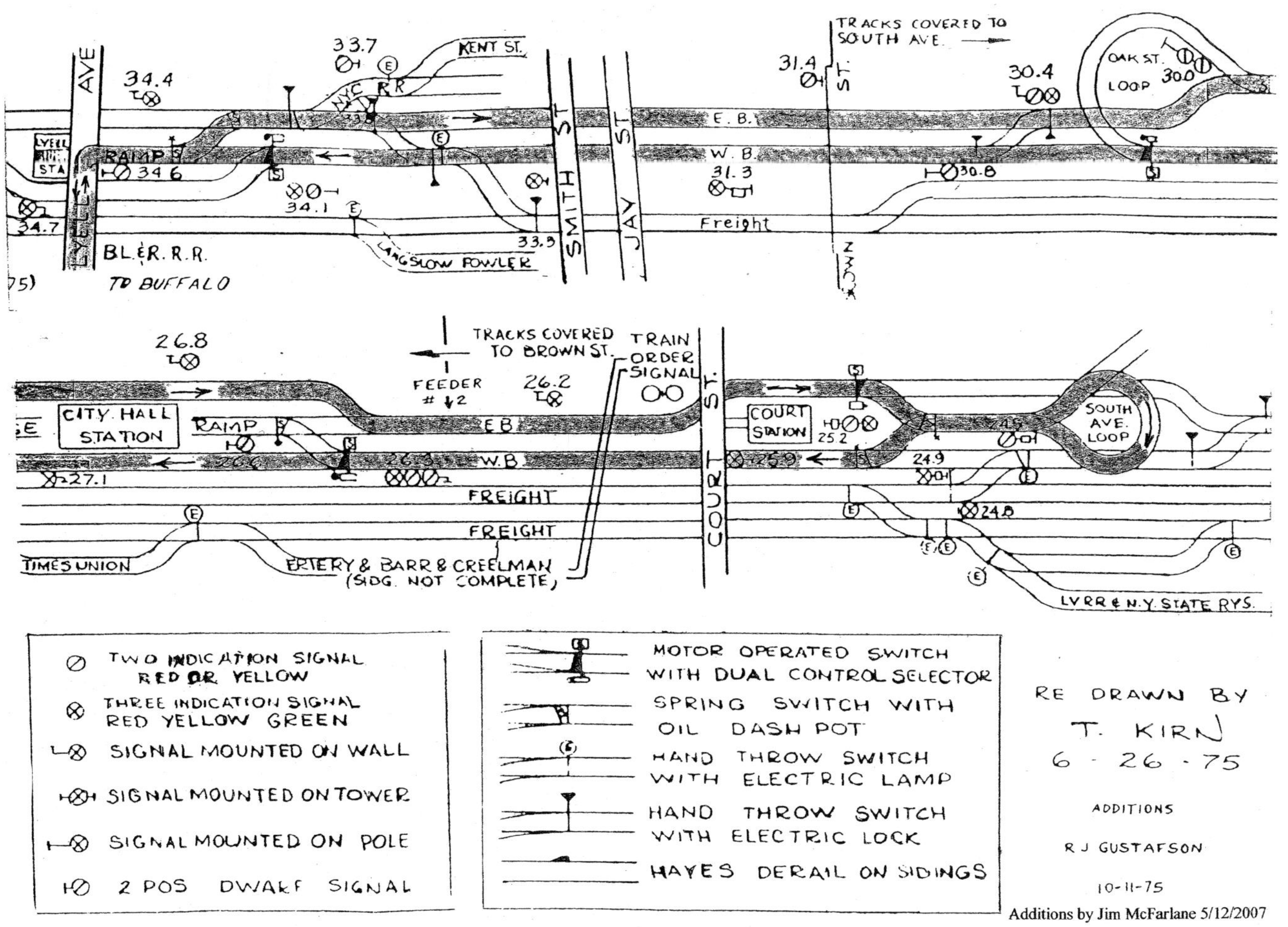

Additions by Jim McFarlane 5/12/2007

Courtesy of Tom Kirn

house together with the freight cars of the Rochester & Syracuse. The New York State Railway's freight cars occupied tracks on the south side of the freight house. RL&B freight car mileage from the Glide Street loop at the city line to the Union Freight Terminal was 1.79 miles.

At this late date, it is not known if any efforts were ever considered to introduce light-weight cars on the RL&B. The big cars continued to pound the road until the end of service in 1931. The running time for locals from terminal to terminal established in 1909 was about 2 hours and thirty minutes. This prevailed until the end. In the early years, hourly service included several daily Limited runs. This frequency was reduced toward the last days to a schedule of a local car approximately every two hours with a morning and an evening trip running Limited between Rochester and Albion, and then local between Albion and Lockport.

In the year 1929, the RL&B operating ratio exceeded 100% for the first time. In other words, its operating revenues did not cover its operating expenses and taxes. The number of passengers carried had fallen from over 2,000,000 in 1914 to 768,840. The fleet of cars, which ran up 966,428 car miles in 1929, was beginning to show its 20 years of age. While the passenger business had decreased through the 1920s, the company's freight traffic had increased nicely. Tons of freight carried in 1914 were 4616 and in 1929 were 16,737. This tonnage would drop drastically as the connecting interurbans were discontinued. The New York State Railways line to Sodus Bay was discontinued on June 27, 1929. The Rochester & Eastern cars to Canandaigua and Geneva stopped running on July 31, 1930. The Rochester & Syracuse lasted until June 27, 1931.

The last cars on the Rochester, Lockport & Buffalo Railroad were run April 30, 1931. All equipment was scrapped except for a few car bodies that became local camps or chicken houses. The body of RL&B car 206 has been rescued and is presently awaiting restoration at the Rochester and Genesee Valley Railroad Museum at Industry, New York, some ten miles south of Rochester.

7 A Short Trip to Marion

Newark & Marion Railway

The Newark & Marion Railway was the longest lived of any of the properties controlled by the Beebe Syndicate. The little 8.19-mile line connecting the village of Marion with the rest of the world at Newark continued to operate as a freight-only branch of the Pennsylvania Railroad System and its successors until 1984. Although chartered as an electric railway, the motive power was "temporarily" steam for the next 50 years.

Organized May 4, 1900 by local interests, construction of the Newark & Marion was begun November 12, 1901. Beginning at a track connection with the Northern Central Railway in the Village of Newark, the new line extended west following the northerly side line of Pearl Street and parallel to the New York Central main line for about a mile and a quarter to the valley of Ganargua Creek. There it turned north and crossed the NYC on a riveted through-truss bridge. The line then followed the same creek northwesterly to East Palmyra and thence through the Red Creek valley to Marion. The track was standard gauge, laid with 70-pound rail on chestnut and oak ties, 2,816 to the mile. The curves were easy and the grades were slight. As of 1912, the only railroad building on the line was the station at Marion. At the time of Federal Valuation in 1917, the Interstate Commerce Commission valued the property at $146,521.00, an indication of the size of the line.

Completion of track laying to Marion and a local church fair were causes for a celebration. On December 14, 1905, the construction locomotive hauling a passenger car donated by the Pennsylvania Railroad made a series of round trips to Newark. The road was finally opened for business February 26, 1906.

All the motive power on the little road was leased except, perhaps, the first steam locomotive. An 0-4-4T Baldwin of 1892 vintage from the Long Island Rail Road was used in building the N&M. Owned by the contractor, the Syracuse Railroad Construction Company, it was kept by the railroad after construction was completed and was given the number 1. Numbers 2 and 3 were 0-4-0 yard switchers. Number 2 was built in 1881 at New York Central's 31st Street shops on New York City's west side line and number 3 was built at its East Buffalo shops in 1889. Each subsequent locomotive arrived on the N&M as a replacement of the one before and each was a hand-me-down, principally from the Pennsylvania Railroad. Apparently there were only six steam locomotives that ever bore the N&M name and were given an N&M number. In its 1912 report to the New York State Public Service Commission, the Newark & Marion reported having one locomotive under lease and one combination passenger-mail-baggage car. Diesel locomotives from the Pennsylvania Railroad's fleet replaced steam power

Here are the alpha and omega of locomotives numbered and lettered for the Newark & Marion and the Marion railways. All the steam power on this 8-mile pike came second-hand from the New York Central or Pennsylvania railroads. Number 1 opened the road in 1906. Number 6 arrived on the property in 1925. Note the headlights and pilots on both ends of each locomotive as there were no turning facilities at Marion.

Facing page: *N&M #1 was an 1892 Baldwin 0-4-4T, originally built for the Long Island Rail Road.*

Above: *Marion Railway #6, a second-hand 2-6-2 Vulcan, was leased from the Pennsylvania Railroad until 1931.*

on the N&M beginning in April 1954.

Initially, the passenger service consisted of three round-trips daily between Marion and the Northern Central (later PRR) station in Newark. Running time varied between 35 and 45 minutes. Fare was 35 cents one way. Being of the same general management as the Rochester, Syracuse & Eastern, the Marion line shared in much of the larger road's advertising. RS&E tickets were on sale at the Marion station. Frequent excursions were run between Marion and points on the Beebe lines. Close passenger connections with the electric line were made at Newark's Northern Central station, located just a few hundred feet off of East Union Street. Transferring passengers left the RS&E cars at the foot of East Miller Street for the short walk up to the NC station at the corner of Miller and Hoffman streets. The Newark & Marion Railway had one mile of trackage rights over the Northern Central to bring its trains to this NC station.

From the start, the N&M depended on carload freight service for its revenue. The village of Marion was central to a large and prosperous dairy and farming area of Wayne County and their products provided most of the tonnage carried by the N&M. Interchange was made with the Northern Central and the New York Central at Newark. In 1907, gross revenue from freight operation was a modest $7,850. By 1927, it had risen to a respectable $41,853. Annual passenger revenues in the early years grossed $5,000, but dwindled to less than $500 in 1927. Passenger service was discontinued in 1929 or 1930.

It was originally intended that the Newark & Marion would be electrified by extending north in North Main Street from Union Street in the village of Newark, to Marion. The electrification never happened because the West Shore Railroad refused to grant grade crossing rights for an electric road at the North Main Street crossing of the steam road's main line.

The Beebe Syndicate planned an extension of the N&M northward from Marion through Williamson to Poultneyville on Lake Ontario. For this extension, a subsidiary company, the Newark, Williamson & Northern Railway Company was incorporated in 1914. However, these plans never got off the drawing board.

In 1915, the Newark & Marion went into receivership, at which time control by the Beebe Syndicate ended. At the foreclosure sale, local interests bid $34,300 for the railroad property and acquired it. The Marion Railway Corporation was incorporated May 5, 1917 as successor to the N&M so operation of the line continued.

On May 4, 1930, the capital stock of the Marion Railway was acquired by the Pennsylvania Railroad for $140,000. It should be remembered that the Northern Central Railway had been leased to the Pennsylvania Railroad in 1911 and had been operated directly by PRR since July 1, 1914.

Two more corporate changes occurred in the extended life of the N&M property. The PRR became part of Penn Central on February 1, 1968. PC was succeeded by Conrail on April 1, 1976. Although the little line had now lost its corporate identity, it continued to do a branch-line business at the same old stand for another 54 years. All service on the branch to Marion ended on July 1, 1984.

ODHOUSE.

A Branch to Auburn 8

Auburn & Northern Electric Railroad
Empire United Railways
Empire State Railroad

The Auburn & Northern Electric Railroad was an 8.17-mile single-track electric line that connected the city of Auburn with the main line of the Rochester, Syracuse & Eastern Railroad at Port Byron. Chartered September 14, 1904, grading was begun the following year. I. M. Luddington was the contractor. The Auburn & Northern Construction Company was in charge of the complete building of the line.

The A&N was completed and placed in operation June 28, 1908, just a few weeks before the RS&E arrived in Port Byron from the west. The A&N cars entered Auburn along State Street running over its own tracks as far south as Seymour Street. From Seymour to Dill Street, the tracks were owned by the Auburn & Syracuse Electric Railroad, Auburn City Division. The tracks on Dill and Water streets were owned by the Auburn & Northern as were those on the one-mile Clark, Jefferson and Orchard Street line and one track on West Genesee Street for three blocks west of State. These track details appear more clearly on an accompanying map of the Auburn City Lines.

The A&N was built on private right-of-way between the two terminals. Since the road was built by the Beebe Syndicate as a connecting link between two of their major properties, construction was very similar to that of the RS&E. The overhead was pole and bracket type carrying 550-volts dc. The rail was 70-pounds-to-the-yard laid on untreated ties on gravel ballast. Power was purchased from the Auburn & Syracuse power house at Auburn except for the northern end which was fed from the RS&E substation at Port Byron.

Facing page: *Auburn & Syracuse cars were occasional visitors to Port Byron on the A&N line. In this real photo postcard view, A&S car 54 was northbound on Main Street as it approached the RS&E station.*
Shelden S. King collection

Above: *This c1908 view was posed to show off the Union Switch & Signal installation on the Auburn & Northern line between Auburn and Port Byron. The car on the siding appears to be RS&E 110. A&N 10 is holding the main.*

H. A. Myers, photographer

In this 1910 real photo postcard view, Auburn & Northern car 51 was standing on the connecting track with the RS&E at Port Byron station. The RS&E main line tracks lay between the two high-tension poles seen in back of car 51.

As originally planned, the A&N was to build a line westward from Auburn to connect with the Geneva, Waterloo, Seneca Falls & Cayuga Lake Traction Company. Because of expensive construction in the Cayuga Lake area and the sparse territory between Auburn and Seneca Falls, the line was never built. The A&N's local line on Clark Street and the second track on Genesee Street westerly from the end of the city's double-track at State Street were apparently a part of their proposed extension to Seneca Falls. The A&N local lines were built in 1905 and placed in operation the following year. A year later, a track with diamond turnouts was laid in Dill Street and a turnout was installed to serve an off-street freight house. Diamond turnouts were equilateral switches located at each end of a short passing track in streets having a single track car line. Of course, one diamond turnout was usually found wherever a single track in the street changed to double track.

The A&N completed installation of automatic block signals along their entire road in August of 1908. There were six signals furnished by Union Switch & Signal Company. Each pair protected the sections of track between the three sidings, at mile posts 0.41, 2.57 and 4.12 as measured from Port Byron. Rochester, Syracuse & Eastern Railroad employees' timetable 47, dated September 25, 1916, details the principal mileage points on the A&N.

Standard octagonal highway shelters were provided at Stops 1, 2 and 3. A fourth one at Throopsville, was 10- by 15-feet in size (one extra panel on two opposite sides) on a 20- by 20-foot platform. These were the same style shelter used on the RS&E, the Syracuse, Lake Shore & Northern and the Auburn & Syracuse. The shelters at Stops 1 and 3 were short-lived as they were destroyed by fire. Replacement buildings were less opulent.

The A&N offered hourly service. Cars from Port Byron looped through Dill, Water, North and Genesee streets to the Auburn & Syracuse waiting room at 82 Genesee Street, just a few doors west of South Street. The Dill Street freight station, owned by the A&S, became the passenger terminal for both Port Byron and Auburn & Syracuse interurban cars after the A&S city lines were discontinued in 1927.

Beginning August 10, 1908, the RS&E operated its Limited cars through between Rochester and Auburn. This arrangement continued until the RS&E was completed to Syracuse on December 18, 1909. Thereafter, Auburn passengers had to change cars at Port Byron. In 1915 and 1916, the Empire United Railways, Rochester-Syracuse Division ran Limited cars between Rochester and Auburn every other hour. This service lasted only until the RS&E was taken out of the bankrupt Empire United. Then, it was back to changing cars at Port Byron for Auburn passengers.

The original complement of rolling stock on the Auburn & Northern consisted of three Kuhlman-built 30-foot city cars numbered 1, 2 and 3. They were purchased in 1905 for use on the A&N city lines, State to York and Clark to Orchard, in Auburn. The cars were leased to the A&S and were operated by

Auburn & Northern cars 1-3 were delivered by Kuhlman Car Company in 1905 for use on its 2.34 miles of city lines in Auburn. Soon after delivery, the vestibules were closed in and fenders were added.

Auburn & Northern cars 1-3 in service in Auburn. These cars were leased to the Auburn & Syracuse Electric Railroad for use on the A&N owned tracks in conjunction with the A&S owned city lines. The A&N cars were maintained by the A&S.

its crews in coordination with the other Auburn City Line routes. In 1908, the Company purchased from Kuhlman, car 10, a 53' 6" closed interurban and a mate to the RS&E 117-118 group. Car10 was the A&N's contribution to the Rochester-Auburn Limited 1908-1909 car service. In 1910, the car was absorbed into the RS&E fleet and was renumbered 119. Also in 1910, the A&N bought two 36-foot closed interurban cars from the Auburn & Syracuse (ex-Auburn Inter-Urban numbered 50 and 51), for use in the Port Byron service. Later renumbered 6 and 7, they were sold in August 1916 to the New York

In 1908, the Kuhlman Car Company delivered A&N car 10 to the RS&E interchange track with the West Shore Railroad just east of Newark. It was equipped for service at the RS&E Newark shops. Car 10 was the A&N contribution to the RS&E pool of cars that operated through service between Rochester and Auburn via Port Byron. This through service was discontinued in December of 1909 when the RS&E opened its main line east of Port Byron to Syracuse. Car 10 had been built as a mate to RS&E cars 117-118. In 1910, it was taken into the RS&E fleet and renumbered 119.

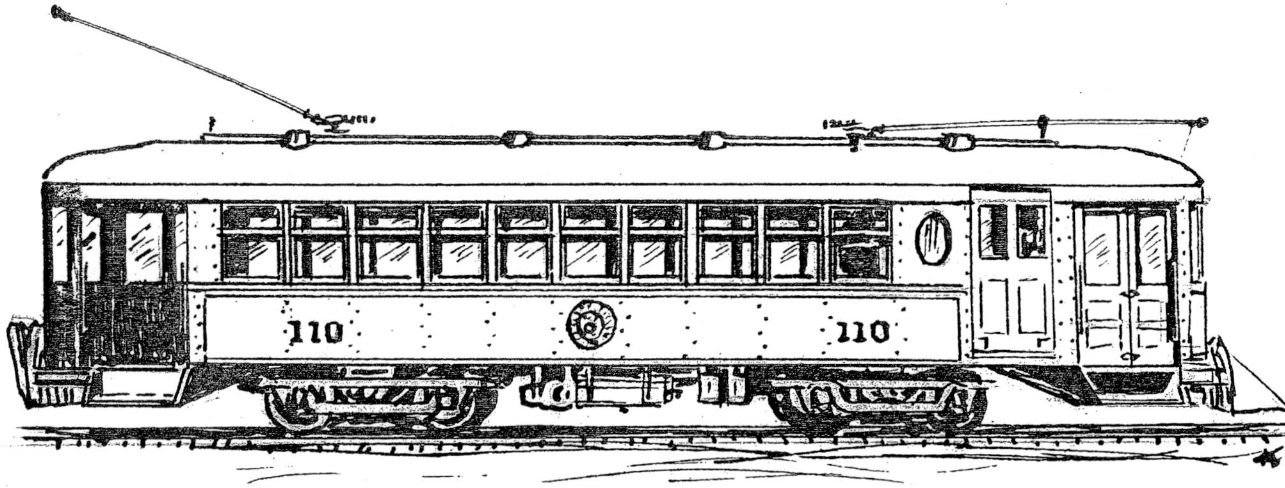

This pen & ink sketch of Geneva, Seneca Falls & Auburn Railroad car 110 was drawn by George Krambles in 1943 for an illustration in CERA Bulletin 44 entitled "The Interurban Lines of Central and Western New York State." After the bulletin was published, George returned my pictures and other artifacts, including his original pen & ink sketch of GSF&A car 110. In 1925, the Empire State Railroad purchased cars 110 and 111 from the Geneva, Seneca Falls & Auburn Railroad to replace two ES cars that had been lost in fires. The two cars, renumbered 215 and 217, saw service on the ES Auburn - Port Byron Division.

State Railways, Utica Lines where they became 388 and 390. The A&N never owned any freight, work or snow fighting equipment. The servicing of, and repairs to, their five cars was performed in the Auburn & Syracuse shops in Auburn.

There are no records available to indicate the disposition of the A&N city cars 1, 2 and 3. It is known that they were still under lease to the A&S in 1917.

Records show that in July or August 1916, an agreement was made with the RS&E to lease one passenger car and one freight car to the A&N on a "per hour" basis. Only one passenger car was needed to operate the complete interurban schedule between Auburn and Port Byron. Beginning in late 1917, the necessary cars for this service were supplied by the Empire State Railroad (the reorganized A&N).

The Auburn & Northern operated under its own name until February 18, 1913 when it became a part of the Empire United Railways, Inc. By 1916, the Empire United was on the rocks, corporately speaking. The RS&E was withdrawn from the EUR and was reorganized separately. This left the Auburn & Northern and the Syracuse, Lake Shore & Northern Railroads. They were reorganized as the Empire State Railroad Corporation on October 27, 1917. The A&N became the Auburn - Port Byron Division of the Empire State Railroad, by which name it was known until the last of its operation.

During the 1920s, the Auburn - Port Byron Division offered virtually hourly service throughout the day. A second-class train was scheduled for one round trip daily except Sunday.

Being a north-south oriented line, the A&N was

Charles R. Lowe collection

This picture shows the track layout on Dill Street, Auburn. The switch in the immediate foreground was the east switch to a single track wye in State Street. The car pictured was either 215 or 217 of the Empire State Railroad (successor to the Auburn & Northern) and was standing at the end of track opposite the Auburn freight and passenger terminal about 1928.

particularly susceptible to drifting snow. Motorman LeRoy Gaston recalled one occasion when a big rotary plow needed four hours to make the 8-mile trip from Port Byron to Auburn. Gaston also recalled seeing numbers of "unwilling" passengers on his cars from time to time. In the early days he often had 12 or more prisoners from Buffalo. They were handcuffed in pairs and were accompanied by three deputy sheriffs. They boarded his car at Port Byron. Prison guards met the car when it stopped adjacent to the Auburn State Prison on State Street.

On August 3, 1930, the Rochester & Syracuse inaugurated a through chair car service between Syracuse and Auburn via Port Byron. Five round trips were made daily. This was a substitute for the Auburn & Syracuse via Skaneateles line which had been abandoned several months earlier. Then on January 1, 1931, the R&S leased the entire Auburn-Port Byron Division from the Empire State Railroad so as to better supervise and coordinate the service between Rochester, Syracuse and Auburn. When the Empire State Railroad discontinued all service on June 24, 1931, their Auburn-Port Byron Division continued to operate until June 27th when the Rochester & Syracuse suspended operations completely.

The last day on the Auburn-Port Byron Division was an eventful one. On the final trip into Auburn, car 121, with motorman Corry Heald and conductor LeRoy Gaston, had an accident. An auto with three drunks in it ran head-on into car 121as it was heading in State Street toward the Dill Street terminal. Neither vehicle was traveling at high speed and no one was seriously injured. An Auburn local police car arrived on the scene shortly and the drunks were carted off to jail. Even so, car 121 left Auburn on time at 11:30 P.M. with only a half dozen passengers for its final trip to Port Byron and then on to Newark shops.

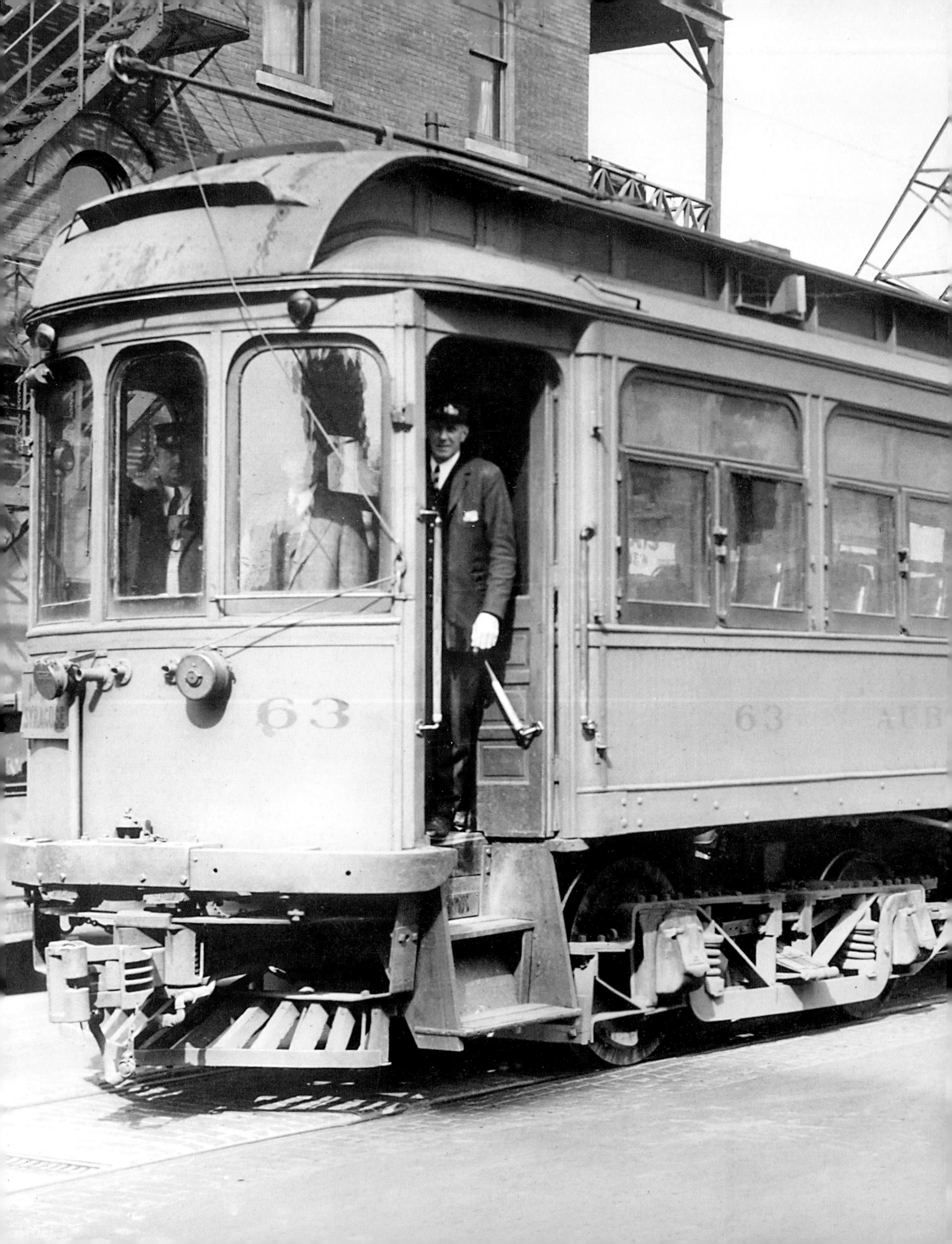
SYRACUSE
63
63 AUB

From the Finger Lakes to Syracuse 9

Auburn & Syracuse Electric Railroad

The third largest city of those served by the Beebe Syndicate's electric lines was Auburn, home of the Auburn & Syracuse Electric Railroad. This company was made up of two distinct parts, the Auburn City Division and the Interurban Division.

Auburn City Lines

The city lines had their beginnings on April 15, 1871 when two horse-drawn railways, the Auburn & Owasco Lake Railway Co. and the East Genesee Street & Seward Avenue Railway Co. were formed. Both were owned by the same interests. D. M. Osborne was their president. The A&OL was the first to begin operations. Its 1.25-mile line was opened on September 17, 1872. Five cars and six horses were required to operate the line that ran from Columbus Street on West Genesee through the center of town and out Owasco Street. A&OL horse cars took passengers to the east pier dock on Owasco Lake where they changed to the steamer *Lady of the Lake* for a 90-minute ride to Cascade.

Later in 1872, the East Genesee Street & Seward Avenue line opened. The company owned 4 cars

Above: *This wonderful view from a glass plate negative gives a rare detailed glimpse of downtown Auburn about 1890 - no storm windows to protect against the cold and no power lines in sight. Car 14 is westbound on Genesee Street, Auburn's principal east-west thoroughfare.*

Facing page: *Auburn & Syracuse car 63 posed for an "end of the era" photograph on the single track on East Jefferson Street, Syracuse, just a day or two before its last trip, April 15, 1930. The A&S passenger station on nearby East Fayette Street was on two busy routes of the New York State Railways city lines and there was no crossover in the street in front of the station. Thus the A&S cars headed for East Jefferson Street, the nearest piece of single track, to change ends. This is not a last-day photograph of 63 because the car was facing an afternoon sun and the last car left Syracuse on April 15, 1930 at 11:00 AM.*

In 1890, the Auburn City Railway purchased 33 acres of land at the mouth of the Owasco River and created Lakeside Park. Tracks to the park were laid in Owasco Street along the east side of the river. The park became so popular that, in 1895, a second line to the park was built along the west side of the river creating a trolley loop between Auburn city and the park. A portion of Lakeside Park can be seen in the background of this mid-1890s picture of Auburn City Railway car 27.

In 1903, Auburn City Railway car 33 was re-lettered by its new owner, the Auburn & Syracuse Electric Railroad. The car's number did not change. This picture was taken at Lakeside Park.

and a dozen horses. Theirs was a 2.25-mile line along East Genesee, Perry and Franklin streets. This company used tokens, about the size of a quarter and violet in color that bore the initials "E.G.S. & S.A."

On October 1, 1886, the two horse car lines were consolidated to form the Auburn City Railway Company. An expansion and betterment program was undertaken. The old 30-pound rail was replaced with 42-pound weight. On December 5th of the following year, a short line on Clark Street was opened. (It was abandoned before electrification.) Eight days later, the first cars ran on the new belt line – North to Park, Lansing, Fulton, Seymour and Lewis to Franklin. About this same time, tracks were laid on

Wilbourne B. Cox collection

In 1909, Kuhlman Car Company delivered eight of these 15-bench open cars, 12-19. Traffic between Auburn and the park was heavier than the company's 10-bench single-truck cars could handle.

State Street from Genesee to Seymour and west one block to Cross Street. By 1889, the company owned 5.63 miles of line, 12 closed cars, 4 open cars and 40 horses. The company carried 223,900 passengers that year. Its car barns were at 20 Perry Street.

The first day of electric operation on the Auburn City Railway was January 17, 1891. About that time, the Owasco line was extended to Lakeside Park on Owasco Lake. The company's power station and new car barns were located on State Street at the corner of Chapel. The New York Central Railroad's passenger station was close by.

By 1895, the company accountants were dipping heavily into the red ink bottle and it was at this point that Clifford D. Beebe, a Syracuse financier, gained control of the system. The lines were completely rebuilt once again and three years later, the west-side route to Lakeside Park was opened. At the turn of the century, the ACR was carrying 1.5 million passengers annually. They took in more than $76,000 in fares but still could show only a modest profit of $1,400 for the year. The line was then 12 miles long with 20 motor cars and 5 trailers. Three horses were retained for standby, probably being used to draw work and line wagons.

As the twentieth century opened, almost every electric railway operated an amusement park to encourage trolley travel. The Auburn & Syracuse was no exception. Thirty-three acre Lakeside Park at the foot of Owasco Lake near Auburn, was inherited by the A&S from the Auburn City Railway. It was the largest park owned by the Beebe Syndicate and was the most widely advertised. Special excursions were run from as far away as Marion, 8 miles north of Newark on the RS&E. The regular round-trip fare from Syracuse to the park was 90 cents, but parties of 10 or more went for 60 cents each.

Lakeside Park boasted, "the largest and finest

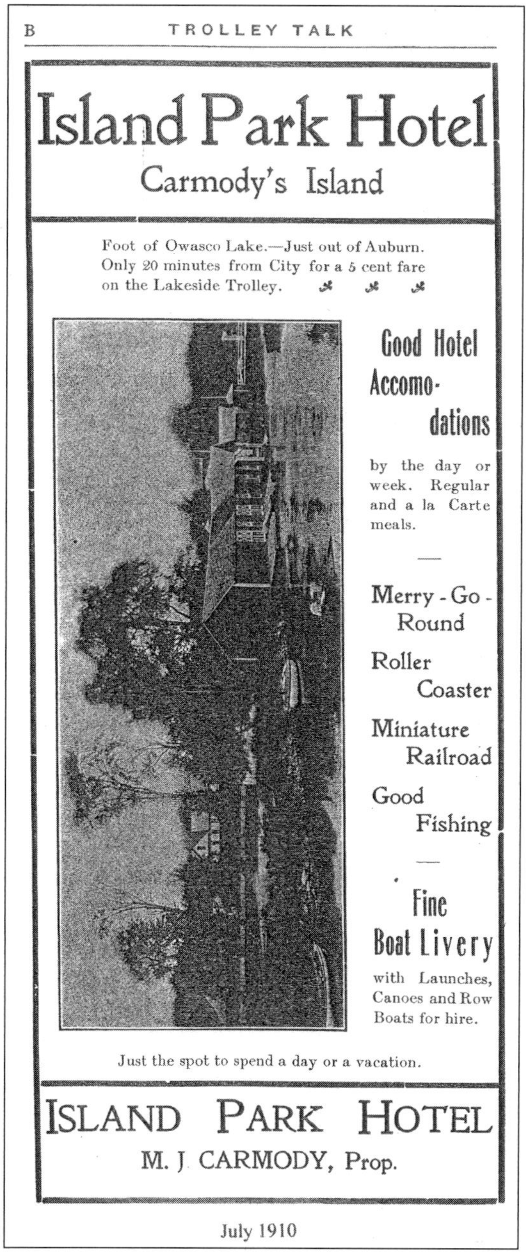
B TROLLEY TALK

Island Park Hotel
Carmody's Island

Foot of Owasco Lake.—Just out of Auburn.
Only 20 minutes from City for a 5 cent fare
on the Lakeside Trolley.

Good Hotel Accomodations

by the day or week. Regular and a la Carte meals.

Merry - Go - Round

Roller Coaster

Miniature Railroad

Good Fishing

Fine Boat Livery

with Launches, Canoes and Row Boats for hire.

Just the spot to spend a day or a vacation.

ISLAND PARK HOTEL
M. J. CARMODY, Prop.

July 1910

Island Park was a 12-14 acre amusement park adjacent to and just west of Lakeside Park. The two parks were separated by a man-made channel of the Owasco River. So far as is known, Island Park was not a Beebe Syndicate enterprise, but it certainly benefited from the street car service from Auburn.

pavilions in the state, containing a large dance hall and restaurant. The veranda will seat 1,000 persons at one time in comfort. An excellent orchestra furnishes music for dancing every afternoon and evening except Sunday, when public concerts are given." Besides the usual recreational facilities, there was an amusement section called Island Park. It even had a miniature railway and a good sized hotel where people could stay for a week if they wished. Motor boating, rowing and canoeing were available for those so inclined.

Another feature of the area was the 5-mile steamboat ride from Lakeside Park to Koenig's Point, a five-acre picnic grove and an adjacent 40-room hotel. Mr. Koenig owned the two steamers on Owasco Lake, the 300 passenger *City of Auburn* and the smaller *Nymph* which carried only 60 passengers. Frequent trips were made. The sailing time was only 30 minutes and the round-trip fare was 20 cents.

This particular view of car 34 was made in connection with an early law suit against the railway. Its location is unknown. Car history on the Auburn & Syracuse City Lines is limited to some data on the A&S roster of equipment and a few pictures such as this one.

Routes and Service in Auburn

In 1916, the Auburn & Syracuse brought in Allen & Peck, Inc., an engineering and management firm of public utilities, to direct all affairs on both the city and interurban divisions of the company. The new General Manager, Talmadge C. Cherry, and the new Chief Engineer, David E. Crouse, both came from similar properties in Maryland. Both men later became principal officers in the reorganized Beebe system.

Rolling stock on the city lines consisted of a dozen 10- or 15-bench open cars and 21 single-truck closed cars, some of them dating back to the Auburn City Railway days. In 1915, the Beebe Syndicate upgraded its city car fleet in Auburn, Fulton and Oswego. The St. Louis Car Company produced 24 double-truck double-end semi-steel city cars. Those assigned to Auburn were numbered 301-312 and those for Fulton and Oswego were numbered 313 -324. Each car was 37'6" long and had a seating capacity of 40. As built, the cars required a conductor and a motorman. But in the early 1920s they were re-equipped as safety cars for one-man operation.

Auburn was first introduced to local bus service on June 2, 1925 when the West End route was established. The A&S-associated Mid-State Coach Lines purchased one 21-passenger Dodge-Graham vehicle. Only one bus was required to give 20-minute service on this 2-mile route which approximately paralleled the Seymour streetcar line. The bus operated on Wall Street, a major east-west cross

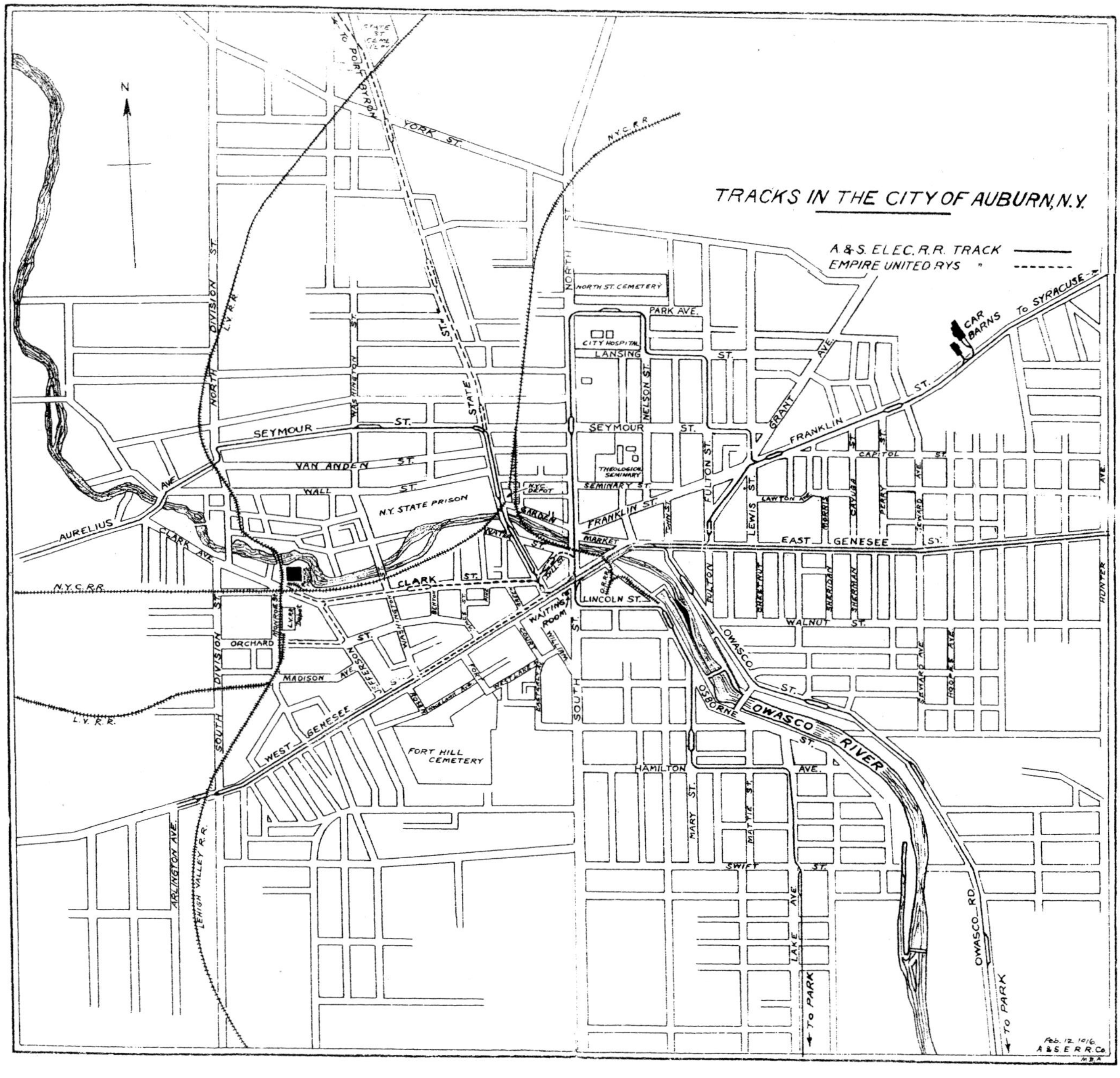

This car is one of four (43-46) Kuhlman cars purchased for the Auburn city lines in 1911. They are thought to have been the last single-truck cars purchased by the company.

Emil J. Kraemer, photographer

In 1915, the Empire United Railways ordered 24 of these cars from St.Louis Car Company. Cars 301-312 were assigned to the A&S for its Auburn city lines and 313-324 went into service on the EUR's Oswego and Fulton city lines.Originally built as two-man cars, they were later equipped as one-man safety cars.

street two blocks south of Seymour. When first begun, 8-cent tickets on the bus were not accepted on street cars and street car tickets were not good on the bus. However, transfers to and from city street and interurban cars were available to bus passengers.

On October 17, 1925, the company discontinued electric car service on its North Street Belt line. Buses operated by the Mid-State Coach Lines were substituted. Prior to that date, 8 city routes had been served by electric cars:

Genesee Street - The "main line" extended 2.64 miles from the eastern city limits (Hunter Avenue) westerly to the Columbian Rope Company at the

H. E. Yury, photographer

The date was October 15, 1927. At least six of these safety cars were lined up on Genesee Street, Auburn for this "final day" photo shoot. This was the last day for street cars in Auburn. William J. Lee, A&S General Freight and Passenger Agent is on the extreme left. E. A. Pelton, Superintendent is fourth from the left. The man on Pelton's right appears to be representing the local constabulary. All twelve cars in this series (301-312) were sold to the New York & Queens County Railway, Flushing, NY.

Lehigh Valley Railroad crossing.

Owasco Street to Lakeside Park - (East side line) Out Owasco Street from East Genesee Street, 2.83 miles to Lakeside Park.

Second Ward line to Lakeside Park - (West side line) From the Common Center at South and Genesee streets, 3.11 miles to Lakeside Park.

Grant Avenue - 1.12 miles from Fulton and Genesee out Grant Avenue and Franklin Street to Marvin Avenue.

North Street - Part of the Grant and the North street lines made up the Belt Line. Cars operated in both directions around a loop of East Genesee, Fulton, Grant, Lewis, Seymour, Fulton, Lansing, Nelson Park and North streets. The loop was 2.28 miles long.

State Street - North on State from Genesee to York, 1.46 miles. The track between Seymour and York streets was owned by the Auburn & Northern but local service was furnished by A&S.

Seymour Street - On State from Genesee to Seymour thence west to the city line, 1.97 miles.

Clark Street - A one-mile line out Clark from State to Jefferson to Orchard and the Lehigh Valley Railroad station. There was a short spur that continued up Clark Street to the A&S power house. This Clark Street line was built by the Auburn & Northern but the local service was provided by the A&S. The Grant and State street lines were operated as one route as were the Owasco and Seymour lines.

Red figures began to appear on the company's income statements after 1924. Beginning in 1925, the operating income was not covering the operating expenses. By the end of 1926, the deficit was over $87,600. Prospects of improving the situation were dim so the company decided to give up the local street railway operation.

The last car operated Saturday evening October 15, 1927. Buses of the Cayuga Omnibus Corporation took over all operations in the city including those of the Mid-State Coach Lines. The *Auburn Advertiser-Journal* had this to say concerning the end of trolley service, "It was the 'end of the line' for the trolleys when they left the Common Center at South and Genesee streets at midnight last Saturday night. And before the last runs were started, the cars were lined up with their operators, many of whom had been in service the greater part of their lives."

Most of the city cars were single-truckers and of such advanced age that they were scrapped. However, 301-312 were sold in 1930 through a second-hand car dealer to the New York & Queens County Railway. They were renumbered 1-12 and they ran another seven years before being scrapped.

Stephenson-built cars 1 and 2 were the original equipment on the Auburn Inter-Urban Electric Railroad when the road opened January 1, 1901. This side-of-the-road trolley extended 7.1 miles from Auburn eastward to the village of Skaneateles.

The Auburn & Syracuse Interurban

In the early 1900s, local electric railways everywhere were expanding into the countryside. The newly formed Auburn Inter-Urban Electric Railroad was building eastward from Auburn along Franklin Street to Skaneateles. This 7.1-mile road-side trolley line was opened for business the first day of January 1901. Their original car equipment consisted of two motor passenger cars and one snow plow. The passenger cars, numbered 1 and 2, were single-truckers built by the Stephenson Car Company. They were later renumbered 39 and 40 and were used on the Auburn City lines. Later the same year, the AI-U purchased cars 50 and 51 from Stephenson. These were 36-foot closed interurban passenger motors. They were sold to the Auburn & Northern in 1910.

The Beebe Syndicate, then in control of both the Auburn City Railway and the Auburn Inter-Urban Electric Railroad, had plans in the works for extending the latter from Skaneateles into Syracuse, so on September 30, 1902, the two companies were formally consolidated as the Auburn & Syracuse Electric Railroad. Construction of the extension was begun at once, and the road was opened into Syracuse June 23, 1903. Terminal to terminal mileage was 27.10. [MP mileage noted hereafter was measured from Auburn.]

Unlike the Auburn – Skaneateles section, which followed the curves and grades of the adjacent highway, the new line was of standard high-speed interurban construction with heavy rail on stone ballast. The line was graded for double-track but operations began with only one. By 1906, the second track had been laid between West Lake Road, Skaneateles and the Syracuse city line except for a short piece of single-track at Marcellus station and the gauntlet track on the long steel trestle over Nine Mile Creek and the Marcellus & Otisco Lake Railway just west of Marcellus.

A&S cars entered Syracuse over the Dudley line of the Syracuse Rapid Transit Railway Company for a three-mile run into downtown. Their first station was on the south side of Clinton Square in front of the Weiting Opera House. Cars laid over on a stub track in the street. The ticket office was later moved to 340 West Fayette Street near the New York Cen-

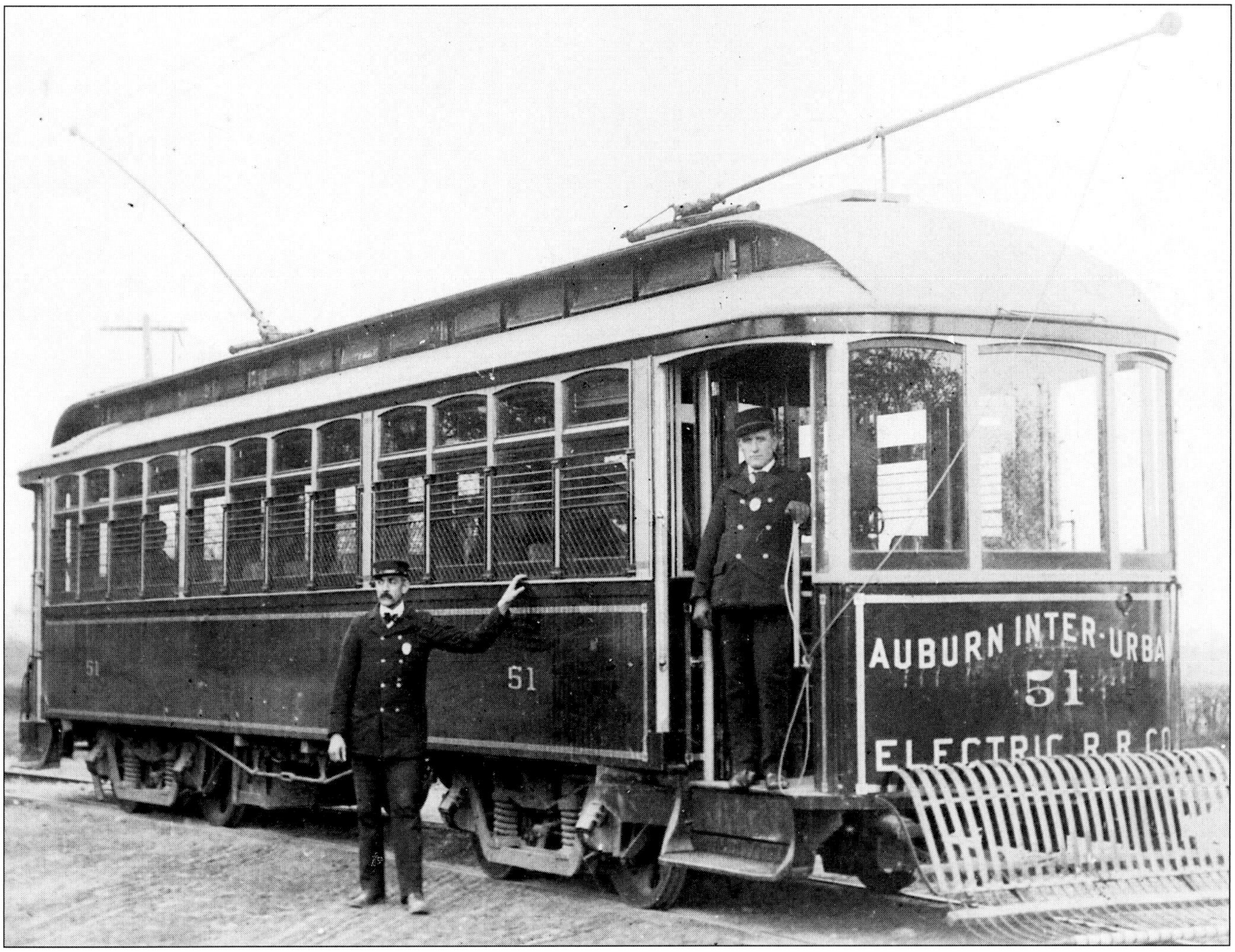

Cars 50 and 51 were products of Stephenson Car Company. In 1903, the Auburn Inter-Urban was acquired by the newly formed Auburn & Syracuse Electric Railroad and was extended eastward from Skaneateles to Syracuse as a double-track high-speed railway. Heavier and faster A&S cars soon replaced cars 50 and 51. In 1910, they were sold to the neighboring Auburn & Northern for local service between Auburn and a connection with the Rochester, Syracuse & Eastern Railroad at Port Byron.

Westbound A&S car 54 is approaching the center of Skaneateles village as seen in this postcard mailed in August 1905.

Here is a late afternoon picture of A&S 56 passing through Skaneateles bound for Syracuse, c1908.

Some of the wreckage piled beside the Marcellus station, Stop 24, has the earmarks of a late departed horse-drawn rig's encounter with an A&S car.

tral station. During that time, the cars looped through East Fayette, Warren, Genesee, Salina and back to West Fayette. The timetables showed eastbound arrival times at Salina and Fayette. Departure times were shown at Genesee and Salina. Transfers were issued to and accepted from the Syracuse local lines. Beginning about 1919, the A&S waiting room made its final move to the Eckel Theater Building in the 200 block of East Fayette Street. This space was shared with the Syracuse & Suburban Railroad. The Auburn cars laid over on nearby East Jefferson Street between Montgomery and State streets.

The interurban cars entered Auburn on Franklin Street, rolled past the new car barns to Grant Avenue and in on East Genesee Street. The waiting room was at 82 West Genesee Street, just a few doors west of South Street. Transfers were, of course, exchanged with the Auburn city lines. There was a crossover in Genesee Street near the waiting room so the double-end A&S interurban cars could reverse directions. The Auburn ticket office

This is one of the few views of "excursion" type car 86 in service. The car is eastbound at Marcellus station, Stop 24, about 10 miles west of the Syracuse city line.

William Jubb, photographer

William Jubb was a local photographer in Syracuse in the business of making souvenir postcard views of Syracuse and its environs. Tinted cards of this particular image are frequently found but this view was made from an original print of Jubb's image #159. Note the overhead trolley wires that were usually blanked out on commercial postcards. Here, Auburn & Syracuse car 58 is seen turning south from East Genesee Street onto South Salina Street, Syracuse. The date is about 1904. The A&S cars made a loop through the downtown area. Timetables listed the leaving time for Auburn-bound cars at this particular corner. Arrival times for cars entering Syracuse were shown at a corner two blocks south.

These are 1903 views of the engine room (top) and the switch board, rotary converters and exciters in the A&S main power house in Auburn. After its sale to the Niagara, Lockport & Ontario Power Company in 1912, this plant continued to furnish power to the railway as long as the cars ran.

facilities were moved to the Auburn & Northern freight house area on Dill Street after the local city car lines were discontinued on October 15, 1927.

There was a combination freight and passenger station at Marcellus but only a waiting room at Skaneateles. Some of the crossroad stops on the A&S had the standard Beebe system octagonal shaped shelters for the protection of waiting passengers.

The Auburn & Syracuse built a new power house in Auburn on Clark Street at the head of Monroe in 1903. The plant was so situated that its elevated coal trestle was served from one end by the New York Central Railroad and from the other end by the Lehigh Valley Railroad. Two Westinghouse-Corliss steam engines generated power for the street and interurban lines. It was stepped up to 16,500

A builder's view of Auburn & Syracuse Electric Railroad car 53 at the G. C. Kuhlman Car Company plant in Collinwood, Ohio, April 16, 1903. Shop Order 167 was for six of these 50-foot cars. They were numbered 52-57.

Wilbourne B. Cox collection

A&S cars 58 and 59 were delivered by Kuhlman in 1904. They were not too different from the 52-57 group.

volts ac for transmission to the two substations. One was just east of Skaneateles and the other was at Howlett Hill, eight miles west of Syracuse. Trolley voltage was 600 volts dc. Besides powering the local lines in Auburn and a portion of the Auburn & Northern, the new plant furnished current at 2200 volts ac to the Citizens Light & Power Company for lighting in the city of Auburn. In November 1912, the A&S power plant was sold to the Niagara, Lockport & Ontario Power Company for $226,000. Thereafter, the A&S purchased its power from NL&O at the rate of nine mills ($.009) per kWh delivered and metered at the substations.

Also in 1903, six 50-foot 30-ton wooden closed passenger cars were purchased from Kuhlman for use on the Syracuse interurban division. They were numbered 52 through 57. Each had a seating capacity of 56. They were capable of mile-a-minute speeds. Additional cars were purchased as the service required. By 1915, the interurban division had 19 passenger cars of which two were "Excursion Type" open (85 and 86). The A&S equipped its interurban passenger cars with multiple-unit controls in 1906 for the operation of 2-car trains. This arrangement worked out well east of Skaneateles, but the roadside alignment west of Skaneateles and extensive street running over foreign rails in Syracuse caused that operation to be given up.

The Beebe Syndicate laid plans in 1907 to build a new line west of Skaneateles. The new route was to be an extension of the Auburn local line out East Genesee Street. Planned for private right-of-way, it would have cut 15 minutes from the overall running time of the cars. Some of the necessary land was purchased but several of the farmers along the route had expensive ideas of asking prices for their real estate so the plan was dropped.

Passenger service between Auburn and Syracuse ranged from half-hourly in the early days to hourly at the end. Running time stayed pretty close

About 1914, the A&S hired Emil J. Kraemer, a local photographer, to take a series of pictures of its interurban car fleet. Approximately a dozen exposures were made of car exteriors and interiors at the A&S car barn in Auburn. Cars from three manufacturers are seen, Jewett, Kuhlman and Cincinnati.

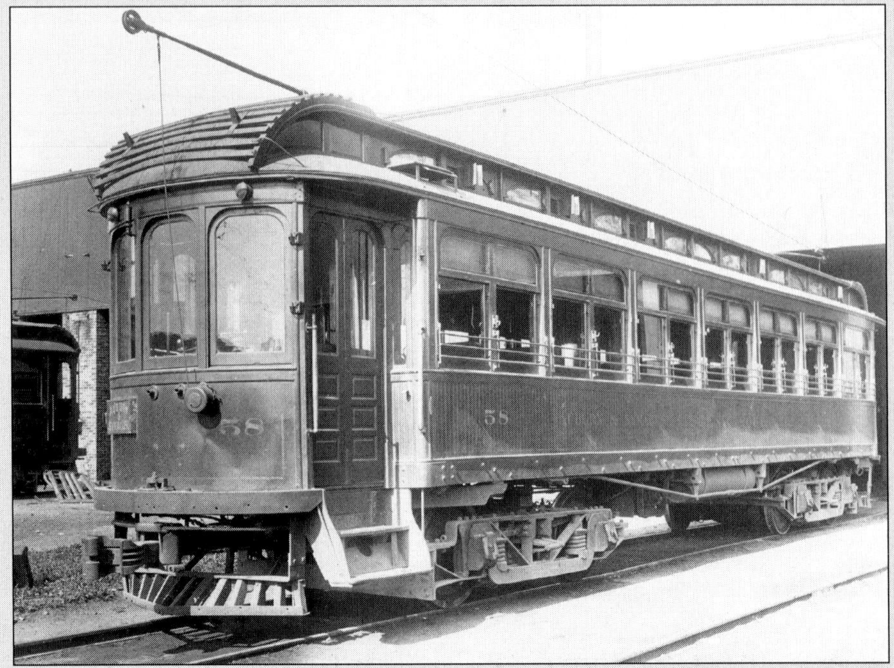

Car 58 came from Kuhlman in 1904. Note the narrowed end platforms and the slim glass plate windows opening into the car.

Here is a flat side view of car 58, built under Kuhlman shop order 247.

The body of car 60, built by Jewett, shop order 160, was mounted on a steel under-frame. The panels below the front windows were elongated by the depth of the under-frame so the car looked to stand a little higher and narrower than the usual interurban cars.

This interior view of car 60 shows the ceiling and clerestory window treatments were more elaborate than the other cars in the A&S fleet.

The steel under-frame is clearly visible in this flat side view of car 60.

Note this 1907 Cincinnati-built car, number 61, had vestibules of full car width, unlike most of the other A&S interurbans.

Car 61 was Cincinnati Car Company's only entry in the A&S interurban car fleet. It was a standard 50-foot 30-ton car.

Car 65 was photographed from all angles, three of the exterior and one interior view.

Cars 62-68 appear to have been a reorder of 58 and 59 with only minor changes being seen. The vestibules were widened to nearly full car width. About this time, the controls were relocated from center to the right-hand side of the vestibule and, of course, the right-hand passenger entrances were closed in.

On many of the A&S cars, the words "Scenic Route" appeared above the company name on each side panel, as seen in this flat side view of car 65.

In this interior view of A&S 65, the backs of the seats appear to be leather. Were the seats completely caned and then mostly covered with leather or perhaps leatherette?

H. E. Yury, photographer
Wilbourne B. Cox collection

This fine view of A&S car 64, Kuhlman 1905, was taken at the Auburn car barn some glorious summer day about 1914. The fake door treatment of the car side at the motorman's position indicates that the motorman's controls had been transferred from the center of each vestibule to the right-hand side.

This tinted postcard is one of the few recognizable pictures of the two A&S "Excursion" type cars, 85 and 86, to be found. They were purchased from Jewett Car Company in 1906 for the specific purpose of transporting passengers between Syracuse and a nearby Beebe Syndicate sponsored amusement park. The uncompleted park was a failure. Being unsuited for regular year-around service, the 85 and 86 were usually found in special or charter service. The view dates to about 1908.

to one hour and twenty-five minutes. The A&S was billed as "The Scenic Route" and so it was. The railway crossed several ranges of hills oriented north-south between the major cities and towns. Grades were not severe but were long. As westbound cars from Syracuse climbed the 1.5 percent grade out of Split Rock heading for Howlett Hill, passengers could look out across the valley toward Onondaga Lake some 5 miles in the distance to the north. The cars then dropped down a two-mile grade of 1 percent to Marcellus. The Nine Mile Creek valley was crossed on a 600-foot-long steel trestle. Automatic signals protected movements over the gauntlet track on the structure. The next three miles were up grade averaging 1.75 percent, a short part of which was 3 percent. Skaneateles Lake could be seen as

Syracuse Post-Standard

Eastbound cars leaving Split Rock, Stop 32, dropped down an average grade of 1.75 percent on the three-mile run to the Syracuse city line. The quarrying operations at Split Rock were located to the rear of this photographer. A row of company houses can be seen in this view.

Onondaga Historical Association Museum & Research Center, Syracuse, NY.

The standard Beebe Syndicate octagonal shelters at country cross road stops were common on the Auburn & Syracuse. Built of chestnut, each of the eight panels was 50 inches wide. The building's foot-print occupied a ten foot square. It would have been hard to find a more handsome crossing shelter anywhere else in the interurban world. Note the electric signal box attached to the door frame for signaling approaching local cars.

the cars passed through Skaneateles village.

A manually operated block signal system governed all train movements on the single-track between Skaneateles and Auburn. The only signal was located at the end of the double-track in Skaneateles village. Each time a car passed the signal, the motorman was required to leave the signal light at the color stated in the timetable (red, white or green). The signal governed westbound movements only. The system was so designed that only one car at a time was allowed between Skaneateles and the Auburn car barn. For instance, the conductor of a westbound car would leave the signal so he could get back out from Auburn after running into the terminal station and picking up a new load of passengers. During the years that the cars ran on a 30-minute headway, there was a timetable meet for most of the trips at Soule (MP 3.10), a double-end siding with spring switches located about midway between Auburn and Skaneateles. Then, the signal at Skaneateles governed the line between it and Soule.

One wreck that occurred on this single-track section during the early years was entirely uncalled for. At this time train orders were verbal, not written. Car 63 left Auburn at 6 P.M. on time and car 61 left Skaneateles at the same time. They were to meet at Soule at 6:13 P.M. according to the timetable. For some unknown reason, the motorman on 63 overran his meet and plowed into 61 a quarter-of-a-mile east of Soule just as 61 was breaking over a hill. Both motormen were killed. From then on, all train orders were written.

Onondaga Historical Association Museum & Research Center, Syracuse, NY.

When the A&S was first opened to Syracuse in 1903, only the eastbound main was in operation. The second track was completed by 1906. Note the right-of-way center line stakes between the power poles. Brackets for carrying the westbound trolley wire were already in place. This is a view of the reverse curve at Sheehans, Stop 25, the first stop east of Marcellus and about 9 miles west of the Syracuse city line.

On May 25, 1910 at 7:30 A.M., passenger car 57 left Skaneateles bound for Syracuse. It was followed out of town by a work extra freight car loaded with laborers. While descending the steep grade east of Wiseman's crossing (MP 10.7), the trolley wheel of the passenger car jumped the wire. The car stopped on a blind curve. The wheel was replaced and just as they got under way again, the extra came around the curve and plowed into them. The ends of both cars were a total loss. Both cars were derailed and the line was tied up for several hours. There were no injuries but everyone was pretty well shaken up.

Probably the most disastrous wreck to occur on the Auburn & Syracuse happened on May 24, 1918 when the early morning eastbound passenger car 66 coming down Split Rock hill slammed into the rear end of two loaded coal cars. One passenger of the standing load was killed outright and all others were injured. The motorman of the passenger car miraculously escaped death at the time only to succumb later. It appears that the eastbound freight train had lost its air when it slowed at Olney (MP 19.5) to put out a flagman. The flagman never got off the moving train. The motorman had called for hand brakes but the train continued to roll down the hill for a mile and a half into the Split Rock area before it was finally stopped. While its crew was trying to set up a move into a siding, the eastbound passenger car sailed down the hill, around the curve and into the stalled freight.

Summer Tourists on the A&S

The Auburn & Syracuse connected two of the major cities in New York state's Finger Lakes district so summer travel to the lakes was particularly heavy. Of the three lakes reached by the A&S, Otisco was the smallest. Passengers for resorts on this lake generally traveled by electric car as far as Marcellus. Here connections were made with the Marcellus & Otisco Lake Railway for a 20-minute ride on a steam train south to the lake shore. The M&OL controlled the Otisco Lake Navigation Company and was the proud owner of the *Fontney* which was a 50-foot 6-cylinder naphtha launch purchased in 1906 from a boat works in Phoenix, NY. A 1909 issue of *Trolley Talk* listed three round trips on weekdays and four on Sundays between Otisco Lake station and Williams. Forest Home, Davis Grove and Lake Side Inn were all popular spots on the lake. A stone road was built southerly along one shore of Otisco Lake in 1913, causing passenger business on the steam road and boat line to dwindle. Boat service ended that season and passenger service on the M&OL ended the following year.

Skaneateles Lake was the summer home for many Syracusans, mostly the wealthier ones who could pack up and move to the lake for the season. There were many beautiful and stately homes built along the lake's shores. Completion of the Auburn

Auburn & Inter-Urban 51, westbound in Skaneateles was crossing over the principal outlet to Skaneateles Lake. The lake steamer Glen Haven *is tied up closest to shore. The steamer* City of Syracuse *was at the far end of the pier. This picture would be dated about 1902.*

& Syracuse electric line put the lake within reach of everyone. The Skaneateles Transportation Company, owned by the Beebe Syndicate, operated two steamboats on the lake, the 600 passenger *City of Syracuse* and the smaller *Glen Haven*. Daily schedules were operated between the Skaneateles dock and the company owned park, Glen Haven, located at the head (south end) of the lake. Regular calls were made at other places including Ten Mile Point.

According to some period advertising, "Every Sunday evening the steamer *City of Syracuse* sails from Skaneateles for a three-hour searchlight trip of 36 miles to the head of the lake and return, making one stop at Glen Haven. An excellent orchestra furnishes music throughout the trip." The regular round trip fare between Syracuse and Skaneateles was 60 cents. The searchlight trip cost 75 cents round trip from Syracuse. Think of leaving Syracuse on the 6:05 P.M. car, transferring to the steamer at 7 o'clock for a cool three hour sail on the lake (for 15 cents) and being back in Syracuse before 11 P.M.

During the week, the *City of Syracuse* "sails at 8 P.M. for a 20-mile searchlight trip to Ten Mile Point and return, stopping at the Point for over an hour for free dancing at the pavilion. Music is furnished by the excellent orchestra carried on the steamer." Ten Mile Point boasted an excellent picnic grounds, nice beach, a picturesque gorge nearby and good fishing. In the days before the auto and hard surfaced roads, the electric cars sure did a whale of a business.

Lakeside Park in Auburn was so successful that Clifford Beebe made plans for a second amusement park on the A&S, this one closer to Syracuse. In 1905, he purchased 24 acres of hill-top land adjacent to Stop 31, Olney, just three miles west of the Syracuse city line. Named Edgecliff Park, it had a commanding view of Onondaga Lake five miles to the north. To serve the new park, the A&S purchased two "Excursion" type passenger cars (85 and 86) from the Jewett Car Company of Newark, Ohio. These two cars had open sides with center aisles, passenger entry and exit through closed vestibules, and could be fitted with side panels for winter use. Their carrying capacity of 68 per car was 20% greater than that of the standard A&S interurbans.

Construction of Edgecliff Park was begun but was never completed. The company finally concluded that the anticipated business just was not there. Syracuse people were flocking to the several beach resorts on Onondaga Lake, all being served by another Beebe road, the Syracuse, Lake Shore & Northern. After World War I, cars 85 and 86 were generally used for charter and heavy weekend trips.

Emil J. Kraemer, photographer

In early 1915, the then seldom used Marcella *became a parlor car, was renamed* Syracuse *and was assigned to the Empire United Railways new Rochester - Syracuse extra fare parlor car service. The car was de-motorized because its two 75 hp motors prevented MU train operation. This picture of* Syracuse *was taken at the Auburn shops of the A&S, probably in the fall of 1916, after the EUR parlor car service had been discontinued. Note the experimental Merrick Roller Bearing journals on both trucks. The only other Beebe car so equipped was Syracuse & South Bay passenger car 20.*

The Auburn & Syracuse owned the *Marcella*, a very substantial private car bought by Beebe in 1903. A more complete description of it may be found in Chapter 4 of this book under "Parlor Cars." It was one of the finest of its type that had been produced up to that time. In 1909, the *Marcella* was converted into a parlor car and was assigned a Limited run between Auburn and Syracuse. Beginning on August 22nd of that year, it left Syracuse at 9:55 A.M., 4:25 P.M. and 7:55 P.M. just ahead of the regular cars. A charge of 25 cents was made for each seat in addition to the regular fare. All 24 seats were reserved in advance and only the capacity of the car was sold. Smoking was permitted on the observation platform only. It was a well patronized service as far west as Skaneateles for a time but after a few seasons, the car was pulled off and thereafter used only for special and charter runs. The Limited service was, however, continued into the early 1920s using regular cars. Limited runs were only 5 or 10 minutes faster than the locals so they were never particularly popular.

Of interest are some of the cash fares that were charged on the Auburn & Syracuse. The adult cash fare on the Auburn city cars was 5 cents, though in later years it was increased to 7 cents. A chartered car between any two points on the city division cost $5. The last fares charged for such service were $7 one-way and $14 round-trip.

An interurban conductor's passenger tariff for 1918 shows that the cash fare from Auburn to Skaneateles was 20 cents, to Marcellus 41 cents, to Split Rock 62 cents and to Syracuse 76 cents. One could charter a car for a trip from Syracuse to Auburn for $30. Round-trip was $47.50. During World War I when special service was being operated between Syracuse and Split Rock, books containing 7 special rate round-trip tickets were sold for $1.68 each. They were good only on the special cars provided.

In the last tariff issued January 1, 1922, the cash fare between Auburn and Syracuse was 92 cents, 10 cents more than the ticket fare. A ticket from Skaneateles to Auburn cost 25 cents and to Marcellus 21 cents. Excursion rates from Syracuse to Lakeside Park were $1 in lots of 100 and were 75 cents for children. Chartered car rates over the whole road were $42.66 one-way and $85.32 round-trip.

A&S 100 was one of two 49' 4" express cars delivered by Jewett Car Company in 1902. Unfortunately the car was destroyed in a fire in Syracuse in 1906.

Express & Freight Service

Express service on the A&S was slow to get started. The Jewett Car Company had furnished two 49-foot express cars. Two daily trips were operated until the last few years when the service was reduced to one round trip. Bundled newspapers were carried on passenger cars at the rate of 25 cents per 100 pounds. The Auburn & Northern freight house on Dill Street in Auburn was shared with the Auburn & Syracuse. The A&S freight house on West Fayette Street, Syracuse was shared with the New York State Railways, Oneida Line, and, before 1911, with the Rochester, Syracuse & Eastern and the Syracuse, Lake Shore & Northern.

The A&S had one very prosperous rail-served industry located on its line. The Semet-Solvay Company (later the Solvay Process Company) operated a limestone quarry at Split Rock, 5.66 miles from Syracuse. The stone was delivered to their plant in Solvay (near Onondaga Lake), several miles away by an overhead gravity bucket system. Coal for heating the buildings at Split Rock was delivered by the A&S in carload lots received from a track interchange with the Marcellus & Otisco Lake Railway at

Auburn & Syracuse work car 110. During World War I, this car was assigned to handle revenue freight traffic interchanged with the Marcellus & Otisco Lake Railway at Marcellus to and from Split Rock Quarries near Syracuse. In 1918, the loads being moved exceeded the capacity of 110 so the job was taken over by a newly acquired Baldwin-Westinghouse 50-ton locomotive A&S 105.

The Auburn & Syracuse rotary snow plow, number unknown, saw action just east of Skaneateles in the winter of 1910.

George M. Wright, photographer

Charles Robinson found the ex A&S 105 alive and well soon after its 1965 arrival at the Connecticut Trolley Museum in East Windsor, CT. No markings identifying any of its previous owners were apparent in this view.

Inset: *This Baldwin-Westinghouse Class B 50-ton freight locomotive came to the Auburn & Syracuse in the summer of 1918. The principal industry it served, Split Rock Quarries near Syracuse, went out of business in 1919 so 105 was sold. After operating on five different electric lines in southern Ontario, Canada, the locomotive finally wound up at the Connecticut Trolley Museum at East Windsor, CT.*

Charles C. Robinson, photographer

Slate Hill (13.16 miles from Syracuse), just south of Marcellus village. Car 110, used for this work, was simply a motorized flat car with a cab on each end. Its hauling capacity was about two loaded coal cars.

In the summer of 1918, the A&S purchased a 50-ton Baldwin-Westinghouse Class B freight locomotive, number 105, to handle the freight between Marcellus and Split Rock. After the war, the Split Rock quarry was closed. The 105 was sold in 1919 to the Hydro-Electric Power Commission at Niagara Falls, Ontario as their locomotive E-21. In 1924, it became number 2 on the Toronto & York Radial Railway. After a short period of time on the Chatham, Wallaceburg & Lake Erie, the locomotive appeared in 1927 on the Niagara, St. Catharines & Ontario Railway as its second number 18. Its next move was in 1940 to the Oshawa Railway where it appeared as number 18 in Canadian National colors. Its next owner was an individual who eventually willed it to the Connecticut Trolley Museum at East Windsor, Conn. Still operational, this locomotive, as yet unnumbered, is the only remaining piece of electric railway equipment that saw service on the Beebe system of electric railways.

During the First World War, the Split Rock Quarry plant was converted into an ammunition plant. Passenger traffic from Syracuse was so heavy that the A&S installed 12 trolley wheel-actuated 3-color Nachod block signals to space trains between Syracuse city line and Split Rock. Excursion cars 85 and 86 shuttled the Split Rock workers to and from Syracuse. On occasions, Syracuse double-end "pay-as-you-enter" type city cars were leased as well.

Sunset on the Auburn & Syracuse

After the Auburn street railway system folded, the interurban division of the A&S struggled on. It was the same old story. People had, for the most part, forsaken the electric cars for the private auto and the hard surfaced roads. Once again, it was apparent that the interurban's earning capacity could not support its heavy capital investment. In the spring of 1930, the entire physical property of the A&S was put on the auction block. It was purchased

The date was Tuesday April 15, 1930 and the time was 9:30 AM. Car 63 was the last interurban to leave Auburn for Syracuse. W. J. Lee, superintendent, Gordon Winters, motorman and Hiram Titus, conductor, posed for the finale. The car was standing on Dill Street facing west. The curve of track in the foreground was the lead to the A&S freight house at 6-8-10 Dill Street.

H.E. Yury, photographer

Auburn & Syracuse car 63 is seen inbound on Gifford Street, Syracuse, on April 15, 1930. This very last car on the A&S was due at the Syracuse terminal at 10:55 AM and to leave for Auburn at 11:00 AM.

A. W. Delano, photographer

for $250,000 by Fred L. Emerson, president of Enna Jettick Shoes, Inc. He retained Lakeside Park, the only valuable parcel in the sale. The park still exists as Emerson Park but is now home to an agricultural museum and a summer theater. He gave the car barn site on Franklin Street to the City of Auburn for a high school location. Much of the right-of-way was sold to Cayuga and Onondaga Counties. The latter county paid $10,000 for all its A&S right-of-way including the ill-fated Edgecliff Park 24-acre site. A current AAA map of Greater Syracuse and Onondaga County shows Edgecliff Park to be located on Kasson Road about one mile south of Genesee Street, in the Town of Camillus. Apparently the county actually developed the same 24 acres into a simple park. The balance of the A&S physical property was sold in April 1930 to H. E. Salzberg Company of New York City. They scrapped the line. There was no re-sale value for the 25-year-old wood interurban cars so they were all burned.

The sale to Enna Jettick Shoes, Inc. was finally confirmed by the Courts at 9:30 A.M. the morning of April 15, 1930. The shut down of all rail operations began within the hour. Here is how the *Auburn Advertiser-Journal* spelled out the end:

> The last car, number 63, manned by conductor Hiram M. Titus, who had helped survey the roadbed, and motorman Gordon Winters, left the Dill Street station in Auburn at 9:30 A.M. April 15, 1930. They arrived in Syracuse at 11 A.M., left Syracuse at 11:10 A.M. and reached Auburn at 12:35 P.M. The company was sold to Enna Jettick Shoes, Inc. Some 60 railroad employees each received $50 checks from W. K. Zinsmeister of Syracuse, treasurer of the A&S, given because of the end of their railroad employment. Fred L. Emerson, president of the shoe company matched the railway's gifts with checks of his own. The local press recorded that more people than had made the trip in a trolley car in many a day rode down on the final run to and from Syracuse. On the final trip out, car 63 picked up 47 fares and on the way back 59 according to the figures that appeared on the register as conductor Titus pulled the cord.

20 SYRACUSE, LAKESIDE 20
& BALDWINSVILLE
RAILWAY.

North to Lake Ontario 10

Syracuse, Lakeside & Baldwinsville Railway
Syracuse, Lake Shore & Northern Railroad
Empire United Railways
Empire State Railroad

Syracuse, Lakeside & Baldwinsville Railway

The interurban electric railroad between Syracuse and Oswego had its beginning in the Syracuse, Lakeside & Baldwinsville Railway. Chartered July 16, 1896 as the Onondaga Lake Railroad (name changed to SL&B in December 1897), the SL&B was opened from Syracuse 6.66 miles to the Maple Bay–Long Branch area (at the north end of Onondaga Lake) on July 22, 1898. The 13.92-mile line was completed to Baldwinsville September 24th of the following year. It was a typical single-track roadside trolley line that served the various summer resorts along the west shore of Onondaga Lake. Pleasant Beach, Rockaway Beach, Maple Bay and Long Branch Park were very active at that time.

Long Branch was a large and well-known amusement park situated on the outlet to Onondaga Lake. It opened in 1882 and was originally served by a spur off the nearby Lackawanna Railroad. When the SL&B was laying track through the area, it constructed a loop through the park to help handle the crowds from Syracuse more efficiently. Long Branch Park outlasted the electric cars for it continued in operation until 1938.

Another early and very popular attraction on the Lakeside line was White City. Opened May 30, 1906, this summer amusement park was located on the west shore of Onondaga Lake at Stop 5, nearly four miles north of downtown Syracuse. Over time, White City gradually decreased in popularity; its last season was 1915.

In 1900, passenger equipment of the Syracuse, Lakeside & Baldwinsville consisted of 19 motor cars (11 open and 8 closed) and 6 single-truck 10-bench open trailers. Service equipment included a box

Facing page: *A head-on view of double-deck 15-bench open car of the Syracuse, Lakeside & Baldwinsville Railway. The picture was taken about 1900 at the company's car shops located 4.5 miles north of Syracuse.*
John Gibb Smith, Jr. collection

Above: *Syracuse, Lake Shore & Northern car 200 was northbound at the Phoenix station. The 200 was less than six months old when this summer of 1909 picture was taken.*

Syracuse, Lakeside & Baldwinsville car 2 was crossing the Seneca River as it left Baldwinsville for Syracuse, 12 miles to the south. This view dates to the early 1900s.

Syracuse, Lakeside & Baldwinsville Railway double-deck 15-bench open car 19 was standing on the loop track at Long Branch Park about 1900. Long Branch, located 7.29 miles north of Syracuse, was a very popular amusement park and was a great source of revenue for the railway for many years.

motor work car and two double-end snow plows. Seven of the 11 open motor cars were double-truck with double-decks, built by Jackson & Sharp in 1899. They were 15-bench cars with a double bench running the length of the car on the second deck. Each car could carry 100 people. The men called them "whales" because they could carry such a whale of a load. In the 1904-1907 period, the top decks were removed leaving rather weird looking open cars with flat roofs.

The SL&B originally generated its own power. Two 400-kW Walker generators were rope-driven by two 450 horse-power Green & Wheelock steam engines. The power house and adjoining car barn were adjacent to the main line just north of Nine Mile Creek, 4.5 rail miles north of Syracuse. This barn was a one-story brick building and contained six tracks. Its storage capacity was 28 cars. The electric line's only track connection with a steam railroad was located here as the Lackawanna Railroad main line from Syracuse to Oswego passed in the rear of the car barn property. Carloads of coal for the power house were delivered at this point. In November 1906, the railway switched to power from the Oswego River Power Company and the Oswego River Power Transmission Company in anticipation of greater load requirements as the electric line was developing. A new substation was built next to the power house at Nine Mile Creek. The steam station was kept on standby for several years before being dismantled. Of note, Cadwell B. Benson, developer of the Oswego River Power Company had, by 1908, become a vice president and a director of the new Syracuse, Lake Shore & Northern Railroad, successor to the SL&B. He was active in management throughout the life of the company.

By the end of January 1908, the patchwork of several power suppliers and routes had been consolidated and all power came from Niagara Falls, transmitted by the Niagara, Lockport & Ontario Power Company. This company fed all of Syracuse and its street railways. They also controlled the Oswego River hydro plant and had a transmission line from the west to the Baldwinsville area. In December 1912, the NL&O purchased the Rochester, Syracuse & Eastern power plant at Lyons. From that time on, all the power generated at the Lyons power plant was transmitted over the Beebe roads' 33,000-volt high-tension circuits. The power company paid each road annually for this transmission privilege. The Syracuse, Lake Shore & Northern's share was $1,800. Each road paid for its power as measured at each substation, at the rate of seven mills ($.007) per kWh delivered.

The Syracuse passenger terminal was located at Clinton Square on the west side of North Clinton Street just off West Genesee Street. The Lakeside cars stood in the middle of North Clinton Street to load and unload. Their single-track line extended north on Clinton to Noxon (later Herald Place), west to Wallace, north to Belden, west out Belden to Liberty Street, thence north under the West Shore Railroad to what later became State Fair Boulevard. Total street running was less than a mile and a half and was mostly on secondary streets.

H TROLLEY TALK

LONG BRANCH PARK

Foot of Onondaga Lake.

The favorite Resort for Everybody.

Special facilities for entertaining church, lodge and club picnics.

Unexcelled in Central New York as a Day Resort

Reached by the Syracuse, Lake Shore and Northern Electric Line—thirty minutes from Syracuse Terminal Station ten minutes from Lake Shore Junction.

SOME OF THE ATTRACTIONS:

Largest Dancing Pavilion in Central New York.	Barn Accommodations.
Six Up-to-date Brunswick-Balke Bowling Alleys.	New Row Boat Livery.
Gasoline Launches for Excursions.	Russian Toboggan.
Hippodrome.	Photo Gallery.
Restaurant.	Purest Drinking Water.
Shooting Gallery.	Ariel Swing.
Carrousell.	Base Ball Grounds.
	American Box Ball Alley.
	Miniature Lake.

Consult B. Maurer & Co. for picnics.

Address, R. F. D. No. 4, Syracuse, N. Y. Both 'Phones

BOATING AT LONG BRANCH.

B. Maurer's Resort on Onondaga Lake and Seneca River, reached by the Syracuse, Lake Shore & Northern.

July 1910

Looking north along the SLS&N right-of-way from Halcomb Stop 4 toward White City, Stop 5. In this picture, taken November 23, 1906, one can just make out in the distant right several of the buildings, rides and roller coaster at White City. This summer seasonal park was not a financial success. It lasted only from 1906 to 1915.

Syracuse Post-Standard

Syracuse, Lakeside & Baldwinsville Railway double-decker car 18, at the North Clinton Street terminal, was loading for a trip to Long Branch Park and Baldwinsville. c1900.

John Gibb Smith, Jr. collection

In 1899, Jackson & Sharp delivered seven double-deck 15-bench open cars to the Syracuse, Lakeside & Baldwinsville Railway. They were numbered 18-24. They were 46' 2" long and could seat 100 passengers. This flat side view of car 21 was taken at the company's shops at Nine Mile Creek, located 4.5 miles north of Syracuse.

These shop tracks at the Syracuse, Lakeside & Baldwinsville shop appear to be less than normal distance apart. Car 23 was one of the seven double-deck 15-bench open cars, seating 100 passengers. Car 44, a product of Jackson & Sharp in 1900, was a 15-bench double-truck open car. Its seating capacity was 75. The picture was one of a series taken in 1900.

Onondaga Historical Association Museum & Research Center, Syracuse, NY.

Bridge 18 - A company photograph of the RS&E 670-foot steel structure crossing Van Vleck Road (later State Fair Boulevard), the single-track Lackawanna Railroad (Syracuse - Oswego Branch) and Nine Mile Creek. The power house and car barn of the original Syracuse Lakeside & Baldwinsville Railway can be seen through the steel bridge structure. The Burlington Route box car was standing on the interchange track connecting the electric road with the Lackawanna railroad. The RS&E rails ended at Lake Shore Junction with the Syracuse, Lake Shore & Northern Railroad 800 feet beyond the bridge.

A SLS&N northbound car was standing at the Minetto station, a simple freight house with an agent's office at one end. After 1915, the first floor of the building in right foreground was remodeled into a more commodious passenger station. When leaving Minetto for Oswego, the car would enter a 900-foot stretch of West River Road before reentering private right-of-way. A railroad valuation plan reveals that this street detour was made to avoid a large brick factory, home of the Minetto Shade Cloth Company. Cadwell B. Benson had been head of the company for many years. He was also a member and director of the Beebe Syndicate. The shade company was a good customer of the electric line's express service.

Syracuse, Lake Shore & Northern car 209 was southbound at Minetto station in the winter of 1911-1912. At that time, the passenger station was one room at one end of the Minetto freight house. The Oswego River is seen in the background.

Syracuse, Lake Shore & Northern car 62 was standing at the original North Clinton Street terminus in the spring of 1909. The car was signed "Local B-Ville" and the green flags indicated that a second car was to follow on the same schedule. 62 was built by St.Louis Car Company in1899 for the Syracuse, Lakeside & Baldwinsville Railway, predecessor to the SLS&N. In the following June, a new Electric Railway Terminal would open just around the corner on Clinton Square.

This double-track bridge, just north of Syracuse, carried the Syracuse, Lake Shore & Northern tracks over the New York Central's freight line. The adjacent bridge carried State Fair Boulevard highway traffic. The embankment and bridge of the West Shore Railroad was in the far distance. c1909.

About 65 years ago, your author spent a very enjoyable afternoon in Warners, N.Y. visiting Caleb T. Loveless. "Cy" was then one of the oldest living employees who had worked on the Syracuse, Lakeside & Baldwinsville. A keen man for his age, he loved to tell stories. Several of these are recounted in these pages. For instance, here is what it was like when he began work.

"I started work for the SL&B Railway in 1899," he began. "I worked with a pick and shovel to help build the road. That was in the fall. In the next spring, I went to work on the cars. I never did take the exam for motorman. Couldn't get up nerve enough, I guess. Anyway, the boss saw me one day and asked me when I was coming to work. 'Tomorrow morning, boss', I told him. 'All right,' he said, 'take a car out of the barn at 8 o'clock tomorrow morning and bring it into the city.' When I went to get the car next morning, there was a crew all ready to take it. I told the motorman that I was going to take the car in. He said he was going to. I said, 'The boss told me to take this car into the city and I am

SLS&N express car 42 was standing in front of the Fulton passenger station in the winter of 1909. The conductor standing on the snow on the right was Caleb "Cy" Loveless, author of the tales recited in this book.

James I. Barstow collection

SLS&N express car 42 was standing at the end of track in Fulton in the winter of 1909. Frank Steves, conductor, was on the left, Caleb "Cy" Loveless was on the right and Cy's son was sitting on the coupler.

going to do what he says. You can either go in and sit down or not go at all.'

"The boss was in the window of the office when I stopped the car in front of the station. He came down the stairs three at a time. He said, 'I was only joking when I saw you yesterday. I thought you were fooling, too.' 'I never joke,' I said, 'so here is your car.' 'Well,' he said, 'these men can take their regular car. You bring one down from the barn at 4 o'clock this afternoon.' So from that time on and for 19 years, I was motorman on freight cars, work trains and in passenger service."

James I. Barstow collection

The Syracuse, Lakeside & Baldwinsville Railway was predominately a 5-mile side-of-the-road trolley between Long Branch Park and Baldwinsville. In this view, one of the original 1899 St.Louis Car Company products, numbered 6-13, was southbound, passing the Frank Van Ness farm, midway between Baldwinsville and Long Branch. When the Syracuse, Lake Shore & Northern Railroad took over the SL&B in 1905, the first major project was to relocate all of this roadside line. The work was finished in January 1908.

The Syracuse, Lake Shore & Northern Railroad Emerges

The SL&B was strictly a passenger-carrying line serving the lake resorts and the New York State Fair Grounds and, as such, was much too dependent on seasonal traffic. Consequently, on December 12, 1903, the company was forced into receivership. The line was sold at foreclosure sale September 8, 1905, and the new owner, the Beebe Syndicate's Syracuse, Lake Shore & Northern Railroad, took over control and all operations the very next day.

The new company began to rebuild immediately. South of Long Branch, the line was reballasted with 6 inches of limestone from the neighboring Solvay Process Company and was double-tracked in its original location. From Long Branch to Baldwinsville, a new alignment closer to the Seneca River, was chosen and the old roadside track was torn up. The new double-track was laid all the way to and through Baldwinsville village except for the 260-foot long Syracuse Street bridge over the Seneca River which carried a single track. The work was completed in July of 1910.

Meanwhile, the northern terminus was being pushed closer to Lake Ontario.The new alignment crossed the Oswego River and Barge Canal at Phoenix on a double-track bridge 733 feet long. The structure consisted of four 94-foot deck-truss spans and a through-truss 357 feet long. Two substations were constructed, one two miles north of Baldwinsville and the other one mile south of Fulton.

This view of SLS&N right-of-way was looking north from Stop 8, Pleasant Beach, one mile north of Lake Shore Junction. Block signal 18 can be seen just beyond the fourth pole from the camera. The Lackawanna Railroad Syracuse - Oswego Branch can be seen on the left.

The Syracuse, Lake Shore & Northern again crossed over the Lackawanna Railroad, Syracuse - Oswego Branch about one mile north of Baldwinsville. This 1908 view is looking north toward Phoenix.

Syracuse, Lake Shore & Northern 2-car train (207-210) southbound passing the Phoenix substation at mile 15.14 as measured from Syracuse.

James I. Barstow collection

There were two Beebe Syndicate classic standard brick substations on the Syracuse, Lake Shore & Northern between Baldwinsville and Oswego. One was at milepost 15.14, three miles south of Phoenix and the second was at milepost 25.18, two miles south of Fulton station. The Fulton substation is pictured here.

James I. Barstow collection

Syracuse, Lake Shore & Northern car 205 was northbound at the Phoenix substation. The sign on the car reads: "Local Car for Oswego and All Stops." Note the smoking section of the car is full of passengers. There were very few non-smokers on this trip.

James I. Barstow collection

Robert O. Waters collection

Syracuse, Lake Shore & Northern car 200 was southbound, on the double-track bridge over the Oswego River and Oswego Canal (against the far shore) at Phoenix about 1912. The river is flowing from right to left under the bridge. An original print of this image was given to Waters by J. E. Motsiff, an early superintendent of the Empire State Railroad.

A 1908 Syracuse, Lake Shore & Northern company photograph of the double-track broken top chord pin-connected truss and 4 deck truss spans crossing over the Oswego River and Oswego Canal at Phoenix.

The Empire State Railroad crossed the Oswego River and Oswego Canal at Phoenix. This view is looking west (railroad south) from the Phoenix end. The special curve at the Phoenix end in the foreground was on a radius of 150 feet so the posted bridge speed of 25 mph was unlikely at this point. c-mid 1920s.

Car speed crossing the Empire State Railroad's double-track bridge over the Oswego River and Oswego Canal at Phoenix was posted for 25 mph. c-mid 1920s.

The Syracuse, Lake Shore & Northern Railroad bridge over the Oswego River and Oswego Canal at Phoenix was indeed an impressive structure. It consisted of 4 deck truss spans of 94 feet each and a single pin-connected broken top arch through truss 357 feet long. Built in 1908, the entire 733-foot bridge cost $100,000.

Passenger service on the SLS&N north of Baldwinsville to Phoenix and Fulton was begun January 6, 1909. Short-turn trips from Syracuse to Phoenix used these 1899 vintage 61-66 series St.Louis Car Company cars. Car 63 is seen at left.

For the first six months of operation into Phoenix and Fulton, the SLS&N used cars from the neighboring and affiliated Auburn & Syracuse. The Lakeshore cars 200-206 series from Cincinnati Car Company were delivered sans trucks and electrical equipment and were not ready to run until July of 1909. In this view, A&S car 50 was northbound at Phoenix. This real photo postcard was mailed in June 1909.

Passengers were plentiful at the Phoenix station in the spring of 1909. Auburn & Syracuse car 50 was northbound for Fulton and SLS&N car 62 was loading for Baldwinsville and Syracuse. The ticket office was in the building in the background.

Louis C. Hennick collection

The baseball players, band members in uniform, flags flying and crowds of people may have been gathering for a July 4th celebration. In this summer of 1909 view, Auburn & Syracuse car 56 and SLS&N 202 were southbound in Phoenix. The green flag on A&S 56 indicates "car following" on the same schedule. The "Fulton" sign on car 56 is contrary to the direction the car was traveling.

SLS&N car 204, signed "Fulton Local," was passing through Phoenix northbound. The sign on a right-hand pole indicates that local cars will stop at this street intersection. No prospective passengers were in sight in this view.

On December 30, 1908, the first car entered Fulton and regular service began 7 days later. For about six months, SLS&N 61-66 series cars and 6 cars of the Auburn & Syracuse were used until the newly arrived 200-206 series cars could be placed in service. A Beebe Syndicate passenger and freight station was opened on East First Street in Fulton on June 1, 1910. It was of the type "B" design because it was set on a narrow lot perpendicular to the street. A siding off the street brought the express cars to the freight platform.

All of the line north of Baldwinsville was graded for double-track but the second track was never laid. A glance at the maps will show that cars could meet or pass in each of the intermediate villages, Phoenix, Fulton and Minetto. In addition, a short passing track was located at Switch 4, midway between Phoenix and Fulton. The company's fourth substation was located in Oswego at the point where the tracks left the right-of-way and entered West First Street.

On July 26, 1911, the road was opened to the Lake Ontario port of Oswego, 38.41 miles north of Syracuse. There were two stations in Oswego. A ticket office was located in leased space at 212 West First Street. The cars continued across the Oswego River on Bridge Street to the "East Side" combination freight and passenger station at 117 East First Street. According to company right-of-way plans, this station and track arrangement appears to have been a duplicate of the one in Fulton. No pictures of the building have surfaced. In 1912, a third station of this type was opened in Baldwinsville.

This picture was posed as an advertisement for Western Electric Company to show its 1909 era "Electric Railway Telephone System, Both Portable and Side-Station Phones of 'Bell' Grade." SLS&N car 200 was standing on the southbound main line just north of Long Branch Park. The headlight was no doubt hung on the rear of the car to dress up the view. The conductor was talking on a Western Electric phone hung on the southern-most catenary tower or trolley bridge of the SLS&N 1907-08 line relocation to Baldwinsville.

both car photos James I. Barstow collection

SLS&N car 202, one of the Cincinnati-built 45-ton cars, was standing on East First Street, Fulton, just north of the end of the company's private right-of-way entering town and south of Fay Street, on September 1, 1910.

This 1908 company photograph of the SLS&N crossing over the Syracuse - Oswego Branch of the Lackawanna Railroad about .8 miles north of Long Branch Park. The view is looking north. The new 5.32-mile line between Long Branch and Baldwinsville was opened January 25, 1908.

SLS&N tracks approaching Stiles bridge over the Lackawanna Railroad. The view is looking south from the passenger shelter at Stop 8, located .8 miles north of Long Branch Park and 8.09 miles north of Syracuse. This picture, in connection with an accident, was taken about 1925.

A construction photograph of the Syracuse, Lake Shore & Northern 1907-08 line relocation was looking south toward Long Branch woods. The image had been enhanced to show catenary bridges and overhead wire construction. In this late fall 1907 view, the second high tension transmission circuit had not been installed.

A 1907 construction photograph of the SLS&N 5.32-mile relocation between Long Branch Park and Baldwinsville. This view, about a half mile north of Long Branch woods, was looking north toward Stiles bridge over the Lackawanna Railroad Syracuse - Oswego Branch. The hangers supporting the trolley wires were originally spaced 10 feet apart as seen here. Experience proved that 30-foot spacing was equally satisfactory. This longer spacing was finally used on the entire catenary installation to Oswego and on the Rochester, Syracuse & Eastern between Weedsport and Lake Shore Junction.

James I. Barstow collection

SLS&N car 207 was standing on East First Street in front of the Fulton passenger and freight station. The time was winter 1910-11. The car had recently arrived in Fulton as evidenced by the snow accumulation on the back windows.

James I. Barstow collection

The SLS&N Fulton terminal was storefront space in the Clark Building on East First Street until June 1, 1910 when its freight and passenger station, one block south, was opened.

Overhead construction between Syracuse and Long Branch and through the villages was of the standard pole and span type. On the balance of the line, single catenary was hung from steel towers designed by Archbold-Brady Company of Syracuse. The towers all spanned the double-track roadbed and were erected by the railway forces. This same design of tower was later used on the RS&E between Weedsport and its connection with the SLS&N at Lake Shore Junction.

Cy Loveless recalled a couple of incidents relative to the rebuilding of the Lake Shore road. "I was motorman on a work train reballasting the track in Baldwinsville. There was double-track through the village streets only. We were in the habit of drawing two gondola cars of stone from the barn [received in interchange from the Lackawanna Railroad] up to the job twice a day, two in the morning and two

James I. Barstow collection

This is one of a series of real photo postcards made of SLS&N cars and crews at the end of the line in Fulton in the winter of 1909. The big new cars were a novelty in town.

James I. Barstow collection

Horse-drawn sleighs were the local personal transportation of choice when the SLS&N first entered Fulton in January 1909. Car 206 was standing opposite the company's terminal station in the Clark Building on East First Street.

For the first five months of operation into Fulton, the SLS&N express cars stood on East First Street at the end of track. Beginning June 1, 1910, a spur into the new SLS&N freight and passenger station was available for loading and unloading the cars.

James I. Barstow collection

SLS&N car 200 had just left Fulton and was headed north toward Oswego. The car was about midway along a mile of double-track between switch #7 and #8. The duplicate high-tension transmission circuits are missing in this picture because their detour around the east side of Fulton city rejoined the railroad right-of-way about six towers ahead of the car in this view.

The Empire State Railroad right-of-way is seen looking south from Stop 20, the first stop south of Phoenix. Block signal 26 at switch #2 can be seen in the distance. This switch was the south end of the double-track through Phoenix village. c-mid-1920s.

This Empire State Railroad photo was taken from Stop 20 showing the approach to the long bridge over the Oswego River and Oswego Canal at Phoenix. c-mid 1920s.

again in the afternoon. That was about all we could handle in the best of conditions. If it rained, we couldn't get the two cars emptied because the section gang absolutely refused to work in the rain. In any case, we had to be off the special work by 5 o'clock at night because there was a Limited car both ways. On this particular afternoon, my conductor insisted that we take up three cars of stone. After some argument, and because he was boss over me, we left for Baldwinsville with three cars of ballast. Because of rain, we weren't through till a little after 5. At the end of the double-track [about two miles north of Long Branch] was a red and white signal. Each car had to stop and set the signal so as to protect cars on the single-track. We just sat on our track and waited for the car to come north from Long Branch. We were on the northbound track and for lack of time had not gone out on the single-track to get over on the southbound side. Pretty soon the Limited came in sight but I could see as it got closer that it wasn't going to stop for the switch. My conductor was on top of the loaded car and when he saw what was going to happen, he gave me a back-up motion. I gave her a couple or three notches. If there had been two empties as there should have been, I could have gotten away. As it was, I blew the

Eugene W. Logan, photographer

The Empire State Railroad between Baldwinsville and Oswego was graded for double-track but only one main track was ever laid. Note that a catenary messenger cable was hung over the second track space, presumably at the time of initial construction, in anticipation of the second track being laid. This undated photo of the mid-1920s was looking south from the Hinmanville crossing, Stop 23. Note the oversize passenger shelter. One extra panel was added to opposite sides of the standard octagonal building in locations where additional passengers were expected.

This accident photo shows the Empire State Railroad right-of-way looking north past the Hinmanville crossing, Stop 23, three miles north of Phoenix and 21 miles north of Syracuse. Note the electric signal box on the left-hand leg of the nearest catenary bridge or tower. It could be lit by passengers waiting for local cars at the crossing shelter.

Eugene W. Logan, photographer

fuses trying to move the heavy load. The wooden passenger car hit the gondola so fast that it split the former in two."

Here is another of Cy's tales in the days prior to the Beebe management. "Before the line was double-tracked between Syracuse and Baldwinsville, most sidings were close enough together that one could be seen from the other. One winter night I was coming down from Baldwinsville to the barn with the snow plow. Now it is hard to see out of a plow, especially on the opposite side from the controls. When we got to Long Branch, we were to meet a northbound regular. It wasn't there and besides, my conductor had sworn that we had passed it further up the line. I was pretty sure we hadn't. He was so sure that we decided to go ahead. There was a long stretch below Long Branch without sidings. Before we started, I stationed the conductor at the rear window ready to haul down the pole if we were running backward and it jumped the line. We were just entering the woods when I saw the headlight of the other car come flickering along the trees. I hollered, jammed her into reverse and started back the way we came as fast as I could make it. We pulled into the siding there without mishap and the regular car came sailing through."

This great picture of a 2-car Syracuse, Lake Shore & Northern train is somewhat of a mystery. It was obviously a special move but why was it photographed on the eastbound track of the RS&E just east of Jordan station? This company image was first published in the June 1916 issue of Brill Magazine. *The lead car 203 is signed "Special" and the second car 202 is signed "Syracuse Local." The board by the rear steps of car 203 reads: "Local Car for Syracuse and All Stops." These beautiful Cincinnati-built cars were relative strangers on the RS&E.*

In 1908, Beebe added to his interurban rolling stock by buying seven handsome 45-ton wood interurban cars from the Cincinnati Car Company. They were numbered 200-206. The cars and their trucks were delivered to the Syracuse & South Bay car shops at North Syracuse for assembly because the SLS&N shops at Lakeland were still under construction. Two years later, five more nearly identical to the first lot were purchased. They were numbered 207-211. These twelve cars, each capable of 60-mph speeds, handled the bulk of the passenger traffic between Syracuse and Oswego as long as the line existed.

In 1908, the Cincinnati Car Company delivered seven car bodies for the Syracuse, Lake Shore & Northern, numbered 200-206, to the North Syracuse shops of the Syracuse & South Bay line. Here they were outfitted with trucks and electrical equipment because the SLS&N shops at Lakeland were still under construction. This portrait of 200 at North Syracuse was taken July 1, 1909.

Wilbourne B. Cox collection

Builder's views of Kuhlman Car Company shop order 427 covering five cars, 207-211, delivered to the SLS&N in 1910. These 53' 10" wood and steel cars were nearly the same dimensions as the 200-206 cars delivered by Cincinnati Car Company in 1908.

A pair of brand new Kuhlman-built cars for the Syracuse, Lake Shore & Northern Railroad, numbers 211 and 208, were standing just south of the Fourth Street crossing at Fulton in 1910. They were facing south. There was a short stretch of double-track in Fulton that ended at switch #5, a short distance south of these cars. This location is known by comparing the tower number (302) painted on the inside of each leg with the Company's 1915 valuation plans.

James I. Barstow collection

Edgar Y. Pattison, photographer

In 1917 the newly formed Empire State Railroad acquired the Auburn - Port Byron branch of the failed Empire United Railways. Car 213, shown here at Port Byron, was originally an open trailer on the Syracuse & South Bay line. It was rebuilt as a closed motor and was assigned to the Auburn - Port Byron run. The picture is dated May 22, 1922.

This flat side picture of SLS&N car 204 was taken at the Lakeland shops on May 15, 1917 in connection with an accident investigation.

Wilbourne B. Cox collection

Cars 218 - 220 were ordered from Cincinnati Car Company in April 1920 by Ford, Bacon & Davis, then managers of the Empire State Railroad. These were the last interurban cars purchased new for the railroad. Weighing 36 tons each, they were also the lightest of the roads 200-211 series by 9 tons each.

Wilbourne B. Cox collection

An end view of Empire State Railroad's 218-220 series cars purchased in 1920. Note the builder's transfer table could accommodate trucks of three different gauges.

Waters - Krambles collection

This posed flat side view of Empire State Railroad car 218 was made at Lakeland shops in the fall of 1920.

This picture of Empire State Railroad car 219 at Lakeland shops appears to have been taken in the summer of 1931after the cars stopped running

George Krambles collection

Empire State Railroad car 219 at Lakeland shops. This view was taken about the time of the road's abandonment in June of 1931.

In 1917, six open cars were brought over from the Syracuse & South Bay road to the Empire State shops at Lakeland. They were rebuilt into closed motor units and numbered 212 through 217. They were assigned local runs on both the Syracuse-Oswego and Auburn–Port Byron divisions. In 1920, Cincinnati Car Company furnished the final additions to the Empire State's fleet. Cars 218-220 were 36-ton steel passenger cars. They were built to Ford, Bacon & Davis specifications. They were somewhat more modern in appearance with squared window tops instead of the arched ones. These cars were not well liked by the operating men as they were cold in the winter and hot in the summer. Besides, as one

This southbound 2-car train on the Empire State Railroad had departed Baldwinsville and was headed for Syracuse. Here are two of the three cars (218-220) purchased from Cincinnati Car Company in 1920. Each weighing 36 tons, these cars turned out to be less satisfactory than the older 200-211 series cars in the heavy weather of central New York state.

of the men pointed out, "they couldn't buck their way through a heavy frost."

On June 1, 1909, the Beebe Syndicate opened a new Electric Railway Terminal in the west end of the Empire House Block on Clinton Square in downtown Syracuse. The ticket office and waiting room occupied the ground floor. The operating and engineering offices were on the floors above. General offices of the company were on the fifth floor of the nearby Syracuse Savings Bank Building until 1928 when they moved into the terminal building on Clinton Square. At the terminal, direct connections were made with cars of the Oneida Railway bound for Canastota, Oneida, Utica and the east, with the Syracuse & South Bay cars for North Syracuse, Brewerton and South Bay on Oneida Lake, and with the Rochester, Syracuse & Eastern cars for points west. All incoming passengers alighted within a few blocks of downtown Syracuse.

At one time, the Auburn & Syracuse cars stopped just across Clinton Square from the electric railway terminal. Later the A&S station was moved to 340 West Fayette Street where quarters were shared with the Syracuse & Suburban Railroad (Syracuse & Eastern Railroad after April 28, 1923.)

50M 7-16-12

AGENT WILL LEAVE THIS STUB ON PARCEL

Electric Railway Terminal

AGENT'S STUB

To be removed from Parcel when called for and forwarded with Parcel Check in Daily Report.

76968

Electric Railway Terminal

SYRACUSE, N. Y.

As a part consideration for the service performed, it is agreed that the value of the article checked does not exceed $10.00 and that the company's liability for loss, due to negligence or otherwise, shall not exceed that amount.

Checking charge FIVE (5) CENTS for each 24 hours or fraction thereof.

PARCEL CHECK

76968

Courtesy Liverpool (NY) Public Library. T. H. Schuelke, photographer

Looking northwest across Clinton Square, Syracuse on May 27, 1928. A Syracuse Northern Electric car with closed trailer 50 was standing in front of the electric railway terminal. Erie Boulevard, extending from upper left to lower right across the picture, was the former Erie Canal location. The canal's former city dock and loading area was now occupied by the rows of parked cars. Through use of the canal ended in 1917 but water was retained for local use until 1923.

The New York State Railways, Oneida Line cars shared a downtown Syracuse interurban terminal with the Beebe roads cars to Rochester, Oswego and Oneida Lake points. Two of these parabolic nose or "windsplitter" cars (530 and 532) were delivered from G. C. Kuhlman Car Company in 1912. Note the third-rail shoes attached to both sides of each truck for contacting the under-running third-rail on the electrified West Shore Railroad (NYCRR) between Syracuse city line and Utica city line. Electric car service to Utica was discontinued December 31, 1930. This posed view advertising Crouse-Hinds "Interurban Trolley Car Carbon Arc Headlight Installation" dates from the early 1920s.

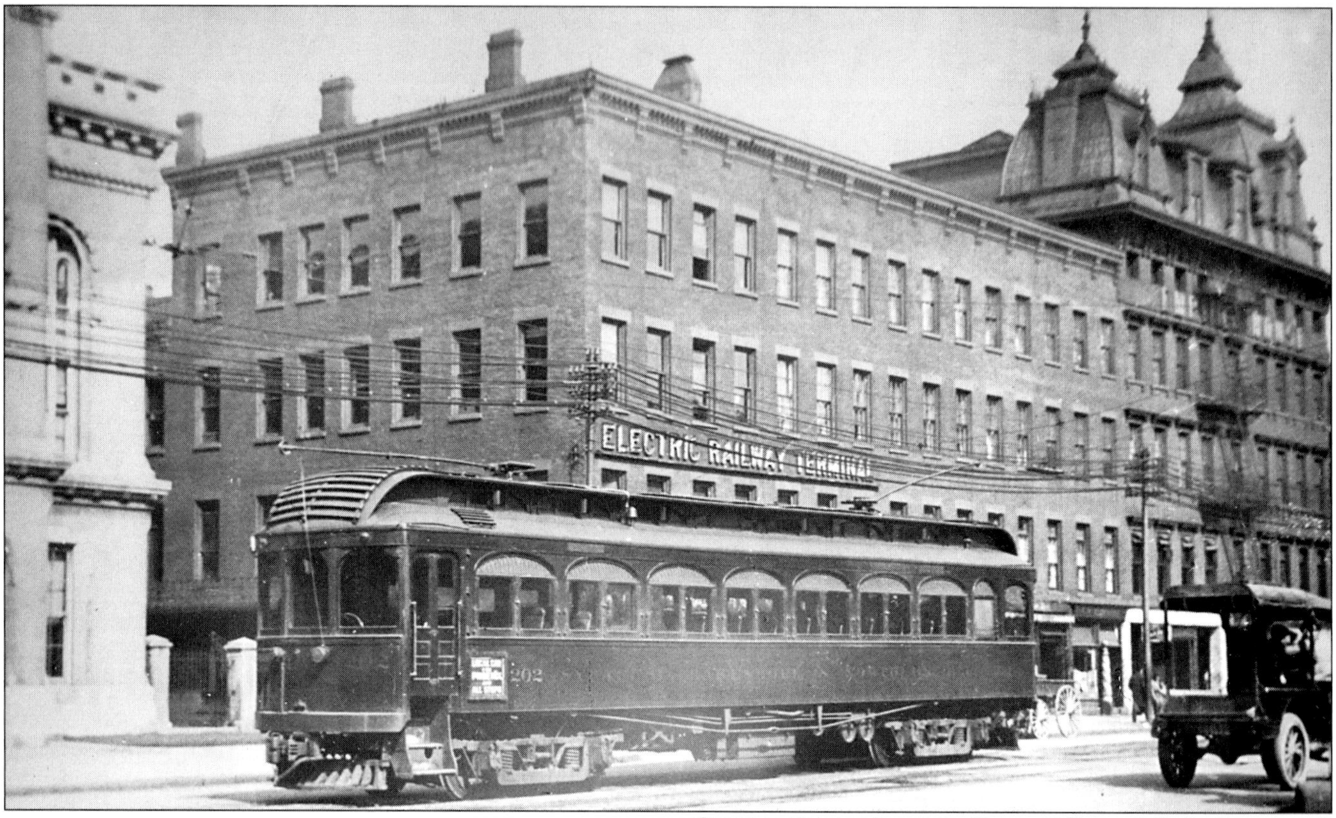

Onondaga Historical Association Museum & Research Center, Syracuse, NY.

Syracuse, Lake Shore & Northern car 202 was departing from the Electric Railway Terminal on Clinton Square, Syracuse. The destination sign reads: "Local Car for Phoenix and All Stops." c1917.

Robert O. Waters collection

The Syracuse & Eastern Railroad was an 18-mile side-of-the-road trolley line reaching Jamesville, Fayetteville and Manlius, all east of Syracuse. There were no physical or financial connections with the Beebe Syndicate roads but S&E's existence as a spoke in the wheel of electric lines with Syracuse as a hub needs to be identified. Car 18, seen above at Orville Junction, was built in the company shops in 1907 by splicing two single-truck Jackson & Sharp cars of 1898 vintage. The picture was taken about 1930. Buses were substituted for electric cars on October 25, 1931.

Until 1923, Clinton Square was divided by the old Erie Canal. Here were located the town docks for canal freight. In 1909, Clifford Beebe was quoted as saying: "If it were not for the canal which makes satisfactory service impossible, I would venture to build an interurban electric railway terminal costing half a million dollars." One is left to wonder what he had in mind. For the general historian and through the courtesy of the Erie Canal Museum in Syracuse, it should be noted that the official Erie Canal service through Syracuse ended in the fall of 1917. Spring 1918 saw the opening of the Erie Barge Canal. The old canal through Syracuse remained full of water, but not part of the system, until 1923 when it was filled in and a principal east-west thoroughfare, Erie Boulevard, was created.

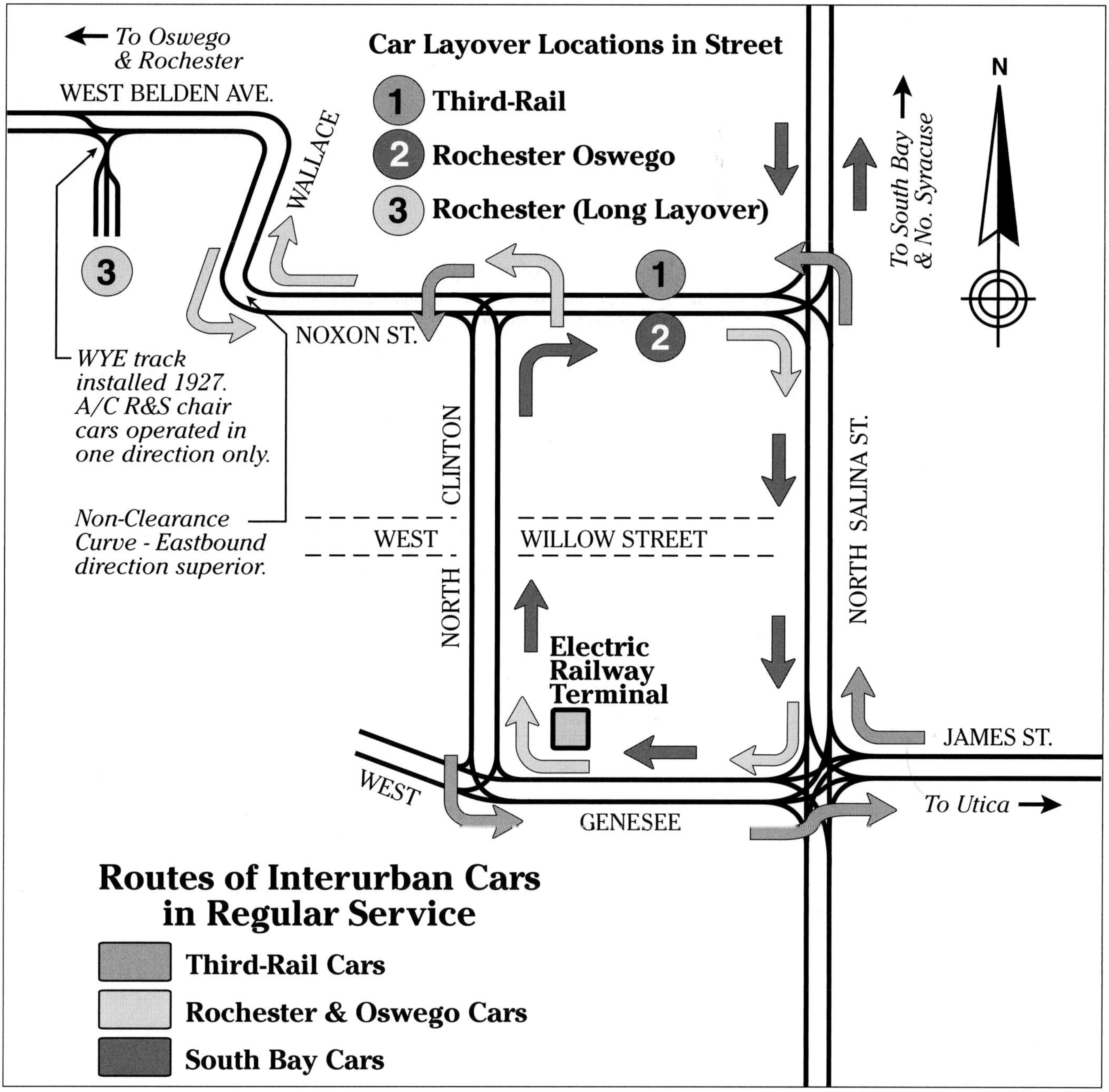

The Rochester, Syracuse & Eastern opened its extension from Port Byron to Syracuse on December 18, 1909. Its cars operated over the tracks of the Syracuse, Lake Shore & Northern Railroad from Lake Shore Junction, 4.40 miles into the Syracuse terminal.

An accompanying map of Syracuse shows the loop that all interurban cars used to reach the passenger terminal. Trackage rights for these cars to operate on North Salina and West Genesee streets were obtained from the Syracuse Rapid Transit Railway (New York State Railways, Syracuse Lines, after 1912.) The tracks in front of the terminal were part of the local West Genesee route, so Beebe's interurban cars with layover time were stored nearby at the Belden Avenue freight house yard. For short spot times, cars could stand on Noxon Street (later renamed Herald Place) between Clinton and Salina. There was a crossover in that block which allowed for some flexibility in spot time storage. After the Oneida third-rail line to Utica was discontinued, the last day of 1930, the west-bound track on Noxon east of Clinton was continuously available for short time storage. All cars of the Beebe roads circled the loop clockwise. The Oneida Line cars ran counterclockwise, entering and leaving the loop at James and North Salina streets.

Pre-World War I travel on the Syracuse, Lake Shore & Northern was fast and frequent. By the summer of 1912, Limited cars were leaving each terminal at 15 minutes past each hour all day long. Local

Here is a June 1911 view of Lake Shore Junction looking north along the Syracuse, Lake Shore & Northern main line. Rochester, Syracuse & Eastern tracks curve off to the left. Note the block signal (#14) on the RS&E governing its eastbound cars as they entered the signaled Lakeshore road enroute to Syracuse. The Lakeland shops were on the photographer's left. The old Syracuse, Lakeside & Baldwinsville shops can be seen in the distance behind the waiting shelter. One of the SLS&N former double-decker cars, 7-13 series, can be seen northbound past signal 13.

R&S passenger car of the 122-129 series (Kuhlman 1910) laying over on track 2 at Belden Avenue freight house, Syracuse, in April or May 1922. The freight cars in the background were two of the five purchased by the Empire United Railways in 1915.

cars, spaced between the Limiteds, also left each terminal every hour with additional early morning and evening trips scheduled. Running time for the Limited was 1:30 and for the locals, 20 minutes more. Empire United schedules for 1915 showed hourly Limiteds making the run in 1:25. Locals were interspersed in the schedule. They took 1:45 to make the trip. The March 7, 1915 EUR timetable also listed seven extra trips each way, daily except Sunday, between Syracuse and Lake Shore Junction to accommodate workers at the Halcomb Steel Company, Stop 4.

About 1911, the company built a freight house on West Belden Avenue on the west bank of Onondaga Creek. The building was of wood frame construction on wood posts to raise the floor to car floor height. The roof and walls were of "corrugated galv. iron." according to Arthur Benjamin, freight house foreman for years. He spoke of the hazards of a metal roof overhanging the freight house platform. He said it was cold working in the freight house in the winter time. However, things would warm up considerably if one of the car crew, while changing trolley poles, accidentally touched one pole to the metal roof while the other pole was still against the wire. The problem was eventually solved by trimming the eaves with wood so an errant pole touched wood instead of metal.

There were three tracks in the Belden Avenue

On Sunday, September 14, 1930, R&S Chair Car 129 Weedsport *was facing east on Herald Place between Clinton and North Salina streets, Syracuse NY. It appears to be on spot time. The terminal station was just two blocks away on Clinton Square.*

Robert V. Mehlenbeck collection

Business was booming in this April 1916 view at the Syracuse Electric Railway Terminal. SLS&N car 206 was the second car of a 2-car train. Those wishing to board were not leaving much room for those wishing to alight. No doubt those standing on the sidewalk were waiting for a car to Rochester, South Bay or for points on the Oneida Line's under-running third-rail line to Utica.

yard. Four cars could be worked on track 1 next to the freight house platform. Tracks 2 and 3 each held two cars that could be worked with "iron bridges" and through the cars on track 1. Three of the Beebe roads operating out of Syracuse (to Rochester, Oswego and South Bay) used this facility as their freight terminal. The Auburn & Syracuse and the Oneida Line of the New York State Railways shared a freight house on West Fayette Street in Syracuse.

The Syracuse freight house was especially busy into the mid 1920s. It handled perishables. Loads of milk were handled from the South Bay road. Best Ice Cream, Syracuse Ice Cream, General Ice Cream, bread from National Biscuit and Cahill Bros. all went on the early morning freights for Fulton and Oswego. For a time, Morsheimer, a Newark beer distributor, wanted his beer shipped on ice. The freight house crew rigged square pans the width of a freight car and sides 18 inches high to hold ice. There were holes in the floor of the freight car to let the water out. During the period of Wells-Fargo operation on the RS&E (1911-1918), its Syracuse agent maintained an office in the Belden Avenue freight house.

A 1915 freight timetable of the Empire United Railways showed two round-trip freights a day between Syracuse and Oswego. Each trip carried a Syracuse-Fulton trailer. It was set off on the northbound trip and was picked up on the motor's re-

Empire State Railroad car 206 with two 15-bench open trailers at the Syracuse Electric Railway Terminal were preparing to leave for points along the west shore of Onondaga Lake and Long Branch Park. c1918.

Syracuse, Lake Shore & Northern cars 14 and 15 were headed for the New York State Fair Grounds about 1915. These cars, produced by Jackson & Sharp in 1900, were part of the original fleet of the Syracuse, Lakeside & Baldwinsville Railway and were originally numbered 1 and 2. The tracks in front of the electric railway terminal were part of the New York State Railways local Solvay - West Genesee route.

Charles O. Dewey, photographer

turn from Oswego. The timetable noted that any train would make unscheduled stops to deliver perishable shipments. By 1926, traffic had dropped off so there was only one round-trip express train advertised.

On Sunday September 15, 1912, a tornado swept through Long Branch Park. Some of the trees were roughed up and the main line was out of service until the downed trees had been cleared off the tracks. There was not too much damage to the dance hall and bowling alley, but the SLS&N waiting room was completely destroyed. A 15-bench open car, number 3, was blown over on its side, and a nearby "whale" (bearing the old SL&B number 24) suffered considerable damage to one end. G. W. Dopp, a motorman, was killed when car 3 landed on him.

The entire Syracuse, Lake Shore & Northern was equipped with 3-position, upper-quadrant block signals similar to those installed on the Auburn & Northern line. They were built and installed by the Union Switch & Signal Company. The block signal system on the Lake Shore reminded Loveless of two stories in particular.

"At some time, I don't remember where or to whom, I had said that I could make a signal clear with a car in the block. One day after the road had been completed to Oswego, I was in the gravel pit with the work train drawing gravel. A car pulled up to the siding, stopped, and quite a bunch of high officials dropped off. They came over to me and one of them said, 'We understand that you can clear a signal with a car in the block.' 'Yes', I said, 'I can.' 'We would like to see it done,' they said. I got some of my men together and told them to go down the line a bit and pile sand on one rail for at least 60 feet. This they did. With the car on the track as the officials had left it, the board was red. Then I ran the car down onto the rail covered with sand. To the amazement of the officials, the board lifted. You see, the sand had acted as an insulator breaking the circuit between the rails and the car axles.

"I maintain that this was the cause of a bad head-on collision on 38 Hill just south of the Os-

It seems the SLS&N suffered the most damage from the September 15, 1912 tornado that swept through Long Branch Park. The 15-bench open car number 3 was overturned killing motorman G. W. Dopp. Car 24, one of the "decapitated" double-deck cars of the old Syracuse, Lakeside & Baldwinsville Railway was damaged. The park's dance hall survived but the railroad's waiting shelter was completely destroyed.

Stop 4, Halcomb, served the nearby Halcomb Steel Company plant. The building was temporarily resting on the short spur and loop that served the New York State Fair grounds. The spur was only in use during the annual Fair Week so the main line switch connection was temporarily installed for that time. This picture was taken November 23, 1906.

This SLS&N publicity picture was taken in the winter of 1910 to show off the brand new passenger cars from Kuhlman Car Company (207-211) and one of the new Union Switch & Signal automatic block signals. The 22 signals on the heavily traveled double-track between Syracuse city line and Long Branch, 5.5 miles, protected cars operating on a 4-minute headway. Ten additional signals were later installed on the 23 miles of single-track line between Baldwinsville and Oswego.

wego car barn. [38 Hill, slightly less than a half-mile long, was on a descending grade for northbound cars between Stop 38 and switch 11.] On August 16, 1913, car 205 was coming north on the single-track just below Oswego. It was a hot day and the sun was very bright. Two young girls were waiting for the car at Stop 38. They were standing on the side of the chalet away from the track in order to be out of the hot sun. The car was practically past before the motorman saw the girls. Then, starting down a 4 percent grade, he gave it the brakes and sanded the track besides. By the time the car stopped, it was all on sand so the block cleared. The southbound regular car, 206, had been waiting at switch 11, so they came ahead when the signal cleared. In the meantime, the northbound car had backed up to get its passengers and then started north again. Both cars were now on the steep grade coming toward each other around a long 3-degree curve. Presently each motorman could see each other through the trees and put their cars into emergency. Many people were injured. This was one of the worst wrecks on the road."

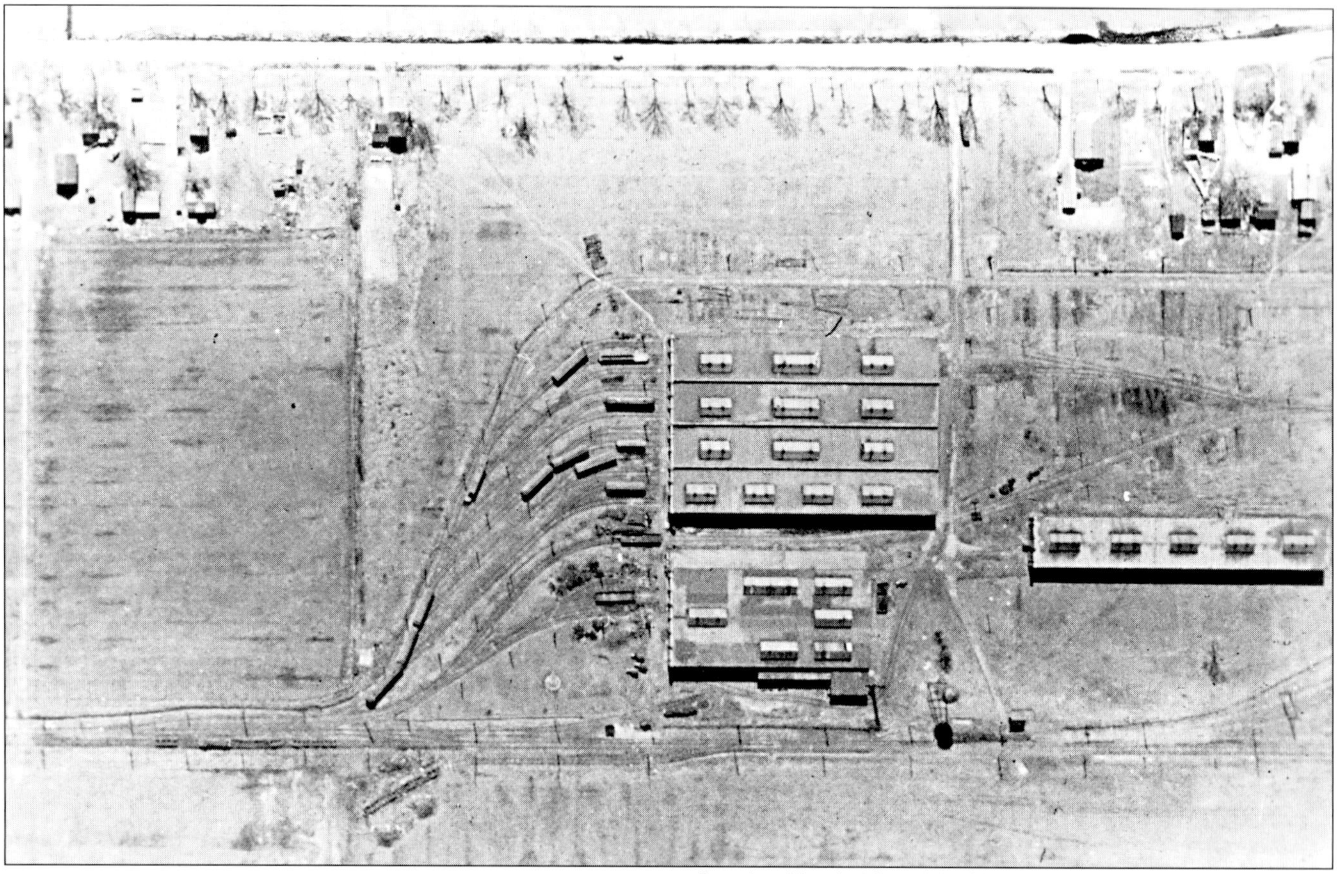

Onondaga Historical Association Museum & Research Center, Syracuse, NY.

This interesting aerial view of the Empire State Railroad's Lakeland car shops was taken in 1932 as dismantling of the car fleet was underway. There were burned out car bodies at the bottom of the picture while a dozen more cars in the yard awaited their fate. Lake Shore Junction, seen in the lower right hand corner of the picture, was the point where the Rochester & Syracuse tracks curved off the Empire State main line. In the intervening years, this entire area has been filled to a depth of 20 feet or more with waste from the neighboring Solvay Process Company and is now occupied by exit 6 of US highway 690 and parking lots for the adjacent New York State Fairgrounds.

Lakeland Shops

The main shops of the Beebe Syndicate lines were located on the Syracuse, Lake Shore & Northern main line at Lakeland, 4 miles north of Syracuse, at the point where the Rochester, Syracuse & Eastern joined the SLS&N. The shops, consisting of three buildings, occupied a 3½ acre plot of ground. They contained over 91,000 square feet of floor space and were surrounded by more than two miles of yard tracks.There, it was possible to put 79 cars under cover at one time. Centrally located with respect to all the Beebe lines, the Lakeland Shops were equipped to handle all work on the Lake Shore road as well as all the heavy repairs for the entire system. The shops were designed by Scheaff & Jaastad of Boston and were built by Edward K. Fenno of Auburn. They were completed in 1910. The total cost of the layout was around $203,000.

The three buildings were the car repair shop, the paint shop and the operating and storage barn. All buildings were of steel, brick and concrete construction. The storage barn and repair shop were side-by-side facing a ladder track while the paint shop was between the buildings and toward the rear of the lot. The paint shop was served from a loop track that ran between the barn and the repair shop and completely encircled the storage barn connecting to the ladder track at both ends.

The repair shop building was 205 feet deep and measured 103 feet across the front. Three tracks occupied one half of the open shop and the other half was a machine and tool section in the rear and office space in the front. A one-story 20-foot wide wing adjacent to the track 3 side of the shop building contained separate rooms for mill work, an armature room, a bake oven compartment, sand rooms, an oil locker room and a stock room.

The three tracks stopped 30 feet from the back wall leaving room for small tools and carpenter shop activities. Each track ran over a heated 4-foot-deep concrete pit. The floors adjacent to the tracks were depressed 18 inches to aid in work around trucks and journal boxes. Hydraulic jacks were used to lift car bodies for changing trucks. The shop had an assortment of overhead cranes, wheel transfers and a turntable to move trucks, motors, etc. into the machine section. Heavy machinery included a 300-

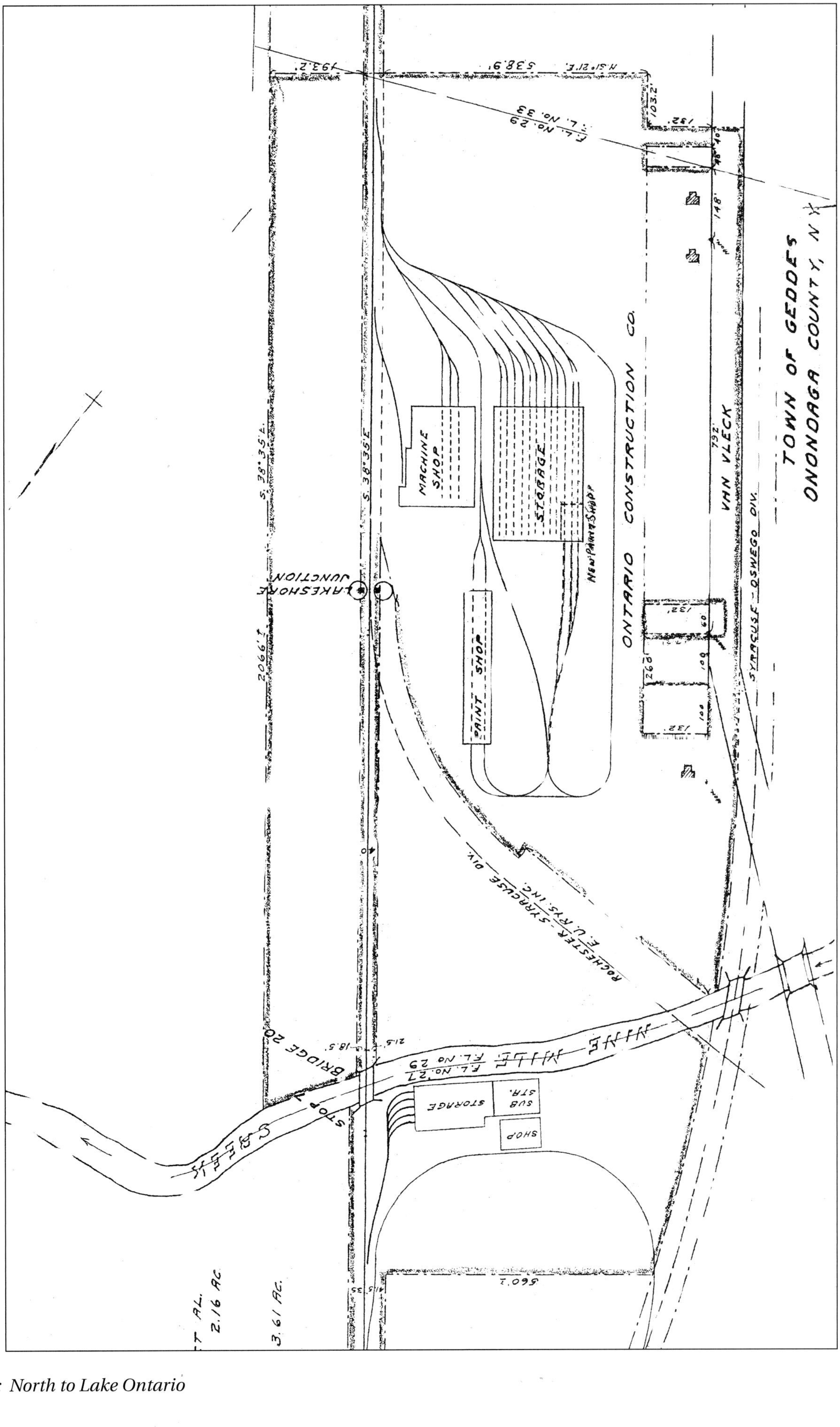

TOWN OF GEDDES
ONONDAGA COUNTY, N.Y.
ONTARIO CONSTRUCTION CO.
VAN VLECK
SYRACUSE-OSWEGO DIV.
MACHINE SHOP
STORAGE
New Paint Shop
PAINT SHOP
LAKESHORE JUNCTION
S. 38°35'E
2066.7
ROCHESTER-SYRACUSE DIV.
E.L.RYS. INC.
NINE MILE CREEK
F.L. No. 27
F.L. No. 29
F.L. No. 33
BRIDGE 20
STOP 7
STORAGE
SUB STA.
SHOP
538.9'
193.2'
560.2
2.16 AC
3.61 AC.

Robert O. Waters collection

Tracks 1, 2 and 3 entered the Empire United Railways car repair shop at Lakeland, near Syracuse. In this 1915 picture, SLS&N car 204 can be seen standing in the doorway of track 1. This picture was one of several company views submitted to J. G. Brill Car Company for publication in its Brill Magazine *series "Interurban Cars and Interurban Centers."*

Earl W. Fletcher, photographer

This is a view of the Lakeland repair shop taken in the summer of 1931, soon after the cars stopped running.

ton hydraulic wheel press, a 48-inch double-wheel lathe and a 43-inch wheel boring mill. It would appear that there was very little car work that could not have been done at the Lakeland shops. Its three tracks had a capacity of 9 cars.

The operating and storage barn measured 184 feet across the front and was 272 feet deep. It was divided into four fireproof bays of three tracks each. One track in each bay ran over a 150-foot inspection pit. Cars entered the building through 12 steel rolling overhead doors. Two of the bays had concrete floors, the others were gravel. This building was used mostly by the SLS&N that owned a large number of summer open cars.

The paint shop was 52 feet wide and 310 feet long. It had two tracks running through its entire length with two track entrance doors on each end. The building was divided into 5 rooms, each separated by tin-clad fireproof doors. The operation of painting a car was a continuous one once the car was taken in. First, the car was run into room 5 where it was stripped of all its furnishings, windows, brass and nickel parts, the metal being cleaned here in acid baths. The car was then hauled into room 1 where it was washed and the trucks cleaned with compressed air. Room 2 was the paint room. In room 3 the striping was added and in room 4 the varnishing was done. The car was then moved into

Robert O. Waters collection

The 12-track operating and storage barn of the Empire United Railways at Lakeland was capable of storing about 60 interurban cars. In this 1915 view, business car 999 was standing on track 6, an SLS&N 200-series car was showing on track 7, an SLS&N 15-bench open car was on track 10 and an open trailer of the Syracuse & South Bay road was on track 11.

This is an enlarged view of car 999 at the Lakeland car shops in 1915. The trucks suspiciously appear to be fitted with third-rail shoes. When built in 1910, the car was wired for under-running third-rail operation over the neighboring Oneida Railway between Syracuse and Utica. No records have surfaced to show that the car ever made such a move.

room 5 where those parts that had been removed were restored. Since there were two tracks through the shop, several cars could be handled at the same time. Notes indicate that at least 15 of the Lake Shore's fleet of summer cars, as well as both city and interurban cars of the Auburn & Syracuse, were to be scheduled through the paint shop during its first year of operation.

The boiler room at Lakeland was attached to the main line side of the repair shop. Carloads of coal were brought in from a track interchange with the Lackawanna Railroad just north of Lake Shore Junction. When the shops were originally built, they were supplied with water pumped from the neighboring Nine Mile Creek into a 50,000-gallon elevated tank. A number of years later, Syracuse city water was extended to the area, so the pumping system was discontinued.

On February 18, 1913, the SLS&N became the Syracuse-Oswego Division of the new Empire United Railways, Inc. During the summer of 1916, in an effort to consolidate the operating forces of the then parent company, the Empire United Railways converted the Lakeland paint shop into a general office building at a cost of about $12,000. The track entrance doors at each end were bricked in and the building was subdivided into suitable office space. A cafeteria was included for all employees at Lakeland. A much smaller car paint shop was created by walling off the rear section of storage barn tracks 13, 14 and 15 and cutting three track entrance doors into the north wall of this bay. Tracks serving this new paint shop were labeled 16, 17 and 18 and were connected into the loop surrounding the barns.

This is a publicity view of Crouse-Hinds Company in Syracuse, to advertise its "Interurban Trolley Car Carbon Arc Headlight Installation." Empire State Railroad car 200 was at the Syracuse Electric Railway Terminal on Clinton Square. The bundles of newspapers stacked in the front vestibule would be set off at various stations enroute to Oswego. c early 1920s.

Empire State Railroad

The consolidation of the Lake Shore road with the Rochester, Syracuse & Eastern and the Auburn & Northern was not financially successful and the general office setup at Lakeland was short-lived. The Empire United Railways was forced into receivership on November 1, 1915 and was sold at foreclosure sale on August 28, 1917. The Syracuse, Lake Shore & Northern and Auburn & Northern properties were reorganized as the Empire State Railroad Corporation, incorporated October 27, 1917. The Empire United receivers, Hendrick S. Holden and C. Loomis Allen of Allen & Peck, completed their work. Ford, Bacon & Davis, engineers, of New York City were hired to manage the new operation that consisted of two disconnected interurban divisions (Syracuse-Oswego and Auburn–Port Byron) and three local city car lines in Auburn, Fulton and Oswego. The operating offices were returned from Lakeland to the floors above the terminal ticket office at 112 West Genesee Street, Syracuse, where they remained as long as the roads operated.

Hendrick S. Holden was the new company's first president and J. C. Nelson was vice president and general manager. When Holden died in November 1918, Nelson became president and general manager. J. C. Nelson had had extensive experience in electric railroad management. He was graduated

G. A. Doeright, photographer

Empire State Railroad car 202 was loading passengers at the Syracuse terminal for Limited stops to Oswego in January 1922.

Empire State Railroad car 206, signed "Oswego", was posing for the photographer at the Syracuse terminal on Clinton Square, Syracuse on June 12, 1931. It was the 2:00 PM local and would make the 38.41 mile run to Oswego in one hour and forty minutes. The car following 206 was Syracuse Northern Electric 4. It was also due out at 2 PM for a 28 minute trip to North Syracuse.

from the University of Alabama as a civil engineer. He also received an electrical engineering degree from Cornell University. In 1902, he became associated with Ford, Bacon & Davis, engineers, in New York City. In April 1916, he was appointed general manager of the Gary & Interurban Railroad Company in northern Indiana, succeeding Alexander C. Miller, resigned. FB&D transferred Nelson to the Syracuse area in July 1917 to manage the newly emerging Empire State Railroad.

For most all of its years, the Empire State Railroad maintained an hourly schedule between Syracuse and Oswego, 1:40 being required for the 38-mile run. Half-hourly service was operated as far as Phoenix, 18 miles north of Syracuse. In addition, several trips were made in the morning and afternoon between Oswego and Minetto. These were known as the Minetto Stub runs.

Stock control of the ESRR was purchased by the Rochester & Syracuse in December of 1922 and

Empire State Railroad car 219, on West First Street, Oswego, was southbound as it crossed the double-track Rome, Watertown & Ogdensburg (NYC) tracks in Utica Street. The RW&O station is seen in the left background. At this point, the 219 was operating on Oswego city's Erie Street line.

On June 25, 1931, the day after Empire State Railroad ceased its Syracuse - Oswego operations, car 203 was moved out of its stall at Lakeland shops for a farewell portrait. Motorman "Ace" Cady performed the honors. It was a beautiful car to the last and in good condition too.

Empire State Railroad car 210 was stopped at the Phoenix station on the afternoon of June 24, 1931. This was the last day of ES operation. Conductor Irving Brand and motorman Robert Patterson stood for their portraits before continuing their trip to Oswego.

James I. Barstow collection

management and engineering of the Empire State was switched to the Peck-Shannahan-Cherry firm. Things ran smoothly for a few years. The company was able to pay all their bond interest through the first quarter of 1927. It even paid quarterly stock dividends on the 6% Cumulative Preferred "A" shares of stock through the fall of 1924. However, such prosperity did not last. On April 29, 1927, General Manager Talmadge C. Cherry was appointed receiver of the Empire State Railroad. The property was sold at foreclosure sale on June 18, 1931 to the Empire State Liquidating Corporation for $125,000.

The last cars between Syracuse and Oswego were operated June 24, 1931. Those between Auburn and Port Byron stopped running three days later when the Rochester & Syracuse connecting service at Port Byron ended. (The R&S had been operating the Auburn–Port Byron division under a short-term lease.) The ESRR property was dismantled in 1932 and 1933 and the affairs of the liquidating corporation were wound up in 1939.

One of the biggest problems on the Empire State Railroad had been snow. The road was laid out in a generally north-south direction and was, therefore, more susceptible to blowing and drifting snow by the prevailing westerly winds weather patterns and its close proximity to Lake Ontario.

The story was told of a passenger car that tried to buck its way through a deep drift near Phoenix one winter. The usual system was to take a run and batter through the drift. Several attempts were made in this particular instance, and the crew thought they were gaining on it. So they backed off nearly a mile and made a run for it. They almost made it when the car came to a sudden halt. The motorman reversed his car for another try but the car didn't move. About that time the conductor came forward to announce that the car's two trucks were sitting on the rails about two poles back and the car body was resting on two feet of hard packed snow.

Cy Loveless had this snow story to tell as a parting yarn. "One day during a bad storm, I had a two-car train headed for Oswego with a standing load in each car. The road was drifting in pretty fast. I would

Snow banks in central New York State were great to look at but were miserable to work through. This is a posed view of the situation just north of Baldwinsville in the winter of 1919-20. Even though signed "Syracuse," car 200 was northbound on the double-track south of the bridge over the Lackawanna Railroad, Syracuse - Oswego Branch.

The company sent a photographer out to record this view of SLS&N car 202, southbound between Fulton and Phoenix. Bear in mind that the window sills of these 200-206 cars were 6 feet above the top of rail and the top of the motorman's door was 9' 6" above the top of rail. This picture was taken in the winter of 1919-1920.

give the cars all they had and hit some of those drifts at 60 miles per hour. We hit them with such a wallop that the snow would fly clear over the top of the cars. I had one of the company officials standing in the front vestibule with me. Pretty soon he commenced to tell me not to hit those drifts so hard. Well, it was a case of hit 'em hard or get stuck. I listened to him until I had had about all I could stand. By this time we were north of Phoenix. Finally I let the cars drift to a stop where I knew we wouldn't get stuck. The snow had a hard crust on it. I opened the vestibule door and the one into the car and announced, 'I am not going to have you tell me how to run my car any longer. Either hit the snow or hit the cushions, one or the other.' He looked at me as if I was joking. 'I mean it,' I said. 'This is as far as this car is going until you do one or the other.' Thereupon the official buttoned up his coat and stepped out into the cold raw air. After closing the doors, I continued on to Oswego without further incident.

"We left Oswego, still with the two cars, and headed for Syracuse on our regular run. Everything ran smoothly until we got to switch number 4 midway between Fulton and Phoenix. There the block was against us and the telephone was dead. We could do nothing but wait. In about a half or three quarters of an hour, I thought I heard the telephone ringing in the box out on the pole. Sure enough it was the superintendent. He said there was a car stuck in a drift down at Stop 22, and told me to go

SLS&N Russell plow 1005 was standing on the southbound track at Minetto station, c1913.

The Fulton & Oswego Falls Railway operated a 1.14-mile horse car line connecting the center of Fulton on the east side of the Oswego River with the Lackawanna Railroad station in Oswego Falls (later West Fulton) on the west side of the river. With the arrival of the Syracuse, Lake Shore & Northern in 1909, the half mile of horse car track on East First Street was electrified. Because of weight restrictions on the Oswego River "Upper" bridge, horse car service to the west side continued for another five years. This post card was mailed in October of 1907.

down and see if we could draw her out. So we went down and found her drifted in solid. We coupled on and made a couple of starts. On the third try, we ripped the whole draw head out of her, just as clean as a whistle. The only thing to do was try and bunt her out. After several attempts, she broke loose and we pushed her back into Phoenix. In the meantime a freight car and a snowplow had come up the line so we loaded all the passengers into the freight car and it headed back to Syracuse with the plow.

"Not knowing when we would eat next, both crews of the passenger cars went into a restaurant near the Phoenix station for something to eat. We ate everything the man had in the place. He pleaded with us to save him something for breakfast but we claimed our money was as good as the next man's. While we were eating, and by the way, it was getting late, who should walk in but the official I had left off in the snow back earlier that afternoon. He bought a box of cigars and passed them around. Then he gathered up all our checks and paid for the whole lot. After that we climbed aboard our cars and headed for home. I ran around the cripple before leaving Phoenix and towed her to the Lakeland shops. There I dropped my second car also, and then went into Syracuse."

The camera was looking north on East First Street, Fulton. The horse car was at the north end of its track, opposite the end of Cayuga Street. This postcard was mailed March 4, 1908 so it would be nearly a year before the first SLS&N cars rolled into the city of Fulton.

City Lines in Auburn, Fulton and Oswego

The Empire State Railroad operated several street railway lines. A one-mile line was owned in Auburn and local cars were operated in Fulton and Oswego. The Auburn line on Clark, Jefferson and Orchard streets was operated by the Auburn & Syracuse as part of its city system until October 15, 1927 when all city railway operations ceased.

The Fulton & Oswego Falls Street Railway Company was a horse car line chartered September 21, 1885. The cars connected the center of Fulton on the east side of the Oswego River with the Lackawanna Railroad station in Oswego Falls on the west side of the river. The track was 1.14 miles long. Four cars and eight horses were owned in 1894. In 1896, the F&OF was consolidated with the Oswego Street Railway to form the short-lived Lake Ontario & Riverside Railway. Three years later the LO&R was dissolved and the F&OF was returned to its original owners under the direction of a receiver. In the spring of 1907, the property was sold to the Syracuse & Ontario Railroad Company, a construction company building the interurban line between Phoenix and Fulton. On June 29, 1907, the S&O was merged with the Syracuse, Lake Shore & Northern Railroad. When the interurbans first arrived in Fulton, only the First Street section of the horse car route was electrified. Horse car service remained on Broadway between First Street and the Lackawanna station because the town's upper bridge across the Oswego River and Barge Canal was considered to be unsafe for electric cars. The bridge was rebuilt in 1911-1913. The remaining portion of the horse car line was then electrified. A more suitable lightweight car arrived from the SLS&N and the "dobbins" were retired. A one-car local service was operated from the Lackawanna station, east on Broadway, north on First Street and across the lower bridge as far as Hannibal Street on the interurban extension to Oswego. The local car line then became 1.48 miles long. This service continued until September 15, 1927 when a local car every twenty minutes became a thing of the past.

The Oswego Street Railway commenced operations on August 23, 1885 with 2.03 miles of line, 25 horses and 5 passenger cars. The single-track main line extended along Bridge Street from East Tenth Street to West Third Avenue, 1.77 miles. A branch on West First Street from Bridge Street to West Utica Street was 0.26 miles long. In 1892, the property was electrified and expanded to nearly 5 miles of line. The J. G. Brill Car Company supplied the motor cars, 7 closed and 5 open.

In 1896, the Oswego company was consolidated with the Fulton & Oswego Falls Street Rail-

One of the SLS&N 61-66 series cars (St. Louis Car Company - 1899) had just arrived in Fulton on a winter day in 1909. The line had just opened in January of that year so some of the people on the sidewalk may have just been curiosity seekers. The motorman was about to swing the single trolley pole around in preparation for the next trip south to Phoenix, Baldwinsville and Syracuse. These cars served all of the Syracuse - Fulton line until the Cincinnati-built 200-206 series cars arrived in the late summer of 1909.

way to form the Lake Ontario and Riverside Railway. The new company began construction of a connecting link of the two properties and built southward, up the east side of the Oswego River as far as Seneca Hill which was at the end of the river bridge to Minetto. No tracks were ever laid south of Seneca Hill and this line became part of the Oswego city operations. Service ended December 14, 1918 as Minetto patrons preferred the faster and presumably more comfortable interurban cars on the west side of the river.

The L&OR was short-lived. On February 1, 1900, a new Oswego Traction Company took over. The system, by 1904, consisted of 10 route-miles. There were two routes that overlapped for 5 blocks in the center of town. From Oswego Beach on the west side of the city to Seneca Hill, the route was 7.5 miles long. From Erie and Hawley streets on the southwest side to Mitchell and East 15th streets on the northeast side, the route was 2.5 miles long. Oswego Traction car equipment consisted of 10 closed motor, 13 open motor trailers, 1 sweeper and 1 snow plow.

In June of 1907, the Beebe Syndicate purchased a controlling stock interest in the Oswego Traction system and on August 20, 1908, the SLS&N bought the company for $100,000 at its foreclosure sale.

In 1915, the Empire United Railways acquired

Empire United Railways

SYRACUSE-OSWEGO DIVISION

FULTON CITY CAR SERVICE

SOUTHBOUND			DAILY	NORTHBOUND		
Leave Hannibal Street	Leave Trolley Station	Arrive D. L. & W. Station		Leave D. L. & W. Station	Leave Trolley Station	Arrive Hannibal Street
....	6 00	6 10		6 10	6 15	6 20
6 20	6 25	6 30		6 30	6 35	6 40
6 40	6 45	6 50		6 50	6 55	7 00
7 00	7 05	7 10		7 10	7 15	7 20
7 20	7 25	7 30		7 30	7 35	7 40
7 40	7 45	7 50		7 50	7 55	8 00
8 00	8 05	8 10		8 10	8 15	8 20
8 20	8 25	8 30		8 35	8 40	8 45
8 45	8 50	8 55		8 55	9 00	9 05
9 05	9 10	9 15		9 15	9 20	9 25
9 25	9 30	9 35		9 35	9 40	9 45
9 45	9 50	9 55		9 55	10 00	10 05
10 05	10 10	10 15		10 15	10 20	10 25
10 25	10 30	10 35		10 35	10 40	10 45
10 45	10 50	10 55		11 00	11 05	11 10
11 10	11 15	11 20		11 20	11 25	11 30
11 30	11 35	11 40		11 40	11 45	11 50
11 50	11 55	12 00		12 05	12 10	12 15
12 15	12 20	12 25		12 25	12 30	12 35
12 35	12 40	12 45		12 45	12 50	12 55
12 55	1 00	1 05		1 10	1 15	1 20
1 20	1 25	1 30		1 30	1 35	1 40
1 40	1 45	1 50		1 50	1 55	2 00
2 00	2 05	2 10		2 15	2 20	2 25
2 25	2 30	2 35		2 35	2 40	2 45
2 45	2 50	2 55		2 58	3 03	3 08
3 10	3 15	3 20		3 20	3 25	3 30
3 30	3 35	3 40		3 40	3 45	3 50
3 50	3 55	4 00		4 00	4 05	4 10
4 10	4 15	4 20		4 25	4 30	4 35
4 35	4 40	4 45		4 45	4 50	4 55
4 55	5 00	5 05		5 05	5 10	5 15
5 15	5 20	5 25		5 30	5 35	5 40
5 40	5 45	5 50		5 50	5 55	6 00
6 00	6 05	6 10		6 10	6 15	6 20
6 20	6 25	6 30		6 35	6 40	6 45
6 45	6 50	6 55		6 55	7 00	7 05
7 05	7 10	7 15		7 15	7 20	7 25
7 25	7 30	7 35		7.35	7 40	7 45
7 45	7 50	7 55		7 55	8 00	8 05
8 05	8 10	8 15		8 15	8 20	8 25
8 25	8 30	8 35		8 35	8 40	8 45
8 45	8 50	8 55		8 55	9 00	9 05
9 05	9 10	9 15		9 15	9 20	9 25
9 25	9 30	9 35		9 35	9 40	9 45
9 45	9 50	9 55		10 02	10 07	10 12
10 12	10 17	10 22		10 22	10 27	10 32
10 35	10 40	10 45		10 45	10 50	10 55
11 00	11 05	11 10		11 10	11 16	....
Light face type denotes A. M.				Black face type denotes P. M.		

MARCH 7, 1915

11

Charles R. Lowe collection

Chicago, North Shore & Milwaukee Railroad car 313 was a 1915 product of St. Louis Car Company and came complete with maximum traction trucks for service on the city lines in Oswego, New York. In 1918, 313 and a mate 315 were sold by the Empire State Railroad to the "North Shore" line. Retaining their original numbers, these cars were rebuilt for 1-man operation in Waukegan, Illinois. The cars provided a total of thirty years of service in two states before being reduced to scrap metal in 1945.

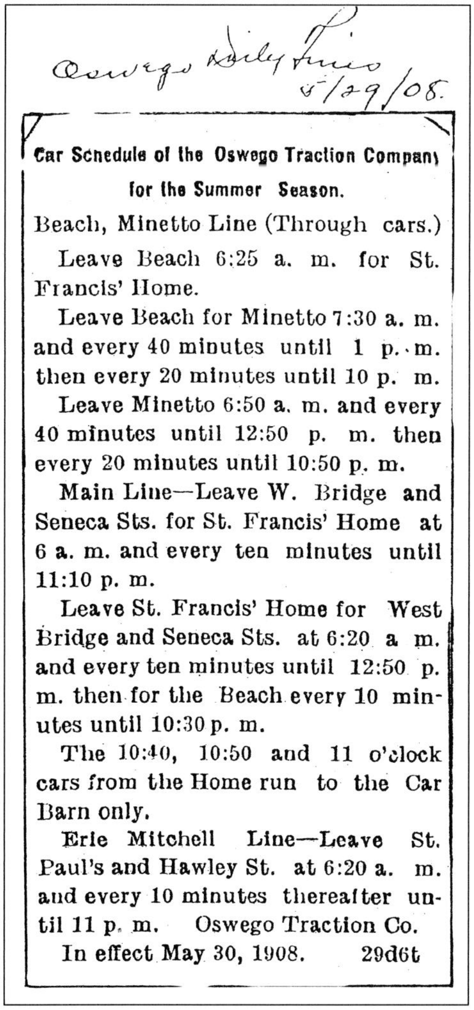

Oswego Daily Times 5/29/08.

Car Schedule of the Oswego Traction Company for the Summer Season.

Beach, Minetto Line (Through cars.)

Leave Beach 6:25 a. m. for St. Francis' Home.

Leave Beach for Minetto 7:30 a. m. and every 40 minutes until 1 p. m. then every 20 minutes until 10 p. m.

Leave Minetto 6:50 a. m. and every 40 minutes until 12:50 p. m. then every 20 minutes until 10:50 p. m.

Main Line—Leave W. Bridge and Seneca Sts. for St. Francis' Home at 6 a. m. and every ten minutes until 11:10 p. m.

Leave St. Francis' Home for West Bridge and Seneca Sts. at 6:20 a. m. and every ten minutes until 12:50 p. m. then for the Beach every 10 minutes until 10:30 p. m.

The 10:40, 10:50 and 11 o'clock cars from the Home run to the Car Barn only.

Erie Mitchell Line—Leave St. Paul's and Hawley St. at 6:20 a. m. and every 10 minutes thereafter until 11 p. m. Oswego Traction Co.

In effect May 30, 1908. 29d6t

24 double-truck city cars from St. Louis Car Company. Twelve of them, numbered 301-312, went to the Auburn city lines and the other twelve, numbered 313-324, were assigned to the Fulton and Oswego city lines. The Oswego car inventory of this size car was reduced in June 1918 when cars 313 and 315 were sold to the Chicago, North Shore & Milwaukee Railroad for service on its Waukegan city lines. These cars retained their original numbers and operated till scrapped in 1945. One more car was sold to an unknown party. Three cars of this class were lost in the Oswego car barn fire February 2, 1920. Those six cars were replaced by six Osgood-Bradley single-truck Birney safety cars numbered 401-406. The remaining six cars of the 313-324 series were equipped with safety-car features and were renumbered 411-416. All 12 safety cars were equipped for one-man operation.

The city car barn on West Bridge Street was rebuilt after the 1920 fire. A new barn for overnight storage of interurban cars was constructed adjacent to the company's Oswego substation on West First Street. The barn was a simple one-track building capable of housing two standard interurban cars.

The Oswego city lines were discontinued April 21, 1927. All twelve safety-equipped cars were sold to a New York scrap metal firm. The six double-truck cars, 411-416, turned up on the Jamaica Central Railway on Long Island as 601-606. The fate of the six single-truck cars is unknown.

SYRACUSE

The South Bay Line to Oneida Lake 11

Syracuse & South Bay Electric Railroad
Syracuse, Watertown & St. Lawrence River Railroad
Syracuse Northern Electric Railway

Syracuse & South Bay Electric Railroad

Several unsuccessful attempts were made to connect Syracuse and Oneida Lake with a trolley line. One of the first was the Syracuse & Oneida Lake Electric Railway Company chartered in May 1895. Two routes were surveyed; the first was through Liverpool and Three Rivers to Phoenix, and the second was through North Syracuse to South Bay on Oneida Lake. Neither was built.

By 1904, the Syracuse & South Bay Railway Company had appeared on the scene with substantially the same promoters as the S&OL. This time construction got underway. The double-track line was half-finished and the rolling stock was on hand, stored in the brand new North Syracuse car barn, when the promoters ran out of money. Work was suspended early in 1907. The property was sold at foreclosure sale February 21, 1907. The purchaser was Clifford D. Beebe who then formed the Syracuse & South Bay Electric Railroad. Construction resumed and the 12-mile line was opened August 27, 1908.

It was a great piece of railroad. High-speed passenger cars operated over a 100-foot wide private right-of-way nearly all the way from the Syracuse city line to Oneida Lake. From the station at North Syracuse to South Bay, 5.5 miles, the two tracks were laid on an absolutely straight line with very little change in gradient. 85-pound rail was used and the track structure was supported by rock ballast.

Unlike the other electric lines of the Beebe Syndicate, the Bay Road was designed to handle freight in carload lots. An interchange track at the Syracuse city line connected the electric road with the end of a New York Central siding serving the extensive Crouse-Hinds Company plant. There was no other railroad entering North Syracuse so all freight destined for that community traveled over the Syracuse & South Bay line. The company also planned to develop a freight business between Syracuse and points on Oneida Lake. Some winter ice was shipped from the lake but freight traffic did not turn out to be extensive. Freight moved in 1912

Onondaga Historical Association Museum & Research Center, Syracuse, NY.

Facing page: *Syracuse Northern Electric car 6 is seen northbound on North Salina Street, Syracuse. It is signed "North Syracuse." The first 2.5 miles of any SNE trip from the Clinton Square terminal were on New York State Railways tracks in city streets. This picture was taken on July 18, 1928.*
Courtesy Liverpool (NY) Public Library. T. H. Schuelke, photographer

Above: *Syracuse & South Bay car 16, southbound, was approaching Cicero, Stop 10, about three miles north of North Syracuse station. Cicero people were more conveniently accommodated after November 1912 when the Bay Road opened its branch to Brewerton. The branch was built by a subsidiary company, the Syracuse, Watertown & St. Lawrence River Railroad.*

A Kuhlman Car Company builder's photo of Syracuse & South Bay baggage/express cars numbered 1 and 3, odd numbers only. These cars were 48 feet long and each weighed 30 tons. One of them was used as a line car.

Wilbourne B. Cox collection

Syracuse & South Bay express car number 1 in work train service on the double-track main line somewhere between North Syracuse and South Bay on Oneida Lake. The Bay Road owned four second-hand 30-foot flat cars. Loaded car number 10 is seen in the foreground.

There are several things of interest in this company photograph of Syracuse & South Bay car 20. The cars were purchased in 1905 from the Kuhlman Car Company by a failed predecessor of the Bay Road. They arrived on the property bearing the wrong railroad name and were stored in the car barn until the road was ready to use them. In 1916, the Beebe Syndicate management arranged for tests of roller bearings on the trucks of two cars of its associated roads - parlor car Syracuse, *a trailer on the Rochester - Syracuse Division of Empire United Railways and passenger car 20 on the Bay Road, as seen at right. The Merrick roller bearings were produced by the Railway Roller Bearing Company of Syracuse. The experimental tests were apparently short-lived as no other pictures of these roller bearing trucks have surfaced.*

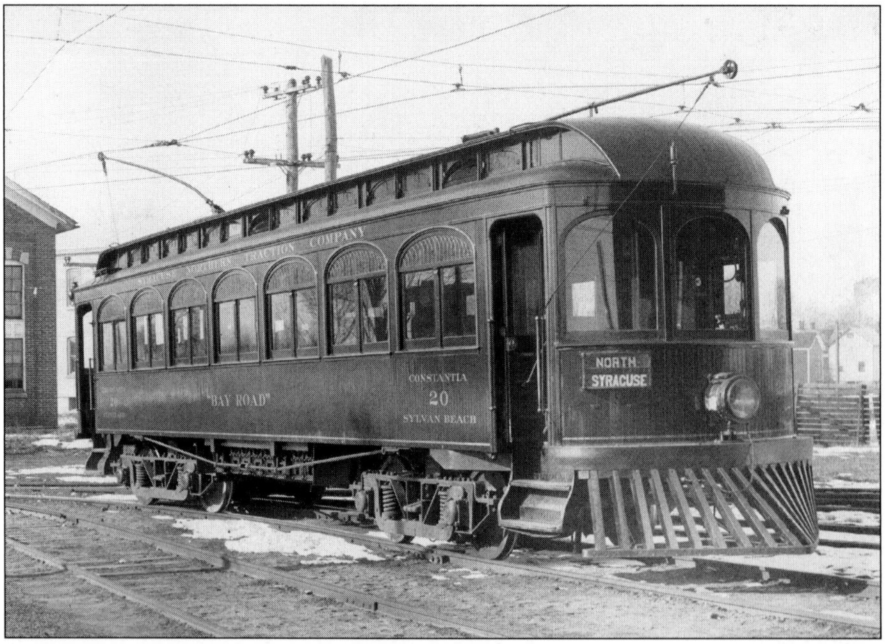

This is a sample of the passenger equipment of the Syracuse & South Bay line. The picture is dated spring 1909 because two of the cars of the Syracuse, Lake Shore & Northern Railroad can be seen behind trailer "K." The brand new SLS&N car bodies were delivered to the Bay Road shops for assembly of parts because the SLS&N shops at Lakeland were still under construction.

Robert O. Waters collection

A Kuhlman Car Company builder's photo of Syracuse & South Bay center aisle open trailer. There were ten cars in the series, lettered "A" - "L." Letters F and I were omitted to avoid confusion in reporting. The cars were 52'-11" long and each seated 60 passengers.

Wilbourne B. Cox collection

A Kuhlman Company builder's photo of Syracuse & South Bay car 6. There were ten single-end cars in the series, numbered 2 - 20, even numbers only. Each 48-foot car weighed 35 tons and could seat 56 passengers. The four names painted on each car side were ports of call on Oneida Lake reached by steamers from the electric road's pier at South Bay.

amounted to 835.85 tons. Most of these trips were deliveries to small enterprises in North Syracuse.

The company's rolling stock consisted of ten motor passenger cars, ten trailers and two motor baggage cars. The ten motors were single-end double-truck 48-foot interurbans. They all bore even numbers beginning with number 2. Each car was divided into passenger and smoking compartments, and each had a total seating capacity of 56. The ten double-truck trailers were modified open cars, 52' 11" long overall. Each seated 60 passengers. These cars bore letters rather than numbers. The letters "F" and "I" were omitted so the series ran from "A" through "L". All cars were built by G. C. Kuhlman Car Company in Cleveland. All the passenger and express cars came incorrectly lettered "Syracuse Northern Traction Company."

Hourly service was scheduled for the 12.39-mile run between Syracuse and South Bay. Cars operated over the tracks of the Syracuse Rapid Transit Railway Company's (New York State Railways, Syracuse lines after 1912) Wolf Street line from Clinton Square in downtown Syracuse to Seventh North Street. Here the Bay Road cars left the streets and entered their own right-of-way. A loop was provided at South Bay as the cars were all single-end.

The Syracuse & South Bay maintained its shops and power station at North Syracuse. Power was purchased from the Niagara, Lockport & Ontario Power Company and was stepped down to the trolley potential of 550 volts dc. The duplicate 33,000-volt transmission line extended from a point on the Syracuse, Lake Shore & Northern near Solvay across Hiawatha Boulevard and Free Street in Syracuse to the Bay Road at Seventh North Street, thence north along the company's right-of-way to the North Syracuse substation.

Courtesy of Liverpool (NY) Public Library. T. H. Schuelke, photographer

A late day view of a southbound Bay Road car standing on the southbound main track adjacent to the North Syracuse car barn.

This 1907 company photo shows the passenger station, substation and a 6-track car barn of the Syracuse & South Bay Electric Railroad at North Syracuse, all under construction. The sign on the car barn proclaims Frank B. Gilbreth to be the builder. The road opened for business August 27, 1908.

The completed car barn, substation and passenger station at North Syracuse are shown here from the street side. A loop track encircled the car barn as all Bay Road passenger cars were designed for single-end operation , even though each car had a trolley pole on the front end.

James I.Barstow collection

Syracuse & South Bay express car number 1 is seen passing the North Syracuse car barn. The car is northbound on the double-track line to South Bay. From the car barn to South Bay, the line was one tangent 5.5 miles long. This postcard dates to 1908.

Onondaga Historical Association Museum & Research Center, Syracuse, NY.

This is an early view of the North Syracuse passenger station and substation. Car 6, standing at the platform, was southbound for Syracuse. Two company flat cars were on the company's gravel pit track, left background. The side track in the immediate foreground was one end of a loop track encircling the car barn. The tracks behind the pump car were leads to the six-track barn.

Syracuse, Watertown and St. Lawrence River Railroad

In April 1911, the Syracuse, Watertown & St. Lawrence River Railroad Company was formed to extend electric railway service north from North Syracuse to Brewerton and Central Square. Brewerton was located at the extreme west end of Oneida Lake. A single-track line left the Bay Road at Stop 9, 1.52 miles north of North Syracuse. The junction was known as Watertown Junction. Skirting the village of Cicero, rails were laid north 6.15 miles to Brewerton. The line was officially opened November 2, 1912. There were stations at Cicero and Brewerton. Cars were turned on a wye near the north end of the line because there was insufficient space for a loop. The Central Square extension was never built.

Onondaga Historical Association Museum & Research Center, Syracuse, NY.

A Bay Road car from Syracuse and North Syracuse is seen approaching the Brewerton Terminal. This village was located at the western end of Oneida Lake and was 14.5 miles north of Syracuse.

The Oneida Lake Terminal Company, a Beebe Syndicate company, built and operated dock facilities at South Bay. As originally planned, the dock was to be an earth-filled loop enclosing a lagoon for small craft. As finally opened about 1909, a 250-foot long pier supported a Bay Road track that was con-

In this posed picture, Syracuse & South Bay car 16, with a trailer, was approaching the Brewerton station. There was no room for a loop track at this terminal so the Bay Road's single-end cars were turned on a wye, one leg of which can be seen in the distance.

Syracuse & South Bay trailer "K" and car 14 were standing at Brewerton station. This village was located at the west end of Oneida Lake where it emptied into the Oneida River.

Syracuse & South Bay car 8 was loading at Brewerton terminal. When leaving for Syracuse, the car would back out of the station area, cross one village street and turn on a wye south of the crossing. These passengers would arrive in Syracuse 50 minutes from leaving time here. In 1915, the company was offering hourly service between Syracuse and Brewerton.

Onondaga Historical Association Museum & Research Center, Syracuse, NY.

This is one of the few pictures of the off-side of a Syracuse & South Bay passenger car. There were no doors on this side. Bay Road cars were all operated single-end even though they had trolley poles on the front end. Possibly they intended to couple two cars back to back at which time the front pole of the second car would be used. No pictures are known of such a train of two Bay Road passenger motor cars.

Syracuse & South Bay car 16 and crew at the South Bay terminal about 1908. When the line to South Bay first opened in August of 1908, a local photographer produced a series of real photo postcard pictures of the cars and crews at the South Bay terminal. This view of car 16 includes a member of the railroad's police force. The hat badges came from Heeren Bros. in Pittsburgh, PA. Conductor badges were black letters on white background. Motormen badges were the reverse.

nected to the railway's South Bay terminal loop so the electric cars could make across-platform connections with the Company's lake steamers *Sagamore* and *Olympia.*

The South Bay Terminal Company also owned a 24-acre island in Oneida Lake. Frenchman's Island was developed as a resort area for picnics and outings. The steamer *Olympia* left South Bay every hour after 10 A.M. to take people to and from the island. The larger steamer *Sagamore,* with a capacity of 600 passengers, operated between South Bay and Sylvan Beach on the eastern shore of Oneida Lake. By 1914, two round trips daily were required to handle the crowds. Period advertisements offered trips "Around the Y" which consisted of rail from Syracuse to South Bay, then a boat trip from South Bay to Frenchman's Island and Brewerton, then rail back to Syracuse, all for 70 cents. A gas-powered launch, *Jean,* was used in this service in 1915.

Excursion service to Oneida Lake and connections with the lake boats across the South Bay pier appear to have faded after the 1915 summer season. The first World War was getting under way in Europe and local travel thoughts were heading in different directions.

The South Bay station and ticket office was the back room of a house on a rise of ground facing Oneida Lake. The railroad's loop track completely encircled the building. c1920.

A Syracuse & South Bay 2-car train at the South Bay terminal, c1909.

The Bay Road's spur to reach its pier on Oneida Lake passed under Shore Road. All cars did not back out onto the pier so a generous paved walkway was provided to connect the pier with the Bay Road terminal station, located over the photographer's right shoulder. This picture was dated July 1, 1909, and was taken when the pier first opened.

William Jubb, photographer

This 1910 tinted postcard of the Bay Road pier shows the steamer Sagamore *taking on passengers for a 1-hour and 45-minute trip to Sylvan Beach at the eastern end of Oneida Lake.*

Syracuse Northern Electric Railway

In 1916, the Syracuse & South Bay and the Syracuse, Watertown & St. Lawrence River railroads were forced into receivership. They were over-capitalized and earnings were insufficient to cover interest payments on their bonds. With Allen & Peck management, the two companies emerged from foreclosure as the Syracuse Northern Electric Railway, Inc., incorporated May 12, 1917. Talmadge C. Cherry was made president. The first SNE timetable listed cars leaving and arriving at the Syracuse terminal hourly with every other car signed Brewerton or South Bay.

One of the first things the new company did was to tear up and sell one of the double tracks between Watertown Junction and South Bay. Six of the Bay Road open trailers were turned over to the Empire State Railroad where they were remodeled into closed cars. Work was done at the ESR Lakeland shops. The cars were numbered 212-217. The first services of these rebuilt cars were to transport soldiers from various points on the former Beebe system to the World War I temporary encampment at the New York State Fairgrounds near Syracuse. Also in 1917, the Bay Road leased combination car 101 from the Rochester & Syracuse Railroad. It was renumbered 22. In 1922, the car was returned to the R&S which changed the number again, this time to 102.

In 1922, the SNE gave serious consideration to the purchase of three light-weight one-man passenger cars. According to a report of the Westinghouse Electric Company, two cars were for use on the main line while the third was to provide tripper service from the Syracuse terminal to North Syracuse. No changes were contemplated in the electrical distribution system. The light-weight cars were never purchased because of lack of available funds. It is now quite evident that because of the Great Depression and the paucity of passengers, such an investment would not have appreciably extended the life of the Bay Road. An interesting feature of the 1922 Westinghouse report to SNE management was the following mileage table:

Syracuse Terminal	0.00
Syracuse city line (jct. with N.Y.S. Rys.)	2.58
North Syracuse	6.87
Watertown Junction	8.39
Cicero	10.18
Brewerton	14.54
Watertown Junction	8.39
South Bay	12.39

This is a close-up of the Sagamore Navigation Company's steamer Sagamore *about 1910. It is hard to tell if they were tying up or casting off from the Bay Road's pier at South Bay.*

Onondaga Historical Association Museum & Research Center, Syracuse, NY.

A late afternoon local was loading at the South Bay terminal c1911. At this time, the Bay Road was running half-hourly service in the summer and hourly in the winter months.

Syracuse & South Bay car 2 with crew at the South Bay terminal about 1908.

Onondaga Historical Association Museum & Research Center, Syracuse, NY.

A 1928 financial report of the company revealed that the gross revenue for the year was $117,739. After all expenses were paid, the net income was a red figure of $642. Over 625,000 revenue passengers were carried that year and nearly 9,200 more were accepted on transfer from the Syracuse lines of the New York State Railways. The following year the company's net operating revenues were $1,583.00 and its operating ratio was 98.33%. Also in 1929, the southbound rails of the double-track between North Syracuse and Watertown Junction were declared surplus and were removed.

In spite of the dearth of traffic generated on the Syracuse Northern Electric, it managed to outlive all the other interurban electric railways in the Syracuse area. The last car was run January 11, 1932, more than six months after the Rochester & Syracuse and the Empire State lines quit and nearly two years after the Auburn & Syracuse folded. The SNE used its own equipment to scrap the line. Carloads of rail and other metals were turned over to the New York Central for shipment at the Crouse-Hinds interchange in Syracuse. Newspaper reports revealed that the last item on the interchange was the SNE

Syracuse & South Bay car 6 with crew at the South Bay terminal about 1908.

Syracuse Northern car 18 at the Electric Railway Terminal on Clinton Square, Syracuse. The car was signed "Brewerton." This picture was taken on the last day of electric car operation, January 11, 1932. Shown here are George Bullard, dispatcher of the Syracuse & Oswego Motor Lines, Herbert Palmer, conductor and Charles Hessler, motorman of the electric car. Hessler's hat badge has survived to date. Numbered 19, it was imprinted "Syracuse & South Bay Electric R.R." so apparently the SNE never issued new badges when the company was formed in 1917.

Robert O. Waters collection

express car that had hauled the scrap trains.

Syracuse Northern Electric Railway, Inc. lived on after the electric cars stopped running. Five ACF 29-passenger buses were acquired. The company, now much reduced in size and having only 9 employees, began operating its own bus service on January 12, 1932, closely matching that of the electric cars. This operation continued for the next five years. Over its fifteen year life, the bonded indebtedness of the SNE had been gradually reduced from an original $175,730 (in 1917) by about two thirds. In 1933, the company's scrap sales helped retire the entire debt. On December 31, 1937, the SNE sold its remaining assets and service routes to the neighboring Syracuse & Oswego Motor Lines. This bus line had been created in 1931 by W. K. Zinsmeister, then treasurer of the R&S, ES and SNE, in anticipation of the Empire State Railroad's demise. Early in 1938, the Syracuse Northern Electric Railway petitioned the New York State Supreme Court for permission to effect a voluntary dissolution of the corporation and by the end of December 1938, the SNE was no more.

ALBION
212

12 The Final Roll Call

Seventy-five years have passed since the last electric cars operating on the Beebe Syndicate lines rolled into their barns. Another seven years would be required to completely liquidate the physical assets of the several corporations. Last service on each of the six Beebe interurbans were as follows: Auburn to Syracuse - April 15, 1930, Rochester to Lockport – April 30, 1931, Syracuse to Oswego – June 24, 1931, Auburn to Port Byron – June 27, 1931, Rochester to Syracuse – June 27, 1931 and the Syracuse Northern Electric Railway – January 11, 1932.

Today, very little remains to remind anyone of the 236 route miles of interurban lines and 25 miles of associated city lines that spread out over the central and western New York state landscape. Most recognizable will be the several locations of bike and walking trails along old right-of-way, a restored and preserved suburban waiting room or two and a few concrete piers or abutments that show where massive steel railroad structures formerly existed. If, when driving along some of the state's secondary highways or byways, a motorist encounters some long sweeping curves and gentle (for the highway) grades, the driver will know in an instant that this particular highway had been built on a section of an old interurban roadbed.

The only known piece of rolling stock still in existence is the 50-ton Baldwin-Westinghouse Class B electric locomotive, number 105 of the Auburn & Syracuse interurban. It now resides un-numbered at the Connecticut Trolley Museum, East Windsor, Connecticut. Sixteen of the steel towers or catenary bridges that supported the overhead wires on the RS&E were donated by the last power company owning them to the Seashore Trolley Museum in Kennebunkport, Maine. Eight of the bridges have been re-erected along the museum's main line. Riding under them in a trolley car will likely give a

James I. Barstow collection

Facing page: *Westbound BL&R car 212, signed Albion, is seen on State Street, Brockport, about 1909. The village of Brockport, 15 miles west of the Rochester city line, was within commuting distance of Rochester. In 1930, the railway was still scheduling seven round trips from downtown Rochester in addition to the eleven round trips to Lockport.*

SLS&N car 202, southbound, is climbing a 1.1 % grade out of Minetto. The passenger shelter at Stop 34 is showing in the distance. Note the Empire United Railways emblem painted on the side of 202 just below the window sills. Very few pictures of passenger cars bearing this emblem are known. The emblem can be more clearly seen on the builder's view of EUR express car 64 on page 88. This picture is dated c1914-1915.

M. C. Howard, photographer

This real photo post card shows passengers boarding eastbound car 111. In the distance, a westbound local is approaching the Port Gibson stop.

warm fuzzy feeling to anyone who can still remember seeing the real thing in action.

Present day visitors to Emerson Park on Owasco Lake in Auburn will have no idea that the park was originally developed in the 1890s by the local street railway company to attract riders from the city. And then there is the strange story of Edgecliff Park, 24 acres of high ground about three miles west of the Syracuse city line on the Auburn & Syracuse interurban. Beebe bought the land in 1905 for an amusement park but abandoned the project, undeveloped, a few years later. Onondaga County's purchase of the abandoned A&S right-of-way in 1930 included the Edgecliff Park lot. The county apparently preserved the land as a park site for "Edgecliff Park" appears on a current edition of the AAA map of Greater Syracuse and Onondaga County New York.

The smaller communities in central and western New York state were not left stranded without public transportation when the electric cars stopped running. Local bus services took over. Cayuga Omnibus Corporation, operating the Auburn city bus lines, opened a route to Syracuse via Skaneateles and Marcellus. Eastern Greyhound Lines added local service to all points between Lockport, Rochester and Syracuse, essentially following the interurban routes. The Syracuse & Oswego Motor Lines, established in 1931, covered the area previously served by the Empire State Railroad to Oswego. The Syracuse Northern Electric ran its own bus service for about five years after the electric cars quit. In December 1937, the S&OML purchased the SNE and added the Syracuse – Brewerton – South Bay routes to its system.

In concluding this history of electric interurban railroads in central and western New York state, several questions should be asked and possible answers suggested:

1. Should the interurbans have been built in the first place?
2. Did their operation contribute to the betterment of the area through which they ran?
3. Could the interurbans' existence have been prolonged for a few more years?

The answer to the first question is "probably yes." The interurbans were designed to haul passengers. In their years of operation through the close of World War I, the electrics very handily captured the steam roads' local passenger business, for the interurbans provided frequent high speed service between all the villages along their lines as well as direct access to the center of the nearest cities.

The answer to the second question is also "probably yes." The electric cars were accepted eagerly by their surrounding population. Their frequent service tended to bring the villagers and local farmers out of their muddy roadways and relative isolation. The electrics brought neighbors closer together and interurban travel introduced the locals to the outside world. Local trade and commerce increased. As of June 30, 1912, the six Beebe electric

One of the RS&E "short cars" (97, 98 or 99) posed for this real photo post card view on Main Street, Newark, NY in the summer of 1906. Likely, the automobile in the view was also posed, a harbinger of things to come, even while the interurban was in its infancy.

lines and the associated steam-operated Newark & Marion Railway were employing over 1400 workers with an annual payroll of over $713,000. This all contributed to the economy of the eight counties of New York state through which the Beebe lines operated.

The automobiles began showing up in increasing numbers by 1908 – even before the three largest of the Beebe interurbans had been completed. The autos were not considered a threat to the electrics until the early 1920s when the New York State Department of Public Works began creating hard-surfaced roads. This changed the dynamics of rural life in central and western New York, all to the detriment of the interurban railway industry. People soon began to desert the electric cars in favor of the free-wheeling freedom of the highways.

The answer to the third question is a resounding "no." For proof, look across the country. The entire electric interurban industry expired within sixty or seventy years of its inception. A few mid-western lines were able to extend their lives by finding capital funds or equipment trust credits to upgrade their 35-year old plant and buy new and modern cars. But most companies were perennially short of capital budget cash so they resorted to home-made rebuilding jobs on their cars. Few of the interurbans ever built were able to cover operating and fixed charges with fare box revenues over an extended period of time. Too little, if any, planning had been done by the promoters of interurban lines to provide for the movement of freight in carload lots. Two of the Beebe roads, the Buffalo, Lockport & Rochester and the Rochester, Syracuse & Eastern, were built in such close proximity to major steam railroad systems that they were hardly in a position to attract freight-producing industries. Beginning in 1925, the abandonment of passenger-carrying interurban railroads across the country increased at an alarming rate. According to Professors George W. Hilton and John F. Due in their book, *The Electric Interurban Railways in America,* 16,110 miles of interurbans were built in the U.S. between 1889 and 1959. Major nation-wide abandonments occurred in the 1925-1939 period, 3285 miles (20.3%) between 1925 and 1929, 5116 miles (31.8%) in the 1930-34 period and 2612 miles (16.2%) in the 1935-39 period. All 261 miles of the Beebe lines were included in the 1930-34 period. The last interurban line in New York state was the Jamestown, Westfield & Northwestern Railroad. It ceased electric operation on November 30, 1947.

When the timeline of land transportation history in our country is viewed, the wonderful system of electric interurban railroads will appear only as a blip or perhaps as a passing hallucination. During their twenty-five to thirty years of operation, the Beebe Syndicate interurbans carved a niche in the lives of the people and commerce in central and western New York state, and recording that niche has been well worth the effort in preparing a book such as this.

Bibliography

General reference publications including various issues of the following:

American Street Railway Investments — 1894 -1910, McGraw Publishing Co., New York
Brill Magazine — 1907-1927, Philadelphia
Electric Railway Journal — McGraw Publishing Co., New York
Electric Traction Weekly — Kenfield-Davis Publishing Co., Chicago
McGraw Electric Railway Directory — 1918, 1924, 1931, McGraw Publishing Co., New York
McGraw Electric Railway Manuals — 1911-1914, McGraw Publishing Co., New York
Moody's Public Utility Manuals — various years
New York State Public Service Commission Annual Report for 1912 — Volume 2
Poor's Manual of Railroads — various years
Poor's Manual of Public Utilities — various years
Street Railway Journal — McGraw Publishing Co., New York

Finally, it is fitting to record the following members of the Beebe lines family, all now deceased, who, in one way or another, contributed much to my working knowledge of their railroads:

Morton B. Avery, Assistant Chief Engineer, all roads except RL&B
Arthur Benjamin, Foreman Syracuse Freight House, R&S, ES, SNE
Ada Campbell, Weedsport Station Agent, R&S
Murray Campbell, Assistant Superintendent, SNE
John H. Cain, Superintendent, BL&R
Harry J. Clark, Traffic Manager of all roads
Alexander H. Cowie, Esq., President, R&S and ES
David E. Crouse, Chief Engineer, all roads except RL&B
Paul E. Emerson, first Superintendent, RS&E
W. C. Felton, Chief Substation Operator, R&S
Washington Ferris, B&B Master and Roadmaster, all roads
Fred Kitts, Syracuse Office (in early years)
W. J. Lee, Superintendent of Transportation & Traffic of A&S city lines
J. J. McCarthy, Engineering, all roads except RL&B
Alan P. Norris, last Superintendent, R&S, ES, SNE
E. A. Pelton, Chief Inspector and then Supt. of Transportation, A&S
M. D. Stafford, Assistant Treasurer, R&S, ES
Harry Stanton, Freight & Passenger Agent, R&S, ES
Walter Summers, Line Foreman, ES
Frank Wade, Master Mechanic, all roads except RL&B
E. M. Waring, Syracuse Office, clerical staff

Trainmen—

Auburn & Syracuse (A&S): **Andrew Carrigan, Hiram Titus** (Conductor #1)
Empire State RR (ES): **Russell Davis, Ward Davis, Albert Hasner, Ed Hasner, Caleb Loveless, Robert Sawyer**
Rochester & Syracuse (R&S): **George Feller, Ed Hart, Corry Heald, Coles Holland, Vincent Kennelly, Harley Lounsberry, Erwin Thomas, Thomas Slater**
Rochester, Lockport & Buffalo (RL&B): **Robert J. Gunnison, L. B. Harner, John Shear**
Syracuse Northen Electric (SNE): **Paul Cook, Charles Hessler**

Rosters of Equipment

The detailed rosters included in this history give as clear and complete a picture of the rolling stock situation on the various railways as is known 75 years after the last car ran. There are a number of unknown quantities in these listings which tend to make some statements questionable. Probably some of the answers will never be known, but one sure way to find a few is to put what is known into print.

It appears to have been common practice to juggle car numbers, trucks, motors and control equipment on related electric railway properties. Also, there was some official transferring of freight and passenger cars between the associated companies. Most of the heavy repair work was done at the Lakeland shops, just outside of Syracuse, so equipment swapping was a relatively simple matter.

Very few official rosters of equipment of any of the Beebe lines have survived and those that do exist were made some years apart and were not always consistent. The rosters that follow represent a careful sifting of the known facts plus the recollections of many of the men who spent the best years of their lives on the properties.

Included here are rosters of the five companies active at the time of their abandonment. Each of these listings include equipment of their predecessor companies:

Empire State Railroad (includes Syracuse, Lake Shore & Northern RR and Empire United Rwys.)
Rochester & Syracuse RR (includes Rochester, Syracuse & Eastern RR and Empire United Rwys.)
Auburn & Syracuse Electric Railroad (includes Auburn Inter-Urban Electric Railroad)
Rochester, Lockport & Buffalo Railroad (includes Buffalo, Lockport & Rochester Rwy.)
Syracuse Northern Electric Railway (includes Syracuse & South Bay Electric Railroad)

Rosters of Auburn & Northern Electric Railroad and Syracuse, Lakeside & Baldwinsville Railway are included because sufficient information is available. Rosters of the Auburn City Railway and the Oswego Traction Company have not been prepared because of insufficient information.

Any positive corrections or additions to these rosters that can be offered by readers will be sincerely appreciated by the author.

EMPIRE STATE RAILROAD ALL-TIME ROSTER

CAR NUMBERS	YEAR BUILT (ACQUIRED)	BUILDER	SEATS	OVERALL LENGTH	WEIGHT	TRUCKS	MOTORS	H.P.	CONTROLS	HEAT	TYPE	REMARKS
						PASSENGER CARS						
1-6	1906	St Louis SO634A	75	42'0"	36,000	St. Louis					Sub	DT 15-bench open trailers
7-13	1899	Jackson & Sharp	75	46'2"	30,000	Peckham	2-WH 101B	40	K6		Sub	DT 15-bench open; ex-SL&B double-deck motors 18-24
14-15	1899	St. Louis	75	42'6"	26,000	St. Louis	2-WH 101B	40	K6		Sub	DT 15-bench open; ex-SL&B 1 and 2; re-numbered in 1906
27-32	1914	Brill	50	32'2"	15,000	Brill	2-WH 1000	35	K2		City	ST 10-bench open; second-hand; not used after 1927
40	1899	St. Louis SO124	40	42'0"			2-GE 1100	25			Sub	DT closed motor combo; ex-SL&B 6-13 series; scrapped 1917
61-66	1899	St. Louis SO124	32	42'0"			2-WP	40			Sub	DT closed motor combo; ex-SL&B 6-13 series; scrapped 1917
200-206	1908	Cincinnati SO775	56	53'1"	90,000	Baldwin	4-W 119	125	L	HA	Int	DT closed wood and steel
207-211	1910	Kuhlman SO427	58	53'10"	90,000	Baldwin	4-W 119	125	L	Elec	Int	DT closed wood and steel; 209 burned at Minetto 1925
212-214	(1917)	Brill	56	52'11"	50,000	Peckham	4-W101B	40	K6	Elec	Int	DT trailers; ex-S&SB; rebuilt as closed motors 1917
215-217	(1917)	Brill	56	52'11"	54,000	Standard	4-GE 203P	50	GEPC	Elec	Int	DT trailers; ex-S&SB; 215 burned on A - PB line, 217 in Oswego fire
215, 217	(1926)	Wason	48	45'6"	22,400	Baldwin	4-W 533X		HL	HA	Sub	ex-GSF&A 110, 111; steel combo; built 1914; cost to ESRR $6,150.57
218-220	1920	Cincinnati SO2525	58	53'7"	72,000	Baldwin	4-W 548C2	100	ALM	Elec	Int	DT closed wood & steel; original cost for all three $80,030.23
307	1905		30	31'1"	16,000	Peckham					City	ST closed trailer; ex-Oswego Traction Company #4
310-312	1911	Kuhlman SO513	30	31'1"	16,000	Peckham	2-GE 1000	35	K2	Elec	City	ST closed wood; assigned to Oswego city lines
313-324	1915	St. Louis SO1052	40	37'6"	34,500	Baldwin	2-GE 200J	40	K36	HA	City	DT closed; 3 lost in Oswego fire 1920; 3 sold; 6 rebuilt as safety cars and re-numbered 411-416
330-333	1914	Brill	50	32'2"	15,000	Brill	2-WH 1000	35	K2	HA	City	same as 27-32 series but assigned to Oswego city lines
401-406	1920	Osgood Bradley	32	27'10"	16,900	Os. Brad.	2-WH 508A		K63B	Elec	City	ST Birney safety; cost $41,665.65; sold 1927 to G.T. Abel, NY City
411-416	1915	St. Louis SO1052	40	37'6"	34,500	Baldwin	2-GE 200J	40	K36	HA	Sub	DT safety cars; sold 1927 to Jamaica Central Railway (601-606)
						FREIGHT AND EXPRESS CARS						
31	1910	Kuhlman		50'0"	72,000	Brill	4-WH 101B	40	K35	Elec	Int	express motor; wood & steel
32	1906	Niles		53'10"	63,000	Brill					Int	express trailer; wood & steel; originally motor #42
33	1914	Kuhlman SO575		53'0"	68,780	Brill	4-WH 333	90	A.B.	Elec	Int	ex-Empire United Railways #63
34	1914	Kuhlman SO575		53'0"	68,780	Brill	4-WH 333	90	A.B.	Elec	Int	ex-Empire United Railways #64

CAR NUMBERS	YEAR BUILT (ACQUIRED)	BUILDER	OVERALL LENGTH	WEIGHT	TRUCKS	MOTORS	H.P.	CONTROLS	HEAT	TYPE	REMARKS
WORK CARS (Empire State Railroad)											
21, 22	(1922)		23'3"	20,000	Western					Work	DT bottom-dump; built 1906; from R&S in 1922
23-25	1908		33'0"	20,000	Western					Work	DT wood flat cars
41	1899	St. Louis SO124	32'0"		St. Louis					Line	DT motor; ex-SL&B 6-13 series; scrapped at Lakeland 1927
43	1906	Niles	53'6"	65,000	Peckham	4-WH 101B	40	K6	Elec	Line	DT wood; rebuilt 1918
209	1910	Kuhlman SO427	53'10"	22,000	Baldwin					Work	DT flat; ex-passenger 209 burned at Minetto 1925; rebuilt 1927
1000	1920		39'7"	80,000	Peckham	4-WH 101B GE57	40 50	K6 K35	Elec	Int	DT rotary snow plow; wood & steel
1001	1920	Russell	42'5"	50,000	Russell	6-WH 101B	40	K10 K6	Elec	Int	DT snow sweeper; sold 1931 to NY State Railways, Syracuse (3014)
1002	1920	Russell	48'9"	60,000	Peckham	4-GE 200J	40	K6	Elec	Int	DT snow plow; wood & steel
1003	1917	McG-Cummings	28'7"	35,000	McG-Cum	2-WH 508A	25	K10	Elec	City	ST snow sweeper; cost $2,315.08
1005	1906	Russell	39'3"	90,000	Russell	4-WH 119	125	HB	Elec	Int	DT Russell snow plow; wood & steel
1007	1900	Taunton	27'0"	35,000	Taunton	2-WH 38B	50	K10	Elec	City	ST wood shear plow in Oswego; may be ex-SL&B
1011	1918	Russell	40'2"	90,000	Russell	4-WH 119	125	HB	Elec	Int	DT Russell snow plow; wood & steel; original cost $7,528.30

Oswego car barn burned February 2,1920
3 city cars lost (313-324 series)
interurban car 217 lost

KEY

A - PB = Auburn - Port Byron Division, Empire State Railroad
ESRR = Empire State Railroad
GSF&A = Geneva, Seneca Falls & Auburn Railroad
R&S = Rochester & Syracuse Railroad
SL&B = Syracuse, Lakeside & Baldwinsville Railway
S&SB = Syracuse & South Bay Electric Railroad

ROCHESTER & SYRACUSE RAILROAD ALL-TIME ROSTER

CAR NUMBERS	YEAR BUILT (ACQUIRED)	BUILDER	SEATS	OVERALL LENGTH	WEIGHT	TRUCKS	MOTORS	H.P.	CONTROLS	HEAT	REMARKS
PASSENGER CARS											
97-99	1906	Niles	46	45'0"	71,500	Brill-MCB	4-WH 306	65	HL	Elec	short cars; generally assigned to Fairport-Culver Road service
100	1906	Niles	46	53'6"	77,000	Peckham	4-WH 119	125	HL	Elec	combo; baggage doors closed off and sides steel plated 1922
101	1906	Niles	46	53'6"	77,000	Brill-MCB	4-WH 119	125	HL	HA	combo passenger & express; leased to S&SB Spring 1917 as their #22
2nd 101	(1918)	Kuhlman SO270	56	48'	70,000	Peckham	4-WH 121	75	HL	HA	purchased second-hand from S&SB (its #8, 10, 12, 14 or 16)
102	(1922)	Niles	46	53'6"	77,000	Brill	4-WH 119	125	HL	HA	this was first 101 returned from SNE #22 and renumbered R&S 102
110	1906	Niles	58	53'6"	84,000	Brill-MCB	4-WH 119	125	HL	Elec	sides steel plated 1922; rebuilt 1927 as Chair Car *Lyons* (seats 45)
111	1906	Niles	58	53'6"	84,000	Brill-MCB	4-WH 119	125	HL	Elec	sides steel plated 1922; rebuilt 1927 as Chair Car *Palmyra* (seats 45)
112	1906	Niles	58	53'6"	84,000	Brill-MCB	4-WH 119	125	HL	Elec	sides steel plated 1922; rebuilt 1927 as Chair Car *Newark* (seats 45)
113-114	1906	Kuhlman SO285	58	53'6"	84,000	Brill-MCB	4-WH 119	125	HL	Elec	
115-116	1907	Kuhlman SO344	58	53'6"	84,200	Baldwin	4-WH 119	125	HL	HA	
117-118	1908	Kuhlman SO383	58	53'6"	84,200	Baldwin	4-WH 119	125	HL	HA	
119	(1910)	Kuhlman SO384	58	53'6"	84,200	Baldwin	4-WH 119	125	HL	HA	originally outshopped in 1908 as Auburn & Northern Elec. Railroad #10
120-121	1909	Kuhlman SO410	58	53'6"	87,000	Baldwin	4-WH 119	125	HL	HA	121 rebuilt by Kuhlman SO527 1912 (converted 4 vestibule doors to 2)
122	1910	Kuhlman SO437	58	53'6"	87,000	Baldwin	4-WH 119	125	HL	HA	rebuilt 1927 as Chair Car *Rochester* (seats 45)
123	1910	Kuhlman SO437	58	53'6"	87,000	Baldwin	4-WH 119	125	HL	HA	rebuilt 1927 as Chair Car *Syracuse* (seats 45)
124-125	1910	Kuhlman SO437	58	53'6"	87,000	Baldwin	4-WH 119	125	HL	HA	
126	1910	Kuhlman SO437	58	53'6"	87,000	Baldwin	4-WH 119	125	HL	HA	rebuilt 1927 as Chair Car *Clyde* (seats 45)
127-128	1910	Kuhlman SO437	58	53'6"	87,000	Baldwin	4-WH 119	125	HL	HA	
129	1910	Kuhlman SO437	58	53'6"	87,000	Baldwin	4-WH 119	125	HL	HA	rebuilt 1927 as Chair Car *Weedsport* (seats 45)
999	1910	Kuhlman SO424		56'0"	90,000	Baldwin	4-WH 119	125	HL	Elec	Beebe Syndicate's Director's Car; owned jointly by all Beebe roads
Rochester	1910	Kuhlman SO424	26	56'0"	90,000	Baldwin	4-WH 119	125	HL	Elec	rebuilt 1915 from *999* into a Parlor Car
Syracuse	(1915)	Kuhlman SO154	24	47'2"	50,000	Peckham*					ex-A&S Parlor Car *Marcella*; used in Parlor Car service as trailer

** car* Syracuse *trucks equipped with Merrick Roller Bearings on a trial basis; manufactured by Railway Roller Bearings, So. Syracuse, NY*

KEY

A&S = Auburn & Syracuse Electric Railroad
SNE = Syracuse Northern Electric Railway
S&SB = Syracuse & South Bay Electric Railroad

CAR NUMBERS	YEAR BUILT (ACQUIRED)	BUILDER	SEATS	OVERALL LENGTH	WEIGHT	TRUCKS	MOTORS	H.P.	CONTROLS	HEAT	REMARKS
FREIGHT AND EXPRESS CARS (Rochester & Syracuse Railroad)											
61	1906	Niles		53'6"	62,780	Brill-MCB	4-WH 119	125	A.B.	Elec	de-motored 1917; re-motored mid-1920s
62	1914	Kuhlman SO575		53'0"	68,780	K-50-E-3	4-WH 119	125	A.B.	Elec	built 1914 for Empire United Railways
63	1911	Russell		50'0"		Baldwin	4-WH 119	125	A.B.	HA	may have been off the property during World War I
64	1915	Kuhlman SO154		47'2"	50,000	Peckham	4-WH 306	65	HL	Elec	rebuilt 1920 from parlor car *Syracuse;* final use as work car
65	1914	Kuhlman SO575		53'0"	68,780	K-5Q-E-3	4-WH 119	125	A.B.	Elec	built 1914 for Empire United Railways
66	1914	Kuhlman SO575		53'0"	68,780	K-50-E-3	4-WH 121	75	ALM	Elec	built 1914 for Empire United Railways, not on R&S after 1928
67	1906	Niles		53'6"	68,780	Brill-MCB	4-WH 119	125	A.B.	HA	
68	1906	Niles	5	53'6"	64,000	Brill-MCB	4-WH 119	125	A.B.	HA	combo passenger & freight; passenger compartment removed 1920
80	1910	Kuhlman SO424		56'0"	50,000	Peckham					rebuilt 1920 from parlor car *Rochester* as a trailer
WORK CARS (Rochester & Syracuse Railroad)											
10-11	(1906)	Western		33'0"	20,000	Western					flat trailers acquired second-hand from railroad construction co.
12	(1922)	Western		33'0"	20,000	Western					flat trailer, origin unknown
21, 22	1908	Western		23'3"	20,000	Simplex	2-WH 121	75			bottom-dump work cars; to Empire State Railroad as trailers in 1922
20-23	(1922)			40'0"							80,000-lb. cap. hoppers; purchased second-hand for ballast service
50	1906	Niles		53'0"	60,000	Brill-MCB	4-WH 119 4-WH 101B	125	A.B. K 6	Elec	overhead line car
1000	1918	Russell		42'5"	50,000	Russell	W328 Brooms 2-WH 121	40 75	K 10 K 6	Elec	DT/DE snow sweeper; sold 1931 to NY State Rwys in Syracuse (3016)
1001	(1919)	Peckham		40'0"	59,000	Peckham	2-GE-74	65	L 4	HA	DT/DE rotary snow plow; renumbered from 1005 in 1919
1002	1906	Russell		34'0"	90,000	Russell	4-WH 119	125	L 3	Elec	DT/DE snow plow; first DE electric plow ever built by Russell
1003	1908	Russell		40'0"	90,000	Russell	4-WH 119	125	L 6	Elec	DT/DE Russell snow plow
1004	1909	Russell		39'0"	90,000	Russell	4-WH 119 2-WH 101B	125 40	L 14 K 6	Elec	DT/DE Russell snow plow
1005	1906	Peckham		40'0"	59,000	Peckham	2-WH 121	90	L 2	HA	DT/DE rotary snow plow; renumbered 1001 in 1919

AUBURN & SYRACUSE ELECTRIC RAILROAD ALL-TIME ROSTER

CAR NUMBERS	YEAR BUILT (ACQUIRED)	BUILDER	SEATS	OVERALL LENGTH	WEIGHT	TRUCKS	MOTORS	H.P.	TYPE	REMARKS
PASSENGER CARS										
1-3	1905	Kuhlman SO286	28	30'0"	16,000		2-unkn		City	ST closed motors; leased from A&N; scrapped about 1915
12-19	1909	Kuhlman SO421	75	41'8"		Brill	4-unkn		Sub	DT I5-bench open; used to Park and occasionally A&S interurban
22-29	1902		28	30'0"					City	ST closed motors; formerly Auburn City Railway cars
30-32	1912	Kuhlman SO538	30	30'0"					City	ST closed motors
33	1902		50						City	ST 10-bench open motor; formerly Auburn City Railway car
34	1902		28	30'0"					City	ST closed motor; open vestibules; formerly Auburn City Railway car
39-40	1901	Stephenson	30	29'0"					Sub	ST closed motors; re-numbered 1907 from Auburn Inter-Urban cars 1-2
41-42	1904	St. Louis SO491	30	30'0"					City	ST closed; 41 later became a line car
43-46	1911	Kuhlman SO513	30	31'0"	16,000	Peckham	2-GE 1000	35	City	ST closed motors
50-51	1901	Stephenson	48	36'0"					Sub	DT closed; built for Auburn Inter-Urban; sold to A&N 1910
52-57	1903	Kuhlman SO167	56	50'0"	60,000	Peckham	4-WH 76	75	Int	DT closed motors; wood
58-59	1904	Kuhlman SO247	56	49'10"	60,000	Baldwin	4-WH 76	75	Int	DT closed motors; wood
60	1904	Jewett SO160	56	50'0"	60,000	Baldwin	4-WH 121	90	Int	DT closed motor; wood; body on a steel underframe
61	1907	Cincinnati SO770	56	50'0"	60,000	Baldwin	4-WH 121	90	Int	DT closed motor; wood
62-68	1905	Kuhlman	56	50'0"	60,000	Baldwin	4-WH 76	75	lnt	DT closed motors; wood
85-86	1906	Jewett SO171	68	51'4"		Peckham	4-unkn		Int	DT open motors; excursion-type, ctr aisle, end entrances, winter side panels
301-312	1915	St. Louis SO1044	40	37'6"	34,500	Baldwin	2-GE 200J	40	City	DT closed steel; converted to Safety cars; sold 1927 to NY & Queens (1-12)
Marcella	1903	Kuhlman SO154	24	47'2"	50,000	Peckham	2-WH 76	75	Int	DT closed; business car; to parlor motor 1909, to parlor trailer *Syracuse* 1915
FREIGHT AND WORK CARS										
99	1901	Stephenson							Sub	ST box motor for Auburn Inter-Urban; later a sand car
100-101	1902	Jewett SO138		49'4"			4-unkn		Int	DT express; 100 burned near Syracuse in 1906
2nd 100	1906	St. Louis					4-unkn		Int	DT express
102	1906						4-unkn		Int	DT express (identity uncertain)
105	1918	B-WH SO48538		85'0"	100,000	Baldwin	4-unkn		Loco	DT 50 ton; hauled interchange freight cars - Marcellus to Split Rock quarry; sold 1919; now at Connecticut Electric Rwy. Museum, East Windsor, CT
110				65'0"					Work	DT Line car *Long Tom*

Snow fighting equipment - 5 DT plows (2 Russell nose, 1 large rotary, 1 shear) also 1 sweeper; details unknown

Note: roster of Auburn City lines is incomplete because of insufficient information.

ROCHESTER, LOCKPORT & BUFFALO RAILROAD ALL-TIME ROSTER

CAR NUMBERS	YEAR BUILT (ACQUIRED)	BUILDER	SEATS	OVERALL LENGTH	WEIGHT	TRUCKS	MOTORS	H.P.	CONTROLS	REMARKS
PASSENGER CARS										
201-215	1908	Niles	49	51'8"	70,000	Baldwin	4-GE 73	75	GE-M	DT/SE; wood; controls at both ends; center drive
500-505	1909	Cincinnati SO1020	49	51'6"	70,000	Baldwin	4-WH 119	125	GE-M	DT/DE; wood; left-side drive
FREIGHT AND EXPRESS CARS										
301-302	1908	Niles		50'7"	60,000	Baldwin	4-GE 207	125	GE-M	DT/DE motors; wood; 301 lost in fire
2nd 301		BL&R shops		50'0"		Baldwin	4-GE 207	125	GE-M	DT/DE freight motor; trucks from old 301
303	1916	Brill		50'0"	36,000	Baldwin				DT/DE steel express motor
400-404	1909	BL&R shops		40'0"	28,000	Baldwin				DT freight trailers; home built
WORK CARS										
100	1908	McGuire-Cummings		47'0"	50,000					DT/DE work car with push plow
101	1908	Smith & Wallace		50'0"	50,000	Baldwin				DT/DE line car
102	1918			28'0"	35,000	McG-Cum				ST/DE sweeper
103	1909	Russell		50'0"	90,000	Russell				DT/DE rotary snow plow; original number at delivery was 400
1201-05	(1908)			23'0"	20,000	Western				high-side center-dump ballast cars purchased second-hand
2001-05	(1908)			33'0"	22,900	arch bar				5 flat cars purchased second-hand

SYRACUSE NORTHERN ELECTRIC RAILWAY ALL-TIME ROSTER

CAR NUMBERS	YEAR BUILT (ACQUIRED)	BUILDER	SEATS	OVERALL LENGTH	WEIGHT	TRUCKS	MOTORS	H.P.	CONTROLS	REMARKS
PASSENGER CARS										
2, 4, 6, 8, 10, 12, 14,16, 18 and 20	1905	Kuhlman SO270	56	48'0"	70,000	Brill **	4-GE 74A	60	L4	DT/SE closed; cars 2,4,6,18, and 20 in service until 1932; one sold to R&S 1918 (their 2nd 101); 4 cars disposition unknown
22	(1917)	Niles	48	53'6"	77,000	Brill	4-WH119	125	HL	DT combination passenger & express; ex-R&S (1st 101); returned to R&S in 1922 as their 102
50	1905	Kuhlman	60	52'11"	41,000					DT closed trailer; rebuilt from open trailer J 1917
A, B, C, D, E, G	1905	Kuhlman SO280	60	52'11"	41,000					DT open trailers; sold to ESRR 1917 (their 212-217)
H, J, K, L	1905	Kuhlman SO280	60	52'11"	41,000					DT open trailers; J rebuilt as SNE 50; H, K and L in service until 1932
EXPRESS AND WORK CARS										
1	1905	Kuhlman SO281		48'0"	60,000	Brill	4-GE 74A	60	L4	DT/DE express car
3	1905	Kuhlman SO281		48'0"	60,000	Brill	4-GE 74A	60	L4	DT/DE express and line car
10-13				30'0"						4 flat cars purchased second-hand
100	1906	Peckham		40'0"	58,000	Peckham				DT/DE rotary snow plow

*** car 20 trucks equipped with Merrick Roller Bearings on a trial basis; manufactured by Railway Roller Bearings, So. Syracuse, NY*

KEY

ESRR = Empire State Railroad
R&S = Rochester & Syracuse Railroad
SNE = Syracuse Northern Electric Railway
S&SB = Syracuse & South Bay Electric Railroad

AUBURN & NORTHERN ELECTRIC RAILROAD — ALL-TIME ROSTER

CAR NUMBERS	YEAR BUILT (ACQUIRED)	BUILDER	SEATS	OVERALL LENGTH	WEIGHT	TRUCKS	MOTORS	H.P.	TYPE	REMARKS
PASSENGER CARS										
1-3	1905	Kuhlman SO286	28	30'0"	16,000				City	single-truck closed motors for A&N city lines; cars leased to Auburn & Syracuse; scrapped 1915
10	1908	Kuhlman SO384	58	53'6"	84,200	Baldwin	4-WH 119	125	Int	double-truck closed; sold 1910 to Rochester, Syracuse & Eastern (119)
50, 51	(1910)	Stephenson	48	36'0"					Int	double-truck closed; from A&S 1910; later re-numbered 6 and 7 sold August 1916 to NY State Railways, Utica lines (388 and 390)

FREIGHT AND WORK CARS

NONE

SYRACUSE, LAKESIDE & BALDWINSVILLE RAILWAY — ALL-TIME ROSTER

CAR NUMBERS	YEAR BUILT	BUILDER	SEATS	OVERALL LENGTH	REMARKS
PASSENGER CARS					
1, 2	1899	St. Louis	75	42'0"	DT 15-bench open motors; 2 motors per car; re-numbered 14, 15 by SLS&N 1906
6-13	1899	St Louis SO124	40	42'0"	DT closed motors; re-numbered six cars 61-66, one as combo 40, one as line car 41 by SLS&N 1906
18-24	1899	Jackson & Sharp	100	46'2"	DT double-deck motors; top decks removed by SLS&N 1904-1907; later re-numbered 7-13
43, 44	1900	Jackson & Sharp	75	42'0"	DT l5-bench open motors; disposition unknown
unkn	1899	St. Louis	50	32'3"	six ST 10-bench open trailers; details and disposition unknown
WORK CARS					
100	1900				ST/DE box motor work car; disposition unknown
	1900				ST/DE rotary snow plow; sent to Oswego city lines 1906; lost in Oswego barn fire 2/2/1920
	1900	Taunton		27'0"	ST/DE shear snow plow; may have become 1007 on Oswego city lines

KEY: SLS&N = Syracuse, Lake Shore & Northern Railroad

BEEBE SYNDICATE LINES - MILEAGE TABLE - 1912

	First Main Track Miles Owned	First Main Track Running Rights	Total Route Miles	Second Main Track	Sidings	Total Track Miles
Auburn to Port Byron	7.74		7.74	0.15	0.32	8.21
on Auburn & Syracuse tracks		0.66	0.66			0.66
Auburn & Northern Electric Railroad	**7.74**	**0.66**	**8.40**	**0.15**	**0.32**	**8.87**
Auburn to Syracuse city line	23.91		23.91	16.28	0.53	40.72
on NY State Railways, Syracuse lines		2.80	2.80			2.80
Auburn city lines	12.14		12.14	2.18	0.62	14.94
on Auburn & Northern tracks		2.34	2.34	0.15	0.18	2.67
Auburn & Syracuse Electric Railroad	**36.05**	**5.14**	**41.19**	**18.61**	**1.33**	**61.13**
Rochester city line to Lockport city line	54.32		54.32	8.30	3.68	66.30
on International Rwy, Lockport city track		1.54	1.54			1.54
on NY State Railways, Rochester lines		2.33	2.33			2.33
Buffalo, Lockport & Rochester Railway	**54.32**	**3.87**	**58.19**	**8.30**	**3.68**	**70.17**
Rochester city line to Lake Shore Jct	79.25		79.25	79.25	0.75	159.25
on SLS&N, Lake Shore Jct to Syracuse		4.40	4.40			4.40
on NY State Railways, Rochester lines		2.63	2.63			2.63
Rochester, Syracuse & Eastern Railroad	**79.25**	**7.03**	**86.28**	**79.25**	**0.75**	**166.28**
Syracuse city line to South Bay	9.58		9.58	9.58	1.88	21.04
Watertown Jct to Brewerton	6.15		6.15			6.15
on NY State Railways, Syracuse lines		2.60	2.60			2.60
Syracuse & South Bay Electric Railroad	**15.73**	**2.60**	**18.33**	**9.58**	**1.88**	**29.79**
Syracuse to Oswego	37.76		37.76	20.21	0.88	58.85
Fulton city line	0.58		0.58		0.04	0.62
Oswego city lines	10.14		10.14	0.17	0.82	11.13
Syracuse, Lake Shore & Northern Railroad	**48.48**		**48.48**	**20.38**	**1.74**	**70.60**
Total Miles - Electric Lines	**241.57**	**19.30**	**260.87**	**136.27**	**9.70**	**406.84**
Newark Jct to Marion	8.19		8.19			8.19
on Northern Central Railway at Newark		1.00	1.00			1.00
Newark & Marion Railway	**8.19**	**1.00**	**9.19**			**9.19**
Total Beebe Syndicate Lines Mileage	**249.76**	**20.30**	**270.06**	**136.27**	**9.70**	**416.03**

These figures may or may not entirely agree with those found in other published sources such as McGraw Electric Railway Manual (Red Book), McGraw Electric Railway Directories and Electric Traction Pocket Lists. Company mileage so reported tended to reflect total track mileage operated including miles of running rights over connecting lines. However, the Buffalo, Lockport & Rochester Railway consistently excluded running rights in its reports to these publishers.

The track miles in this table are based on the detailed figures reported by each railway company to the New York State Public Service Commission, Second District, appearing in their June 30, 1912 Annual Report, volume 2, pages 262-266. Adjustments have been made as follows: 1) included is the 6.15-mile Brewerton branch of the S&SB opened for service Nov. 2, 1912, four months after the Commission's Annual Report was filed; 2) excluded is the Commission's mileage of "second main track" or "sidings" of lines over which the Beebe cars had operating rights; 3) excluded are 0.48 miles of "second track" on Genesee Street, Auburn, that were laid but never operated.

Passes of the Beebe Syndicate Lines

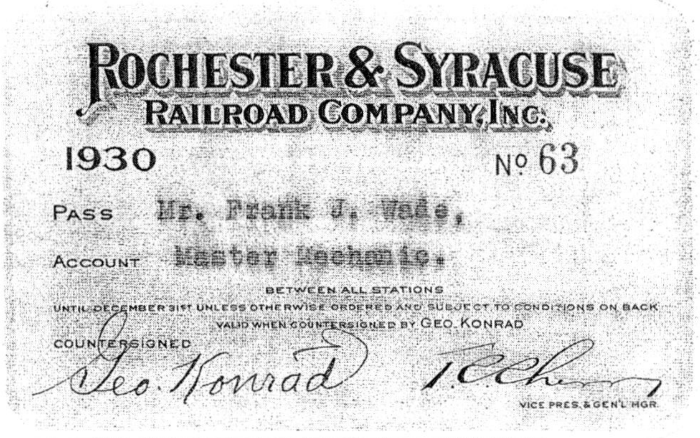

ROCHESTER & SYRACUSE
RAILROAD COMPANY, INC.
1930 № 63
PASS Mr. Frank J. Wade,
ACCOUNT Master Mechanic.
BETWEEN ALL STATIONS
UNTIL DECEMBER 31ST UNLESS OTHERWISE ORDERED AND SUBJECT TO CONDITIONS ON BACK
VALID WHEN COUNTERSIGNED BY GEO. KONRAD
COUNTERSIGNED Geo. Konrad
VICE PRES. & GEN'L MGR.

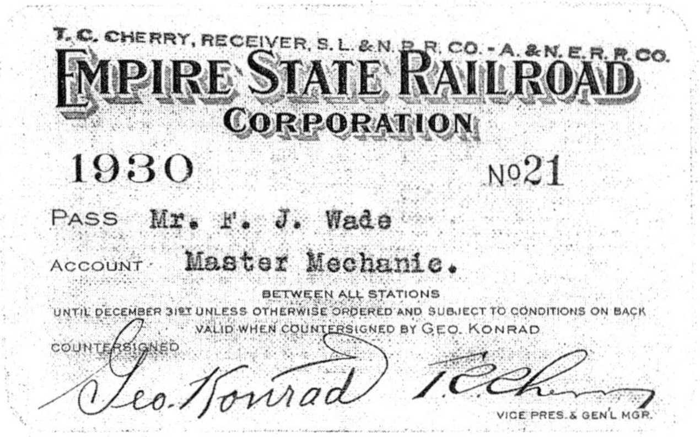

T. C. CHERRY, RECEIVER, S. L. & N. R. R. CO. - A. & N. E. R. R. CO.
EMPIRE STATE RAILROAD
CORPORATION
1930 №21
PASS Mr. F. J. Wade
ACCOUNT Master Mechanic.
BETWEEN ALL STATIONS
UNTIL DECEMBER 31ST UNLESS OTHERWISE ORDERED AND SUBJECT TO CONDITIONS ON BACK
VALID WHEN COUNTERSIGNED BY GEO. KONRAD
COUNTERSIGNED Geo. Konrad
VICE PRES. & GEN'L MGR.

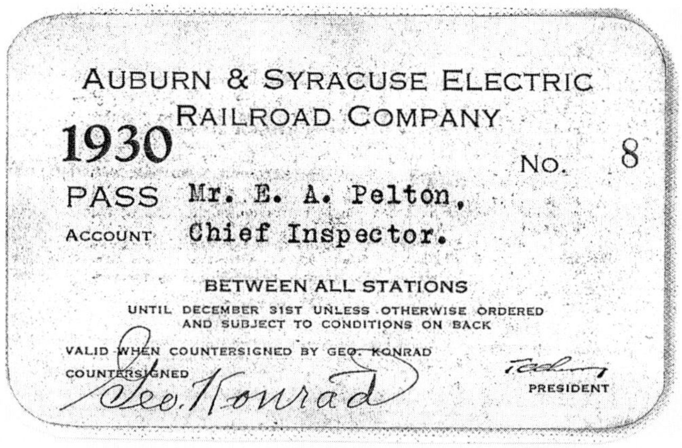

AUBURN & SYRACUSE ELECTRIC
RAILROAD COMPANY
1930 NO. 8
PASS Mr. E. A. Pelton,
ACCOUNT Chief Inspector.
BETWEEN ALL STATIONS
UNTIL DECEMBER 31ST UNLESS OTHERWISE ORDERED
AND SUBJECT TO CONDITIONS ON BACK
VALID WHEN COUNTERSIGNED BY GEO. KONRAD
COUNTERSIGNED Geo. Konrad
PRESIDENT

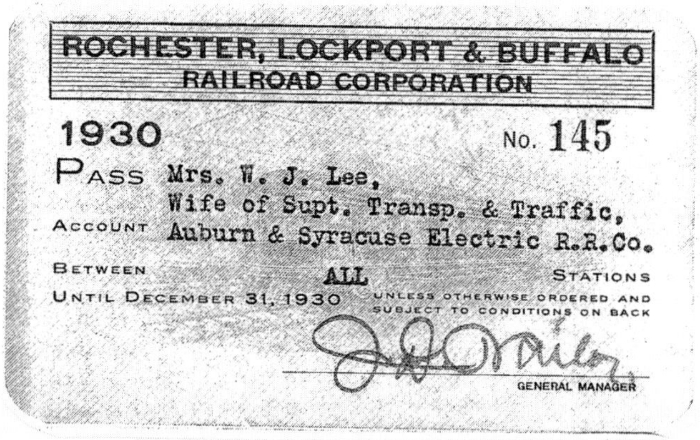

ROCHESTER, LOCKPORT & BUFFALO
RAILROAD CORPORATION
1930 NO. 145
PASS Mrs. W. J. Lee,
ACCOUNT Wife of Supt. Transp. & Traffic,
Auburn & Syracuse Electric R.R.Co.
BETWEEN ALL STATIONS
UNTIL DECEMBER 31, 1930 UNLESS OTHERWISE ORDERED AND SUBJECT TO CONDITIONS ON BACK
GENERAL MANAGER

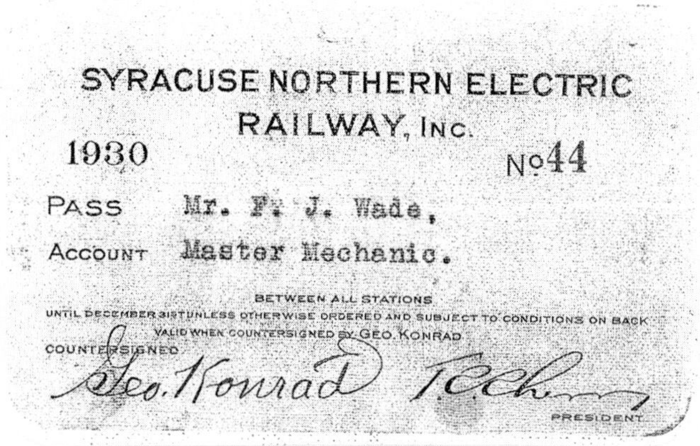

SYRACUSE NORTHERN ELECTRIC
RAILWAY, INC.
1930 №44
PASS Mr. F. J. Wade,
ACCOUNT Master Mechanic.
BETWEEN ALL STATIONS
UNTIL DECEMBER 31ST UNLESS OTHERWISE ORDERED AND SUBJECT TO CONDITIONS ON BACK
VALID WHEN COUNTERSIGNED BY GEO. KONRAD
COUNTERSIGNED Geo. Konrad
PRESIDENT

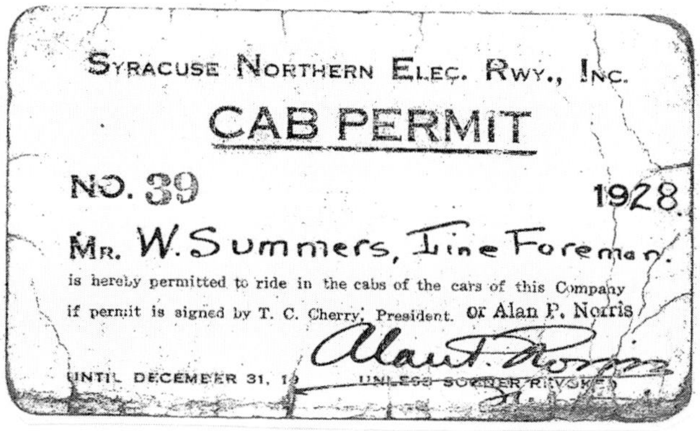

SYRACUSE NORTHERN ELEC. RWY., INC.
CAB PERMIT
NO. 39 1928
MR. W. Summers, Line Foreman.
is hereby permitted to ride in the cabs of the cars of this Company
if permit is signed by T. C. Cherry, President. or Alan P. Norris
UNTIL DECEMBER 31, 19 UNLESS SOONER REVOKED

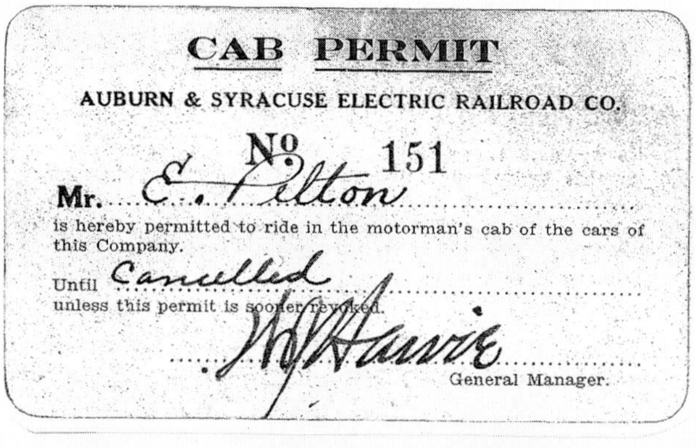

CAB PERMIT
AUBURN & SYRACUSE ELECTRIC RAILROAD CO.
№ 151
Mr. E. Pelton
is hereby permitted to ride in the motorman's cab of the cars of this Company.
Until Cancelled
unless this permit is sooner revoked.
General Manager.

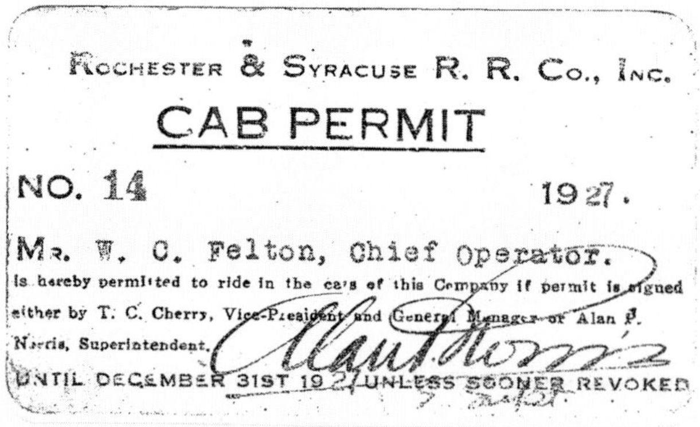

ROCHESTER & SYRACUSE R. R. CO., INC.
CAB PERMIT
NO. 14 1927.
MR. W. C. Felton, Chief Operator.
is hereby permitted to ride in the cars of this Company if permit is signed either by T. C. Cherry, Vice-President and General Manager or Alan P. Norris, Superintendent.
UNTIL DECEMBER 31ST 1927 UNLESS SOONER REVOKED

Successors of the Beebe Syndicate Lines

Index

A

B

C - D

E

F

G - H - I - J - K

L

M

N

O - P - Q

R

S

T - U - V

W - X - Y - Z

Beginning in 1927, the Rochester & Syracuse distributed these car cards for display in local street cars of the New York State Railways to advertise the new R&S Chair Car service. The original card measures 21" x 11".

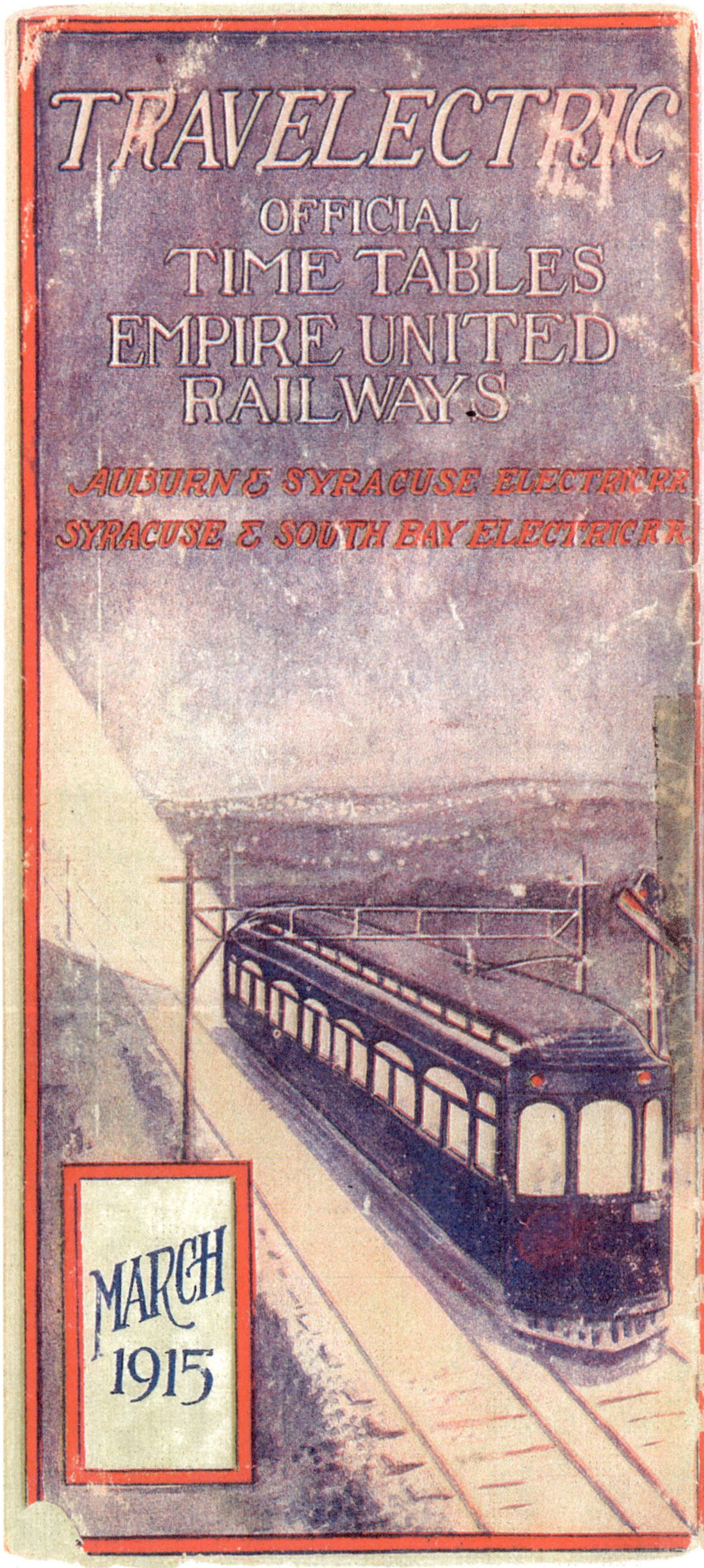
TRAVELECTRIC
OFFICIAL
TIME TABLES
EMPIRE UNITED
RAILWAYS
AUBURN & SYRACUSE ELECTRIC R.R.
SYRACUSE & SOUTH BAY ELECTRIC R.R.
MARCH
1915

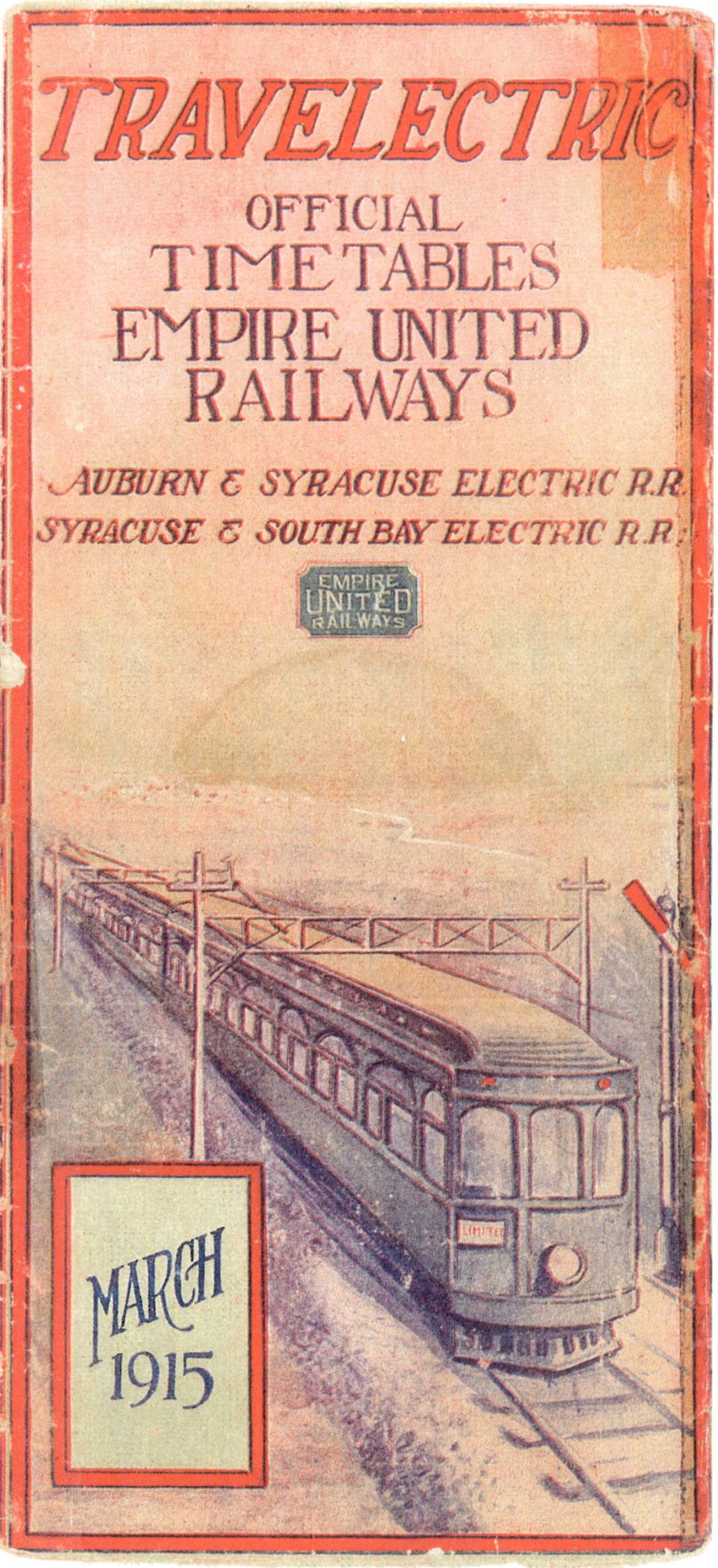
TRAVELECTRIC
OFFICIAL
TIME TABLES
EMPIRE UNITED
RAILWAYS
AUBURN & SYRACUSE ELECTRIC R.R.
SYRACUSE & SOUTH BAY ELECTRIC R.R.
EMPIRE
UNITED
RAILWAYS
LIMITED
MARCH
1915